*A Garland Series*

# British Philosophers and Theologians of the 17th & 18th Centuries

A Collection of 101 Volumes

Edited by
René Wellek

# Richard Price

## A FREE DISCUSSION
## OF THE DOCTRINES
## OF MATERIALISM AND
## PHILOSOPHICAL NECESSITY
In Correspondence With Joseph Priestley

1778

Garland Publishing, Inc., New York & London

1978

Bibliographical note:

this facsimile has been made from a copy in the
Beinecke Library of Yale University
(1973.393)


The volumes in this series have been printed on
acid-free, 250-year-life paper.

Library of Congress Cataloging in Publication Data

Price, Richard, 1723-1791.
  A free discussion of the doctrines of materialism
and philosophical necessity in correspondence with
Joseph Priestley, 1778.

  (British philosophers and theologians of the 17th &
18th centuries)
  Reprint of the 1778 ed. printed for J. Johnson and
T. Cadell, London.
  Includes index.
  1. Materialism.  2. Free will and determinism.
3. Philosophy and religion.  I. Priestley, Joseph,
1733-1804.  II. Title.  III. Series.
[B1382.P73F7 1978]          146'.3          75-11247
ISBN 0-8240-1798-6

*Printed in the United States of America*

A

# FREE DISCUSSION

OF THE DOCTRINES OF

# MATERIALISM,

AND

## PHILOSOPHICAL NECESSITY,

IN A CORRESPONDENCE BETWEEN DR. PRICE,

AND DR. PRIESTLEY.

TO WHICH ARE ADDED,

BY DR. PRIESTLEY,

## An INTRODUCTION,

Explaining the Nature of the CONTROVERSY,
and LETTERS to feveral Writers who
have animadverted on his DISQUISITIONS RE-
LATING TO MATTER AND SPIRIT, or his
TREATISE ON NECESSITY.

---

Together let us beat this ample Field.
————————Be candid where we can,
But vindicate the Ways of God to Man.

POPE.

---

L O N D O N:
Printed for J. JOHNSON, No. 72, St. PAUL'S CHURCH-YARD,
and T. CADELL, in the STRAND.
M.DCCLXXVIII.

# THE

# DEDICATION.

## *To* JOHN LEE, Efq.

### OF

## LINCOLN's-INN.

DEAR SIR,

I TAKE the liberty to prefent to you, not in the character of an *advocate*, but in that of a *friend*, and a *judge*, a production that is in part my own, and in part that of our common and excellent friend Dr. Price. Though you are employed in the practice of a particular profeffion, your education, and ftudies, have by no means been con-

fined

fined to it, but you have extended your inquiries to all subjects that are interesting to *men*, to *citizens*, and to *christians*.

My object in the present publication, as well as in those which have preceded it, is to overturn, as far as my endeavours can effect it, what I deem to be a prejudice of the greatest antiquity, and the deepest rooted, of any that have contributed to debase christianity, and a corruption which, in this philosophical age, calls the loudest for reformation. And though this will necessarily destroy some flattering hopes respecting our prospects after death, they are such as are ill founded; and it will draw our attention more strongly to those *more certain*, though *more distant* prospects, that christianity holds out to us.

Our

# THE DEDICATION.

Our friend, however, confiders my endeavours in a light unfavourable and hoftile to chriftianity, and overturning not fuppofed, but real foundations. As truth will finally prevail over all oppofition, time (though we may not live to fee the iffue) will difcover whether my zeal in attacking, or his in defending, is better founded; and as our intentions, I believe, are equally upright, our difcuffion truly amicable, and confequently *truth*, not *victory*, our object, it will be equally (or, to make allowance for a little human frailty, it will, I hope, be as near as poffible equally) acceptable to us both, on which fide foever it be found. You, who have an equal friendfhip for us both, will not, on this account, be biaffed on one fide more than on the other; and whichever way any of our friends incline, as we are confident we fhall not

lofe

lose their esteem, so, we can assure them, they will not lose ours.

Intricate as the discussion of such questions as these is, there is a peculiar pleasure attending the speculations ; and from the relation they bear to the greatest of all objects, they have a dignity and sublimity in them, and eminently contribute to inspire a *serenity* and *elevation of mind,* which both improves and enlarges it, and thereby enables us to look down upon the trifling but tormenting pursuits of a bustling world.

I have no occasion to describe to you the satisfaction that arises from the rational use of the human faculties, a freedom from vulgar and debasing prejudices, and the habitual contemplation of great and important subjects ; and also from such a course of reading, and such a choice

of

of company, as tends to keep up that *right bent*, and *firmnefs* of mind, which a neceffary intercourfe with the world would otherwife *warp* and *relax*. He who can have, and truly *enjoy*, the fociety of fuch men as Dr. Price, Mr. Lindfey, and Dr. Jebb, cannot envy the condition of princes. Such fellowfhip is the true balfam of life; its cement is infinitely more durable than that of the friendfhips of the world, and it looks for its proper *fruit*, and complete *gratification*, to the life beyond the grave.

I think myfelf happy in being able to call myfelf one of fuch a fraternity; and wifhing to perpetuate, as far as may be in my power, the memory of fuch friendfhips, and efpecially that with yourfelf, which is now of long ftanding, and

has

## THE DEDICATION.

has been ftrengthened by a variety of
ties, I fubfcribe myfelf,

    Dear Sir,

        Your countryman,

            friend, and

                fellow chriftian,

                    J. PRIESTLEY.

CALNE, Aug. 24,
    1778.

THE

# THE

# INTRODUCTION.

THIS work, it will be owned, exhibits an uncommon, if not a fingular fpectacle, viz. that of two perfons difcuffing, with the moft perfect freedom and candour, queftions which are generally deemed of the greateft confequence in practice, and which are certainly fo in theory. The occafion of it was as follows.

When my *Difquifitions*, &c. was printed off, I put it, as I have obferved, into the hands of feveral of my friends, both well and ill affected

b                                            to

to my general hypothefis, that I might
take the advantage of their remarks,
in an additional fheet of *Illuftrations*,
which is accordingly annexed to the
firft volume.   Among others, Dr.
Price was fo obliging as to enter into a more particular difcuffion of
feveral of the fubjects of the work;
and afterwards, imagining that I
meant to write a direct anfwer to
his remarks, he expreffed a wifh that
I would print them at large, together
with any notice that I fhould think
proper to take of them.

This, I told him, did not fall
within my views with refpect to that
particular publication, but that I
would take the liberty to propofe
another fcheme, which I thought
would correfpond with both our
views, and be ufeful to others who
might wifh to fee the arguments on
both fides freely canvaffed, without
the

the mixture of any thing perfonal, or foreign to the fubject, which often conftitutes a great part of the bulk of controverfial writings, and tends to divert the mind from an attention to the real merits of the queftion in debate. It was, that he fhould re-write his remarks, after feeing what ufe I had already made of them in my fheet of *Illuftrations*; that I would then reply to them diftinctly, article by article, that he fhould remark, and I reply again, &c. till we fhould both be fatisfied that we had done as much juftice as we could to our feveral arguments, frankly acknowledging any miftakes we might be convinced of, and then publifh the whole jointly.

To this propofal he chearfully acceded, chufing only that the remarks he had already fent fhould ferve as a bafis, and that, to avoid repetitions,

I

I might refer to my *Illuftrations* in
my firft reply.  He added, however,
certain *Queries*, that by my anfwers
to them he might perceive more diftinctly in what refpects my ideas
really differed from his.  Accordingly I replied to his remarks, and
anfwered his queries, with as much
explicitnefs as I poffibly could ; and
in the courfe of the correfpondence
propofed others to him, with the
fame view, and likewife, in order to
bring into a fmall compafs, my objections to the commonly received
hypothefis.  In this manner, at our
leifure, and without communicating
with any third perfon, we exchanged
our *remarks* and *replies*, till it appeared to us needlefs to advance any
thing farther.  In this ftate we fubmit the refult of our difcuffion to
the judgment of the public, wifhing
that they may attend to it with the
                                    fame

fame coolnefs and candour with which we ourfelves have written.

Our readers will obferve that this difcuffion refpects all the fubjects of my *Difquifitions*, except the doctrine of the *pre-exiftence of Chrift*. But though this be the point to which all that I have written tends ; it being the capital inference that I make from the doctrines of *materialifm, penetrability of matter*, and *neceffity* (thefe being, in my idea, parts of the fame fyftem) Dr. Price thought it was a fubject that had been fo much debated, that it would be needlefs to enter into it.

I will here acknowledge, that in propofing this fcheme, I was not without a farther view, which was, that among fo many angry opponents as I expected, I might fecure a friendly one, and at the fame time one who

could

could not but be acknowledged to be capable of doing ample justice to his argument as any writer of the age. I had pledged myself to go through with this business, replying to every thing that should appear deserving of notice; and it was much more agreeable to me to urge all that I had to say in letters to a candid friend, than in tart replies to an angry disputant. And I thought that, according to the law of arms, and modern honour, when I had fairly engaged with one antagonist on this score, I should be more easily excused encountering another. The reader, however, will find that I have not entirely availed myself of this privilege; for though I have not entered minutely into the argument, which would have been mere tautology, I have noticed such other opponents as have appeared since the publication of my work. And though

I

I think I may now be excufed from replying to any others in a feparate publication, I will promife that, in any new edition either of the *Dif-quifitions* themfelves, or of this work, I will take more or lefs notice of every thing that fhall come out in the mean time, and that fhall appear to myfelf and my friends to deferve it; and I will publifh all fuch *additions* feparately. To do more would, I think, be tedious with refpect to the Public, and unneceffary in itfelf.

As many perfons unverfed in controverfies on the fubject of religion (and I wifh I could not fay the fame of fome who are verfed in them,) will be apt to entertain a confufed notion about the *nature* and *importance* of the queftions that are here difcuffed, it may not be amifs to explain, with fome diftinctnefs, though

it

it fhould be pretty much at large,
what the nature and importance of
them really are, and to give our
readers a plain rule by which to form
a judgment in other cafes of a fimilar nature.

I muft affume as a maxim, that
the object and end of all *fpeculation*
is *practice*, and that, in matters of
religion, opinions are on no other
account worth contending for than
as they influence the heart and the
life. If this be allowed me, I think
I can eafily fatisfy my readers, that
they have no reafon to be alarmed
about the tendency or iffue of this
debate, notwithftanding all the cla-
mour it has, in different ages, and
even at prefent, excited.

That the general interefts of virtue will be effectually fecured by the
belief of a *fufficient recompence in a*
                                    *future*

*future life*, for all that has been well or ill done in this, will hardly be denied. Now this is equally taken for granted both by Dr. Price and myſelf. We even believe this day of recompence to take place at the fame period, viz. at the *general re-ſurrection* ; when " all that are in " the graves ſhall hear the voice of " the ſon of man, and ſhall ariſe; " ſome to the reſurrection of life, " and others to the reſurrection of " condemnation."

The advantage, therefore, that either of our ſchemes can have over the other, muſt ariſe principally from the truth and conſiſtency of ſuch opinions as are uſed in ſupport of the great doctrine of future retribution ; on which account one of us may be ſuppoſed to give a more firm and unwavering aſſent to that practical doctrine, and to be in leſs danger
of

of abandoning it. Or one fet of
opinions may be fuppofed to exhibit
our maker, or ourfelves, in a light
more proper to excite and keep up
a juft fenfe of devotion; confifting
of the fentiments of love, reverence
and truft in God, and alfo to imprefs the mind with a ftronger feeling
of benevolence towards our fellow
creatures.

It muft be added, alfo, that one
fet of moral and metaphyfical principles, by exhibiting every thing
about which we are converfant, and
to which our fpeculations can extend,
in fuch a manner as fhall imprefs the
mind with ideas of *fimplicity, com-
prehenfivenefs, fymmetry, beauty*, &c.
may give the mind more pleafure in
the contemplation of it, and confequently create a ftronger attachment
to it, and in fome meafure heighten
the finer feelings of virtue.

But

But thefe are matters in which the bulk of mankind have certainly very little to do; and as the effect of thefe views of things depends, in a great meafure, upon our own *per-fuafion* concerning them, it cannot be eafy to determine what fyftem of fpeculative opinions has the moft of thefe leffer advantages. We all claim them, and are too apt to think the fyftem of our adverfaries deftitute of them; fo much fo, that we often think it impoffible to contemplate it with any degree of fatisfaction, or without fenfations of pain and difguft. Now the *fact* of this perfuafion being generally *mutual* is a proof that there is a great deal of *imagination* in it. Why then fhould we difpute about thefe matters, with any other difpofition, than that with which we ufually difcufs other fubjects of *tafte*; and we do not quarrel with our neighbours if they happen

not

to think as favourably of our houfes, gardens, pictures, wives, or children, as we do ourfelves,

All that is worth confidering, therefore, in this cafe, is whether any cf the opinions contended for by Dr. Price and myfelf will, if proved to be falfe, weaken our faith in the great doctrine of a future ftate of retribution, or indifpofe the heart to the love of God or of man.

Having ftated thefe preliminaries, let us confider feparately the nature and effects of the different opinions we hold with refpect to the *penetra- bility of matter*, the *doctrine of the foul*, and of *philofophical neceffity*.

That matter has, or that it has not, the property of *impenetrability* has no afpect whatever with refpect to morals and theology ; but as matter

ter being fuppofed to be poffeffed of it, may be confidered as an argument againft its being endued with the properties of *perception* and *thought*, thofe different properties being apprehended to be incompatible

But I think it will be generally acknowledged, that there can be no objection to matter, as I defcribe and conceive of it, being capable of thought, fo that one fubftance may admit of all the properties of man; and its being favourable to this hypothefis is the circumftance that gives me a bias towards it: becaufe it is with reluctance that I can admit the intimate union and mutual action of two fubftances, fo different from one another as *matter* and *fpirit*, are defined to be, in the conftitution of *one being*, *i. e. man.* To fuppofe man to be *all matter*, or *all fpirit*, will, of itfelf, be allowed to be an advantage

tage in point of fpeculation, provided the thing itfelf be poffible, and
agreeable to appearances.

The proper advantage derived from
the doctrine of *a foul*, or the hypothefis of the perceptive and thinking powers of man refiding in a fubftance diftinct from his body, is
that it will not be affected by the
death of the body, but will pafs into
a ftate of recompence when the body
is in the grave. This doctrine is,
therefore, in fact, nothing more than
a provifion againft a failure in the
arguments for the fcripture doctrine
of the *refurrection of the dead*, and
confequently does not affect a chriftian, who, as fuch, firmly believes
that doctrine.

On the contrary, the doctrine of
a foul places the evidence of a future
life on a foundation quite different
from

from that on which revelation places it; which always reprefents the *re-furrection of the dead* (founded on the promife of God, confirmed by the refurrection of Chrift) as the object of all our future hopes, and never fuggefts the idea of the foul, or the percipient and active part of man, being in one place, and the body in another.

The doctrine of a foul is, indeed, generally reprefented as coming in aid of the chriftian doctrine of a future life, and that would be the cafe if it fupplied another argument for *the fame thing*; but here the things themfelves are different: for the confcious ftate of the *feparate foul* is not the refurrection of the *whole man*; and according to the fcripture, the rewards of virtue and the punifh-ments of vice do not *commence* till the day of judgment; fo that the chriftian

chriftian believes *one thing*, and the mere theift *another*.

This, however, has nothing to do with any thing in debate between Dr. Price and myfelf; the difference between us being chiefly this. He fuppofes that the powers of perception and thought refide in an immaterial fubftance, but that the exercife of thefe powers is made to depend on the organization of the body; whereas I fuppofe thefe powers to refide in the organized body itfelf, and therefore *muft* be fufpended till the time when the organization fhall be reftored. This I think can never be conceived to be a difference of much importance, all the *confequences* being the very fame.

The confideration that biafes me, as a chriftian, exclufive of philofophical confiderations, againft the
doctrine

doctrine of a feparate foul, is that it has been the foundation of what appears to me to be the very groffeft *corruptions of chriftianity*, and even of that very *antichriftianifm*, that began to work in the apoftles' times, and which extended itfelf fo amazingly and dreadfully afterwards ; I mean the oriental philofophy of the *pre-exiftence of fouls*, which drew after it the belief of the pre-exiftence and divinity of Chrift, the worfhip of Chrift and of dead men, and the doctrine of purgatory, with all the popifh doctrines and practices that are connected with them and fupported by them.

Among thefe I rank the doctrine of *atonement* for the fins of men by the fufferings or death of Chrift. For I think it will be allowed, that had Chrift never been confidered as any other than a *mere man* (though the

c                        moft

moſt diſtinguiſhed prophet, or meſ-
ſenger from God to man) it would
never have been imagined that his
ſufferings could have had the effect
that has been aſcribed to them, and
conſequently the doctrine of the proper *placability*, and *free-mercy* of
God would not have been impeached.
Alſo, what would it have ſignified
to contend for the tranſmutation of
bread and wine into the real body
and blood of Chriſt, if Chriſt had
been a mere man, and conſequently
his fleſh and blood nothing more
than the fleſh and blood of Moſes,
John the Baptiſt, or any other man.

As a *Chriſtian*, therefore, and a
*Proteſtant*, I am an enemy to the
doctrine of a ſeparate ſoul. One
who believes in a ſoul *may not*, but
one who diſbelieves that doctrine
*cannot* be, a papiſt. At the ſame time
I readily acknowledge that this bias
may

may carry a man too far, even to reject doctrines eſſential to chriſtianity,
though held by papiſts. But this
objection has no weight here.

I ſhall not enlarge upon this topic;
but it would be eaſy to ſhow, that
almoſt every thing that has been re-
preſented as moſt abſurd and miſ-
chievous in the faith of chriſtians,
and what, of courſe, has been the
cauſe, or pretence, of a great part
of the infidelity of the philoſophical
world, in the preſent age, muſt be
laid to the door of this one article.

It is evident, therefore, that a
chriſtian has, at leaſt, no reaſon to
be biaſſed in favour of the doctrine
of a ſoul, and may, without concern,
leave it to philoſophical diſcuſſion.

With thoſe who do not believe
the doctrine of an intermediate ſtate,

and

and myfelf, the difference between *a foul* and *no foul*, in my opinion, nearly vanifhes: for according to them, though it be a fubftance diftinct from the body, it is altogether incapable of fenfation, or action, but in conjunction with the body.

There only remains the doctrine of *neceſſity*, with refpect to which the difference of opinion between Dr. Price and me can be thought of much importance. But even here our difference of opinion is not fuch as to affect our expectation of a future ftate of retribution. For whatever we apprehend to be the *foundation* or *ground* of future recompence, we equally believe both the *fact* and the *propriety* of it. To me it feems fufficient, that men be *voluntary agents*, or that motives, fuch as hopes and fears, can influence them in a certain and mechanical manner, to

make

make it in the higheſt degree *right*,
and *wiſe* in the Divine Being to lay ſuch
motives before them, and conſequently to place them in a ſtate of moral
diſcipline, or a ſtate in which rewards
and puniſhments are diſtributed, ſo
as to correſpond to certain characters,
and actions.  By this means, and by
this means only, can his great object,
the happineſs of his intelligent off-
ſpring, be ſecured.  And one principal reaſon why I reject the doctrine of philoſophical liberty, is that
exactly in the degree in which we
ſuppoſe the mind *not* to be determined by motives, in that very degree do rewards and puniſhments
loſe their effect, and a man ceaſes to
be a proper ſubject of moral diſcipline,

At the ſame time that I ſecure
this great advantage, which is of a
practical nature, I think it is a con-

ſideration

fideration greatly in favour of the
doctrine of neceffity, that, according to it, all *effects*, even thofe dependent on the volitions of men,
have an *adequate caufe*, in their previous circumftances; which, being
known, a being of competent underftanding, may certainly forefee the
effect. On this fcheme therefore,
there is a fufficient provifion for a
plan of *univerfal providence*, comprehending all events whatever; every
thing being what God forefaw and
intended, and which muft iffue as
he wifhes it to iffue, *i. e.* as I fuppofe, in the greateft poffible happinefs of his creation.

Upon this fcheme, therefore, we
have, as it appears to me, every motive that can poffibly influence the
mind of man to exert ourfelves to
the utmoft, to promote our own
happinefs and the happinefs of others,

at

at the fame time that it lays the deepeſt foundation for the moſt intire fubmiſſion to the will of God, and an unbounded confidence in his affection and providential care, with reſpect to all things preſent, paſt, and future. It alſo, in my opinion, takes away all poſſible ground for envy and hatred towards men, and thus gives the freeeſt ſcope to the growth of univerſal benevolence, and of all virtue.

In the eye of Dr. Price, however, this ſcheme, great and glorious as it appears to me, wears a very different aſpect. He thinks we cannot juſtly be accountable for our conduct, and rewarded or puniſhed for it, unleſs we be, in his ſenſe of the word, *agents*, or the proper and ultimate cauſes of our own actions; that, therefore, ſince we are in a ſtate of diſcipline, and a future ſtate of retri-

bution

bution will take place, we muſt
be poſſeſſed of a power of proper
*ſelf-determination*, not ſubject to the
control of any being whatever ; and
that ſince God *does* govern the world,
and has frequently foretold events
dependent upon the volitions of men,
he muſt have a power, incomprehen-
ſible as it is to us, of foreſeeing *ſuch*
events.

This difference, however, though
real, and important, has nothing to
do with any thing that is within the
apprehenſion of the bulk of mankind. Nay the difference between
the doctrines of *liberty* and *neceſſity*
is what few writers appear truly to
have apprehended. No neceſſarian
denies that, in a ſufficiently proper
ſenſe, men have a power over their
own actions, ſo that they can do
what they pleaſe ; and that without
this power they could not be accountable

countable beings, or the proper fubjects of rewards or punifhments.

The charge of *Atheifm* has been
fo much hackneyed in religious controverfy, as to have paffed almoft
into ridicule. It was the common
charge againft the primitive chriftians, and has hardly ever failed to
be urged, on one pretence or other,
againft every man who has diffented
from the generally received faith.
But perhaps no character has fuffered
more generally, and at the fame
time more undefervedly on this account, than that of Mr. Hobbes;
who, notwithftanding his heterodoxy
in politics, appears to me, as far as
I can judge from fuch of his writings
as have fallen in my way, to have
been no atheift, but a fincere chriftian, and a confcientious good man.
See his Life in the *Biographia Bri-
tannica.*

This

The fame tremendous cry of atheifm has not failed to be echoed againft me alfo; but this cry has now been repeated fo often, that, like other echoes, the found is become feeble, and is by no means fo terrific as formerly. In this cafe I think there is fomething unufually abfurd and ridiculous in the charge; becaufe it fuppofes that lefs power is requifite to create and animate mere matter and even to make matter intelligent, than to give life and intelligence to a fpiritual and immaterial fubftance; that the former may ftart up into being of itfelf, but that the latter requires an author.

If I were difpofed to retort upon my adverfaries, I would fay that a man who believes that *one effect* may exift without a caufe (which I maintain to be the cafe with every perfon who denies the doctrine of neceffity)

ceffity) may believe that any *other*
effect, and confequently that *all*
effects may exift without a caufe,
and therefore that the *whole univerfe*
may have none. And what might
I not fay of the Scotch defenders of
the doctrine of *inflinctive principles
of truth*; who, difclaiming *argument*, reft this moft facred article of
all religion upon a fallacious *inflinct*;
and efpecially of Dr. Ofwald, who
even profeffedly, and at large, endeavours to invalidate the only proper
argument for the being of God, viz.
from effects to caufes, and to prove
it to be altogether inconclufive.

I am very far, however, from
charging either the oppugners of the
doctrine of neceffity, my Scotch opponents, or Dr. Ofwald himfelf, with
*actual atheifm*; becaufe, notwithftanding *atheiftical conclufions* may be
drawn from their principles, they
themfelves do not admit thofe conclufions,

clufions, and I am fatisfied that, were they convinced of the juftnefs of thofe conclufions, they would readily abandon the principles from which they were drawn. I claim the fame candid conftruction for myfelf that I allow to others. With the *reafonable*, and the *candid*, I fhall have it; and as to the *uncandid*, I thank God it is of little confequence, except to themfelves, in what light they confider me.

Dr. Price's letter to me at the clofe of this Introduction, and which he obligingly infifts upon my publifhing juft as he has fent it, fhews that *all* thofe who even differ from me the moft in thefe fpeculative points do not think fo ill of their neceffary effects, with regard to *character* and *morals*. Any teftimony of mine in his favour, in return, would be impertinent; or I fhould

cer-

certainly, having much more reafon for it, not exprefs lefs efteem and good-will for him than he has done for me. It is myfelf only, who avow fuch unpopular opinions, that ftand in need of fuch a teftimonial; and, on this account, it fhews confiderable *courage in friendfhip* to act as Dr. Price has done.

If he will allow me to fpeak fo freely, I would fay, that I fee no reafon for fo particular an *apology* as he makes for a feeming want of refpect in his manner of writing; as I really think he has nothing of this kind to apologize for. I am certain I might with more reafon apologize for the manner in which I have expreffed myfelf with refpect to him. But, in my opinion, it is perfectly confiftent with candour, and even with friendfhip, to exprefs the ftrongeft difapprobation of any *opinions*

*nions* whatever; and freely to fay that we think them *inconfiftent, contradictory*, or even *abfurd*, or *dangerous*, if, after an attentive confideration, they really do appear fo to us.

All that candour requires is, that we never impute to our adverfary a *bad intention*, or a *defign to miflead*, and alfo that we admit his *general good underftanding*, though liable to be mifled by unperceived biafes and prejudices, from the influences of which the wifeft and beft of men are not exempt. And where *particular friendfhip* is not concerned, there certainly are occafions that will juftify even great afperity, indignation or ridicule in controverfial writing. This is often the beft method of repreffing extreme conceit and arrogance, joined, as it often is, with as great weaknefs in fupporting a bad caufe,

caufe, even when there is no proper want of fincerity.

A man muft be very criminal in-deed, who can maintain what he, at the fame time, believes to be. ill-founded. There are very few, I hope, fo much abandoned. But there may be a great degree of guilt fhort of this. For the difpofition may be fo vitiated by a wrong bias, that the moft frivolous reafons fhall appear to have the force of demon-ftration, when a favourite hypothefis is concerned, and arguments, in them-felves the moft perfectly conclufive, fhall appear to have no weight at all when urged againft it. The truly candid will confider not the *manner* of writing only, but alfo the *oc-cafion* of it, and all the *circumftances* attending it. What can exceed the indignation and zeal with which Paul often writes, the feverity with
which

which the meek apoftle John expreffes himfelf, or the vehement in-
vectives even of our Saviour himfelf
on juft provocation.

The letters which I have addreffed to my other opponents are
written differently, according as I
felt myfelf difpofed towards them
at the time of writing. I do
not fufpect that any thing will be
objected to the manner in which
I have expreffed myfelf with refpect
to Dr. Kenrick, or Dr. Horfeley;
and my addrefs to Mr. Whitehead is,
I think, as refpectful as he deferves.
I had alfo addreffed a letter to the
anonymous author of *An Effay on
the immateriality and immortality of
the foul*; but as I could not help
treating him with a good deal of
levity and contempt, I was advifed
by my friends not to infert it in the
prefent publication, as not fuiting
the

the gravity with which the reft of the work is written.

Befides, I am not without hopes that this neglect may ferve to keep back other equally ignorant and felf-fufficient anfwerers, and thereby leave the field more open to the truly *able*, who are generally, at the fame time, the moft *candid*. And as the fubject is of great importance, I ftill profefs myfelf ready to argue it with any perfon who fhall appear to me to have ability, and learning equal to the difcuffion; and to fuch a one it would give me but little pain to make any conceffion, or retraction, that I might be convinced was neceffary. They muft, however, go on other ground than that of Dr. Price, who has certainly done all poffible juftice to his argument.

As

As the *Sheet of Illustrations*, sub-
joined to the *Disquisitions*, is frequently referred to in this work,
and as it is suspected that some of
the copies may have been sold without it, it is here reprinted, with
*additions*, written for the satisfaction
of some of my friends, who wished
me to discuss some questions that
they proposed to me.

It may be proper to observe, that
in this publication I confine myself
to the consideration of particular *objections* and *difficulties*; and that the
proper arguments in support of my
hypothesis are to be looked for in the
*Disquisitions on Matter and Spirit*,
and the *Treatise on Necessity*.

A LET-

## A
# L E T T E R

### F R O M

## Dr. P R I C E,

### T O

## Dr. P R I E S T L E Y.

NEWINGTON-GREEN, May 14, 1778.

DEAR SIR,

I AM obliged to you for fending me your laft replies. I have read them with a defire to be as open as poffible to conviction; and even not without wifhing for an opportunity of fhewing candour by retracting any miftakes into which I may have fallen. But more perhaps through

a fault in me, than in you, my views
and fentiments continue the fame.

I muſt leave you to manage the
publication as you pleaſe. You muſt
be fenſible that my *firſt remarks*
were written without the moſt dif-
tant view to publication; and this,
I hope, will be an excuſe for the
incorrectneſſes and want of order
which will be found in them. There
is alſo in ſome parts of theſe firſt
remarks, a turn of expreſſion which
carries an appearance not fufficiently
reſpectful; and which I ſhould have
avoided had I written them with a
view to publication, and been more
on my guard. I know your candour has engaged you to overlook
this, but I cannot reflect upon it
without ſome concern.

I

I fhall be very happy fhould this publication anfwer any valuable ends; but I am afraid the difcuffion it contains will be too dry and metaphyfical to be generally acceptable. Some good ends, however, it may probably anfwer. It will afford a proof that two perfons may differ totally on points the moft important and facred, with a perfect efteem for one another; and it may likewife give a fpecimen of a proper manner of carrying on religious controverfies. There is nothing that offends me more than that acrimony of fpirit with which controverfies in general, and particularly religious ones, are commonly conducted. In religion there is nothing fo effential as charity, candour, and benevolence. How inexcufable then is that cruel

d 3                              zeal

zeal which some religious people indulge; and how melancholy is it
to see them, in the very act of contending for religion, losing what is
most valuable in religion? Will you
give me leave, Sir, here to add,
that your opinions give a striking
proof of a truth, which, could it
be stamped on every human mind,
would exterminate all bigotry and
persecution; I mean the truth, that
worth of character, and true integrity, and consequently God's acceptance, are not necessarily connected with any particular set of
opinions. Many think yours to be
some of the most dangerous possible;
and yet the person who holds them is
known to be one of the best men in
the world; and I ardently wish my
soul may be united to his at the time
when

when *all that are in their graves
shall hear the voice of the son of man,
and come forth*; *they who have done
good to the resurrection of life, and
they who have done evil to the resurrection of damnation.* Our agreement in expecting this awful period
makes it of little confequence in what
we differ.

With great refpect and affection,

I am,

Dear Sir,

ever yours,

RICHARD PRICE.

# T A B L E

## O F

# C O N T E N T S.

## PART I.

*Of the* NATURE OF MATTER.

PART

SECOND

SECT.

ADVER-

# ADVERTISEMENT.

THE Reader has been already informed *(Introduction* p. 36) that a great part of the following Remarks (to p. 178) has been written by Dr. PRICE, without any view to publication. He thinks it neceſſary to add here, that his ADDITIONAL OBSERVA-TIONS (from p. 327 to 359) are the reſult of a deliberate review of the whole con-troverſy, as it had been previouſly printed; and have, therefore, been compoſed, with more care and attention. This controverſy having been made too prolix, he has left every perſon to judge for himſelf, of the force of Dr. PRIESTLEY's Replies to theſe Additional Obſervations, (from p. 363, to p. 405) chuſing to take leave with the ſhort Note at the end of this volume.

# REMARKS

### BY

## Dr. PRICE

### ON SEVERAL PASSAGES IN

## Dr. PRIESTLEY's

### DISQUISITIONS ON MATTER AND SPIRIT.

### WITH

## Dr. PRIESTLEY's REPLIES.

## PART I.

# PART I.

*Remarks concerning* THE PENETRABILITY
OF MATTER.

## THE FIRST COMMUNICATION.

D R. Prieſtley obſerves in *Diſquiſitions,*
(page 2, 3) " *that it is aſſerted that*
" *matter is neceſſarily ſolid, and of itſelf deſti-*
" *tute of all powers whatever, as thoſe of at-*
" *traction and repulſion, &c. or that matter*
" *is poſſeſſed of a* VIS INERTIÆ, *and indif-*
" *ferent to reſt or motion but as it is acted*
" *upon by a foreign power——I do not won-*
" *der* (adds Dr. Prieſtley) *that the vulgar*
" *ſhould have formed theſe notions, &c.*"

## DR. PRICE's Remark,

That matter is *inert,* or that it will continue in that ſtate of reſt or motion which
it poſſeſſes till ſome foreign cauſe alters that
ſtate ; and that this alteration of ſtate muſt
be in proportion to the impreſſed force, &c.
Theſe poſitions are the foundation of all

that

that is demonſtrated by natural philoſophers concerning the laws of the colliſion of bodies. They are, in particular, the foundation of Sir *Iſaac Newton*'s Philoſophy. The three laws of motion with which he begins his *Principia* have no meaning, or evidence, if they are only *vulgar prejudices.* To me they appear to be *ſelf-evident truths*———" That matter is " of itſelf deſtitute of all powers" may be ſaid with much more truth of matter according to Dr. Prieſtley's ideas of it, than of matter according to the common ideas. *Solid* matter has the power of acting on other matter by impulſe, and the effects of this *action*, in all caſes, have been demonſtrated by mathematicians, particularly in the *laws of* motion, and the corollaries, at the beginning of the *Principia.* But unſolid matter, that is, matter which admits other matter into its place without reſiſtance, cannot act at all by impulſe; and this is the only way in which it is capable of acting.—See the next, and ſome of the following remarks.

ANSWER.

ANSWER, *by* DR. PRIESTLEY.

All the laws relating to what has been called the *collifion of bodies* are neceffarily the very fame, whether their feparation from each other be fuppofed to take place at the point of contact, or at any given diftance from it, occafioned by a power of repulfion, extending fo far beyond the real furface. The *laws of motion* are only general rules, to which the facts relating to the approach of bodies to each other, and their receding from each other, are reducible, and are confiftent with any *caufe* of fuch approaching or receding.

Unfolid matter is here faid to admit other matter into its place *without refiftance*; but this is directly contrary to the hypothefis, which makes matter to be a fubftance, which, though penetrable, is poffeffed of a power of repulfion, which, if an approaching body be not able to overcome, effectually prevents it from coming into its place. If it was not poffible for matter to act but by impulfe,

A 3                              it

it could not be true that rays of light are reflected from bodies at a diftance from their furfaces, which Sir Ifaac Newton has fhewn to be the fact.

## Dr. Price.

*Difquifitions*, p. 4. " The refiftance of " matter is never occafioned by its *folidity*, " but by a *power of repulfion*, always acting " at a real diftance from the body."

But fuppofe it folid, or impenetrable, in the common fenfe, could we not conceive of its being brought into contact with other matter; and would there not then be refiftance, and action? Does Dr. Prieftley here mean that one particle of matter can act upon another without contact and impulfe; or in other words, that matter can, *by its own proper agency*, attract or repel other matter which is at a diftance from it? If this is true, a maxim hitherto univerfally received muft be falfe, That *nothing can act where it is not*. If matter can act at the leaft diftance from itfelf, it may at the greateft.

Sir

Sir Ifaac Newton, in his letters to Dr. Bentley, calls the notion that matter poffeffes an innate power of attraction, or that it can act upon matter at a diftance, and attract and repel by its own agency, " an " abfurdity into which, he thought, no " one could poffibly fall."—Shall I here beg leave to refer to what I have written on this fubject in the *Differtations on Providence?* (p. 39, &c.)

## ANSWER.

I do not fay that, fuppofing matter to have folidity, it could not act upon other matter by impulfe; but that there is no evidence *from fact*, that refiftance is ever occafioned by any thing abfolutely impenetrable. It is undeniable, that, in *all known cafes*, refiftance is owing to fome *other caufe*, and therefore it is contrary to the acknowledged rules of philofophizing to fuppofe refiftance in *any cafe* to be owing to this caufe.

The difficulty refpecting matter *acting where it is not* is precifely the fame, whe-

A 4                              ther

ther it be fuppofed to be penetrable or impenetrable. Let any perfon explain how
it is that the fun acts upon the earth, or
how the parts of folid bodies are kept at a
diftance from each other *upon any hypothefis.*
For a more particular difcuffion of this
fubject, I refer the reader to the fheet of
*Illuftrations,* fubjoined to the *Difquifitions.*

At the clofe of this remark, Dr. Price
refers me to his *Differtations on Providence*.
(p. 39, &c.) I have read the whole paffage
with care, but find nothing in it that appears to me to bear harder upon my hypothefis than on the common one. For it
only fhows, though in a very clear and
mafterly manner, that the prefent laws of
nature require an *intelligence,* and an *energy,*
of which what we ufually call matter is
not capable. Now I certainly admit an
intelligent and active caufe in nature, and
have no objection to fuppofing that this intelligent caufe has even more to do in the
execution of the laws of nature than Dr.
Price is willing to allow.

Dr. Price.

## DR. PRICE.

*Difquifitions,* p. 14. " The particles of
" light never impinge on any folid parts in
" paffing through glafs, &c." How does
this appear? All the light never paffes
through glafs. Part of it probably im-
pinges, and is loft. This was Sir Ifaac
Newton's opinion. *Opticks,* p. 241.

## ANSWER.

That the particles of light never impinge
on the folid part of glafs, &c. is evident
from none of them being obferved to be
deflected from their courfe after they have
entered it, provided the fubftance be perfectly tranfparent. Newton's fuppofition
of particles of light being loft by their
impinging on the folid particles of bodies, is neither probable in itfelf, nor coun-
tenanced by any *fact.* The moft probable
effect of fuch impinging would be a re-
flexion, and not a ceffation of motion.

DR. PRICE.

## Dr. Price.

*Difquifitions,* p. 17. " *Matter has in*
" *fact no properties but thofe of attraction*
" *and repulfion.*"

This is frequently afferted in the courfe
of thefe *Difquifitions;* and matter is de-
clared to be nothing but *powers.* And yet
in p. 25, the property of *extenfion* is exprefsly afcribed to matter, *by which it occupies a certain portion of fpace.* And in
p. 19, it is faid to confift of *phyfical points*
only, (that is, fmall parts of extenfion)
*endued with powers of attraction and re-
pulfion taking place at different diftances——*
This is not confiftent; but let us examine
it particularly, and confider what matter is.

Matter, if it be any thing at all, muft
confift of folid particles or atoms occupying a certain portion of fpace, and therefore *extended,* but at the fame time *fimple*
and *uncompounded,* and incapable of being
refolved into any other fmaller particles;
and it muft be the different form of thefe
*primary* particles and their different com-
binations

binations and arrangement that conftitute
the different bodies and kinds of matter in
the univerfe——This feems to have been
Sir Ifaac Newton's idea of matter.   See his
*Opticks*, p. 375, &c.

Mr. Baxter's notion that thefe particles
are themfclves compofed of other particles
which cohere by divine agency; and,
for the fame reafon, thefe others of
others ftill fmaller which cohere by the
fame caufe, and fo on; this notion
appears to me abfurd.   According to
the account juft given, each of thefe particles is a *monad*, or a *folid continuum*, void
of pore, and, as fuch, endued with refiftance and impenetrability, and capable of
receiving and communicating motion by
impulfe, according to the laws of collifion
explained by *Keil*, *Newton*, and others.

If this is not a right account, then matter
muft be either *mere* extenfion; or it muft
be fomething more, which is entirely unknown to us.   If the former is true, then
matter is nothing but fpace.   Inftead of
having

having pores, it is all pore. Like fpace, it muft be neceffary and infinite, and a vacuum muft be impoffible. This was Defcartes's notion of matter, and alfo Spinoza's, who has founded upon it a fyftem of atheifm.

On the other hand, if it is afferted that the elementary parts of matter have in them fomething more than extenfion, but that this fomething, not being *folidity*, is unknown to us, it will follow, that, being ignorant what matter is, we cannot reafon about it, or determine any more concerning it than that, wanting folidity, it is incapable of acting or re-acting in any way on other matter.

It muft not be faid, that the property which matter has more than extenfion, is a power of attracting and repelling. This would be faying that void fpace attracts and repels. Befides, it has been fhewn that the particles of matter cannot, according to any conception of them, have fuch a power. When two particles not in contact, are faid to attract one another, all that is meant, is, that there is fome force that

drives

drives them towards one another, according to a certain law. That force, it is
certain, cannot be their own force, for
the reafon already affigned. It muft then
be the *impulfe* of furrounding particles, or
(if that is not poffible) fome other *foreign*
force. The power; therefore, of attraction
and repulfion afcribed to matter, is demonftrably a *foreign* property. I fay *demonftrably*; for nothing can be demonftrated,
if a pofition can be falfe which is implied
in a maxim fo clear as that, " nothing
" can act where it is not."

In fhort. Matter, according to the idea
of it into which I am enquiring, being
an *unknown extended fomething* which makes
no oppofition to any thing that would take
its place, and not being capable of acting
beyond the fpace which it occupies, can have
no powers. It can be of no ufe. It is as
fuperfluous in nature as Dr. Prieftley in
p. 65, &c. reprefents matter to be according to Mr. Baxter's account—But more
than this may be faid. From Dr. Prieftley's
account of matter it may be inferred, not
only that it is of no ufe, but that it muft
be

be a *non-entity*. It has, he afferts repeatedly, no other property than the power of attracting and repelling; and the argument in *Difquifitions*, p. 5 and 6, obliges him to affert this. But it has been proved that this is a property that cannot belong to it. It muft, therefore, be *nothing*.

Let it, however, be allowed the property of *extenfion*. If not *mere* extenfion, it muft be fomething that has fhape and form, and is circumfcribed within a certain portion of fpace. It muft, therefore, confift of parts. Thefe parts muft be held together by fome power; and the fame muft be true of the *parts* of thefe *parts*, and fo on. But we cannot go on thus *in infinitum*. The exiftence of matter, therefore, is impoffible,

Should it be faid in anfwer to this, that the primitive particles of matter may be extended and figured, and yet not be divifible, or want any attracting force to keep them from refolving themfelves into nothing. Should this be faid, I will fay the fame of

a *folid*

a *solid continuum*, or the *monads* which
conftitute matter, and the argument in *Difquifitions*, p. 5, &c. will be overthrown.

But to return to the affertion that matter
has no other property than the power of
attraction and repulfion. All power is the
power of fomething. What is that fomething in the prefent cafe ?—Is it a power of
attraction and repulfion only that perceives,
thinks, reafons, &c. Is it only powers that
circulate in our veins, vibrate in the nerves,
revolve round the fun, &c.—I will add
what feems particularly worth Dr. Prieftley's confideration. According to his own
fyftem, the attraction and repulfion of matter, (performed with a fkill that gives the
world its order and beauty) cannot be its
own actions. They muft be the effects of
fome action upon it. But of what action
are they effects ? Let this be explained.
If the effects of fuch action as that of ideas
and motives on confcious and thinking
beings, then fince all matter attracts and
repels, all matter muft be confcious and
intelligent.

ANSWER.

## Answer.

It is very poffible that, in defining matter in different places in a large treatife, with a view to different objects, I may fometimes have omitted fome particulars, to which it was not then neceffary to attend. The complete definition is evidently this, viz. that *matter is an extended fubftance, poffeffed of certain powers of attraction and repulfion.*

That " matter wanting folidity muft be " incapable of acting or re-acting in any " way on other matter" cannot be afferted, without taking it for granted, that a fubftance defined as matter is defined above, is in itfelf impoffible. Now, it is rather extraordinary, that the only *proof* of impenetrability fhould be *actual impulfe,* and yet that no clear cafe of actual impulfe can be affigned ; and that a definition of matter framed purpofely to correfpond to *facts only,* fhould be deemed impoffible, that is, *contrary to fact.*

The reafoning in this remark goes upon the idea that matter muft be nothing at all, if it have not the property of *impenetrability,*

*bility*, a property which no one fact requires, and therefore which ought not to be admitted by any philofopher. It alfo feems to have arifen from a want of confidering, that the term *thing*, or *fubftance*, fignifies nothing more than that to which properties are afcribed, and is itfelf abfolutely unknown, and incapable of fuggefting any idea whatever. For when we exclude all properties, we, at the fame time, exclude from our minds all idea of fubftance, and have nothing left to contemplate. Thus, a mafs of gold is defined to be a fubftance of a certain length, breadth, and thicknefs, of a certain colour, weight, &c. But take away all colour, weight, length, breadth, thicknefs, with every other fenfible quality, and where is the fubftance of the gold? Impenetrability is only a property, or fomething that is *affirmed* concerning material fubftances, and therefore muft not be affirmed without proof, any more than penetrability, or any other property. Now what I demand, is, *a proof from fact*, that any material fubftance is impenetrable to other material fubftances. Till this be

B                          produced,

produced, I cannot, as a philofopher, admit
that matter has fuch a property. On the
contrary, analogy obliges me to fuppofe,
that, fince all the evidence of bodies being
impenetrable, when rigoroufly examined,
*i. e.* by actual experiments, (as optical, elec-
trical, &c.) appear to be cafes in which
bodies are prevented from coming into
actual contact by *powers,* acting at a diftance
from their furfaces, that *all* refiftance is of
this kind only.

If the reafoning in the laft part of this
remark be juft, it will not follow that, becaufe all the powers of matter may be ana-
lized into modes of attraction and repulfion,
all particular fubftances muft have the very
*fame modes* of attraction and repulfion, and
confequently that there is no difference between *acids* and *alkalis, metals* and *earths,* &c.
The powers of perception and thought, in
how great a degree foever they be unknown
to us, may be the refult of a certain ftate of
the brain, and certain motions taking place
within it, though they could not refult
from

from matter of a different form, texture, or confiftence.

## DR. PRICE.

*Difquifitions*, page 81 and 104. *Matter has no other powers than thofe of attraction and repulfion*.

What is it that attracts and repels, and that is attracted and repelled? Till I am informed of this, no more is told me of matter, than would be told me of the inhabitants of *Jupiter*, by faying that they have no other powers than thofe of *moving* (or rather *being moved*) *to* and *from* one another. And to make the idea of matter to confift in being thus moved; or to fay, that it has no other power or property, and at the fame time to afcribe to it the powers of thought, fenfation and reafon—This feems to me indeed extraordinary—How totally different are attraction and repulfion from perception, confcioufnefs and judgment? What connexion can there be between them?

B 2              ANSWER.

### Answer.

It is impoffible to know more of matter than can be inferred from the *phenomena* in which it is concerned. The relation that attractions and repulfions bear to feveral modes of thought, may be feen in *Hartley's Obfervations on Man.* But though the *mode* of the connection be ever fo much unknown, the *reality* of the connexion is evident from fact. Perception, and all the modes of thinking, as much depend upon the brain, as the power of giving a blow to a ftick. Is not the *reality* of the union of the foul and body, on the common hypothefis, always afferted, without any perfon pretending to have the leaft idea of the *mode* of fuch an union?

### Dr. Price.

Page 105. " When we attempt to form
" an idea of the fubftance of matter ex-
" clufive of the powers of attraction and
" repulfion which it has, and exclufive of
                    " impenetrability

" impenetrability which it has not, ab-
" folutely nothing is left"—This is very
true, and the juft conclufion from it is,
that matter does not exift.

Exclufive of attraction and repulfion, it
is here faid, matter is abfolutely nothing.
But it has been demonftrated that it does
not attract and repel, therefore it muft be
nothing.  Befides, allow it the power of
attracting and repelling, yet if, as here afferted, it is nothing but this power, it
muft be the power of nothing, and the very
idea of it is a contradiction—What a ftrange
thing indeed is matter according to Dr.
Prieftley's ideas ? Its effence, it feems, confifts in impelling (without touching, or exerting any force that is conceivable) other
matter, *towards* itfelf and *from* itfelf,  Take
this away ; fet it at reft, or remove its
neighbours, fo as that it may have nothing
to act upon, and it becomes nothing.  The
whole of it may be crouded into the very
fpace that is now occupied by the fmalleft
of its component parts, or into any compafs not fo little as a mathematical point,

and in confequence of this, having nothing to attract or repel it would be nothing.

### ANSWER.

What a ftrange thing, indeed, is matter, according to Dr. Price's conftruction of my meaning; but fuch matter as he here defcribes I never had in contemplation. The matter of which I treat is a fubftance poffeffed of certain powers of attraction and repulfion. Thefe powers may be exerted more or lefs, or not at all, according to circumftances. To matter thus defined I cannot conceive that any of thefe remarks do in the leaft apply.

### A QUERY BY DR. PRICE.

If matter is not folid extenfion, what is it more than mere extenfion?

### ANSWER.

If, as Dr. Clarke and Dr. Price fuppofe, *Spirit* be extended, but not folid, what is
*that*

*that* more than mere extenfion? If Spirit can act upon matter, as they fuppofe, it muft have the very power of attraction and repulfion with refpect to matter that I afcribe to unfolid matter. If they chufe to call my matter by the name of *Spirit*, I have no fort of objection. All that I contend for is fuch a *conjunction of powers in the fame thing*, or fubftance, by whatever term it be denominated, as we find by experience always go together, fo as not to multiply fubftances without neceffity,

THE

B 4

THE SECOND COMMUNICATION.

OF THE NATURE OF MATTER, *containing Remarks by Dr.* Price *on Dr.* Prieftley's *Replies to the* firft Communication; *with Dr.* Prieftley's fecond *Replies.*

DR. PRICE's *Obfervations on the Reply,* p. 5.

THE laws of the collifion of bodies, as determined by mathematicians, relate to two forts of bodies; *elaftic* and *unelaftic.* The laws which govern the collifions of the latter fuppofe no repulfion between them; and are founded entirely on the confideration of matter as *folid* extenfion, and confequently *inert,* and endowed with all thofe properties expreffed by Sir Ifaac Newton in his three laws of motion—The laws alfo which govern the collifions of the latter fort of bodies, fuppofe matter to poffefs folidity, or a *momentum* in moving, proportioned to its

quantity

quantity and velocity, independent of its
power of repulfion—For example, When
an elaftic body at reft is ftruck by another
equal elaftic body, the effect of the collifion
will be that the latter will lofe its whole
motion, and the other move forward with
the very velocity which the impelling body
poffeffed before collifion. But if both
bodies were void of folidity, or nothing but
figured and moveable extenfions repelling
one another, the impelling body would
move *back*, and the other would move *forward* as foon as they began to repel one
another. It would be impoffible for them
to enter into the fphere of one another's
repulfion, becaufe they wanted that *folidity*
which gives *momentum*.

It is not, in my opinion, confiftent with
Dr. Prieftley's own fyftem to intimate (as
he feems to do in the paffages in his
*Difquifitions*, to which I have referred in
my firft remark) that " matter poffeffes
" powers", and that it is a vulgar error
to think it " indifferent to reft or motion
" but as it is acted upon by fome fo-
" reign caufe." If matter can move without

out being acted upon by a foreign caufe, it
muft move itfelf; but this Dr. Prieftley
cannot allow. He muft, therefore, fay
that it is entirely a torpid and paffive thing.
This, without doubt, is the matter which
is the object of natural philofophy: and it
is this property that, in my opinion, forms
one of the fundamental differences between it and fpirit.

When I fay that *unfolid* matter will admit
other matter into its place " without re-
" fiftance," I mean, " without any re-
" fiftance given by itfelf;" and I fuppofe
*contact*, which Dr. Prieftley muft grant to
be at leaft *conceivable*. The refiftance arifing from repulfion, being always made at a
diftance, is not the refiftance of the matter
itfelf that is faid to repel, but of fome
foreign caufe: and this I apprehend to be
juft as certain as that nothing can act on
another thing without being prefent to it.
When a ray of light is reflected from a body
*before* contact, it is certainly not that body
itfelf that reflects the light: nor did Sir
Ifaac Newton, who difcovered the fact, ever
mean

mean to affert this; on the contrary, he
has called this an abfurdity which no one
can receive. He profeffes to have difcovered
only certain facts in the conftitution of
nature : the caufes he has left others to inveftigate.

## Answer.

I cannot conceive any difference between
the cafe of *elaftic* and *non-elaftic* bodies, with
refpect to the hypothefis in queftion ; fince
whatever may be fuppofed concerning the
parts of a *folid*, may be faid concerning
that *fphere of repulfion*, which, on the new
hypothefis, is to be fubftituted in the place
of fuch folid parts. It is denied that folidity is neceffary to give *momentum*, fince a
fphere of refiftance may, in certain circumftances, be as impenetrable as any fuppofed
folid fubftance. It is not folidity, but the
*refiftance* occafioned by it that is the immediate caufe of *momentum*.

I readily admit the inaccuracy that Dr.
Price obferves. But I could not mean to give
to a ftone the felf-determining power which
I had

I had denied to man. My meaning through the whole was, that matter, to be what it is, muſt be poſſeſſed of what has been denominated a *power*, viz. attraction, eſpecially that of coheſion. All that I mean by a repulſion at a diſtance from the ſurface of a body, is, that which Sir Iſaac Newton proves to be the caſe with reſpect to light; ſo that whatever ſolution may be found for the difficulty in his caſe, will ſerve for mine. His too is the caſe of an elaſtic ſubſtance.

Dr. Price's *Obſervations on the Reply*, p. 7, 8.

Dr. *Prieſtley*, in his *Illuſtrations*, (ſee the *Diſquiſitions*, p. 350.) ſays, that *Newton* conſidered attraction and repulſion as " pow-
" ers inhering *in* and properly belonging *to*
" matter." With great deference to Dr. Prieſtley's ſuperior knowledge on this ſubject, I would obſerve, that I have never met with any aſſertion in Sir Iſaac Newton's works that can be fairly conſtrued to imply this; and that it is ſcarcely poſſible that he ſhould have uſed any expreſſions which will bear this interpretation, except when

ſpeaking

fpeaking loofely, and by way of accommo-
dation to vulgar conceptions. I have quoted
a paffage from the letters that paffed between him and Dr. Bentley, in which he
fays the contrary very ftrongly. In the
fame letters he fays to Dr. Bentley, " Pray
" don't afcribe the notion of *innate* gravity
" to me." And, in an advertifement prefixed to his *Treatife on Optics*, he informs
the public, that he had, in the fecond
edition of this treatife, added a queftion
concerning the caufe of gravity, on purpofe
to fhew that he did not take it to be an
effential property of bodies. And what he
thought of the attraction or gravitation of
matter he certainly thought likewife of its
repulfion; and would have acknowledged
concerning the repulfion of that æther
which (merely in the way of conjecture
and illuftration) he has fuppofed to be the
caufe of gravity.

Dr. Prieftley here takes notice of the difficulty there is in accounting for the attractions and repulfions of bodies on *any*
*hypothefis*. But the maxim that " nothing
" can

" can act where it is not," proves more than a difficulty in this cafe. It proves that fince thefe attractions and repulfions are always performed at a diftance, and fometimes the *greateſt* diftance from the furfaces of bodies, it is impoffible they fhould be the actions of the bodies themfelves; and confequently, that they are not properties inhering in bodies; or that belong to the nature of matter as matter.

If nothing can act where it is not, matter cannot attract or repel where it is not. It cannot, therefore, have the *power* of attraction and repulfion : and it muft be an abfurdity to include fuch a power in the definition of it; or to make it *an eſſential property* of matter. In fhort, this feems to me the fame abfurdity, that it would be to afcribe to man actions done by a higher order of beings; and when it is afked what he is, to defcribe or define him by thefe.

No light (fee p. 9.) that falls perpendicularly on an uniform tranfparent furface can be deflected in paffing through it. But
how

how does it appear that any fubftance can be made fo tranfparent as to ftop *none* of the light that enters it?

Dr. Price's *Obfervations on Reply*, p. 16.

What has been faid under the laft head is all I would fay with refpect to the firft part of this *Reply*. As to the latter part of it, I would obferve, that we afcribe impenetrability or folidity to matter partly becaufe we find that we never can make one body occupy the place of another without removing it. The reafon of this appears indeed in fome inftances to be, that they repel one another: but in moft inftances no fuch repulfion appears: and the true reafon may be, that they are brought into contact, and will not penetrate one another in confequence of that effential property which we call *folidity*, and which we find ourfelves under a neceffity of afcribing to matter, in order to diftinguifh it from *mere extenfion*, or void fpace. Even in the collifions of elaftic bodies, the probability is, that there is contact and impulfe; and that the reafon of their flying off from one

another,

another, or rebounding, is, that their parts, by impinging, are bent inwards, and afterwards unbent: agreeably to the reaſonings of natural philoſophers. I am, however, of opinion, that we derive our ideas of the ſolidity of bodies, not ſo much from experience, as from another more important inlet of ideas, which I have endeavoured to explain in the firſt chapter of my *Treatiſe on Morals*. But I may be very wrong: and I refer all my diſquiſitions on theſe and other ſubjects, to the candid attention of thoſe who may think it worth their while to conſider them.

When I ſay that " Matter wanting ſo-
" lidity muſt be incapable of acting, or re-
" acting on other matter," I mean, by any action of its own. Two equal ſolid bodies moving towards one another in contrary directions, and with equal velocities, will meet and impinge and ſtop one another: but if *unſolid* they would not act at all on one another, but paſs through one another, juſt as if there had been nothing in their way. Dr. Prieſtley, in a ſubſequent reply, (ſee P. 22) ſays,

fays, if I underftand him, that matter fometimes neither attracts nor repels " according
" to circumftances." It is of *fuch* matter
I here fpeak.—Sir Ifaac Newton calls that
*vis inertiæ* and *folidity*, which he fays experience teaches us to afcribe to all bodies,
even the minuteft, *the foundation of all philofophy*. See his comment on his third rule
of philofophizing.

### Dr. Price's *Obfervations on Reply*, p. 22.

In the paffage which has occafioned the
remark to which Dr. Prieftley makes this
reply, it is faid, that matter without the
power of attraction and repulfion is nothing;
and in p. 5, &c. he afferts, that this power is
neceffary to the very being of matter. I
muft infift upon it that matter cannot poffefs
this power; and that, confequently, according to Dr. Prieftley's account of matter,
it is *nothing*. Let it be as clearly proved
that matter cannot poffefs *folidity*, and I
will fay the fame of my own account of
matter.

C       Dr.

Dr. Prieftley, in this reply, feems to acknowledge that, in particular circumftances, matter neither attracts nor repels : and it is very obvious that there muft be fuch circumftances ; how then can attraction and repulfion be its effential property ? Would not one think that if it is effential to it to attract, it cannot be alfo effential to it to repel ? What is matter when it neither attracts nor repels, different from void fpace ? I wifh for a direct anfwer to this queftion. How does matter know *when*, and *where*, and with *what precife degree of force*, at different diftances, to attract and repel other matter ? Or were there a poffibility of its being *knowing* enough for this, how can it have the *power*, when perhaps the matter it is faid to act upon, is at the diftance of millions of miles from it ? Even the Deity knows all things, and acts upon all things, only by being prefent with all things. " Deus eft om-
" niprefens (fays Newton at the end of
" the *Principia*) non per *virtutem* folam,
" fed per *fubftantiam ;* nam *virtus* fine *fub-*
" *ftantia* fubfiftere non poteft." But I have
perhaps

perhaps repeated thefe arguments too often :
and however decifive they appear to me, I
am afraid Dr. Prieftley will think I mean
to teaze him, and to wrangle with him.
But I am as far as poffible from having any
fuch intention.

I am glad to learn from his Reply (p. 8.)
that he approves of the reafoning I have
ufed in the *Differtation on Providence,* to
prove that the laws of nature are derived
from an intelligence, and a conftant energy,
of which matter is not capable.   With this
is connected a truth the moft important and
joyful of all truths : I mean, that there
exifts an All-wife Providence, or a benevolent and perfect direction of all events.
Our agreement in thefe things fhould make
us regard lefs our differences on other
points.

In anfwer to a query of mine which follows this reply, Dr. Prieftley afks, p. 22,
" If *fpirit* be extended, what is it more than
" mere extenfion ?" I anfwer, confcioufnefs,
perception, thought, &c. If this is likewife what matter is *more* than mere ex-

tenſion, then *matter* and *ſpirit* are the ſame ;
and our controverſy is at an end.   But the
truth ſeems to be, that not extenſion, but
ſolidity, inertneſs, figure, diſceptibility, &c.
are the properties which diſtinguiſh matter :
and that, on the contrary, ſenſation, perception, ſimplicity, ſelf - determination,
judgment, &c. are the properties which
diſtinguiſh ſpirit.   I am entirely in the
dark with reſpect to the *extenſion* of ſpirit,
and therefore chuſe to enter into no diſpute
about it.   All I am ſure of, is, that it poſſeſſes locality.   The *manner* I do not comprehend.

### A N S W E R.

If certain effects invariably take place in
any caſe in which bodies are concerned, as
on their mutual approach when placed at a
given diſtance, the analogy of language requires us to ſay, that thoſe bodies are poſſeſſed of the power of approaching or attracting one another.   But by ſaying that
bodies have certain properties, philoſophers,
I apprehend, only mean to expreſs the unknown cauſe of the known effects.   As to
real

real *agency*, a neceffarian can allow of no
more than one proper feat or fource of it.

If, in any cafe, " no light can be de-
" flected in paffing through an uniformly
" tranfparent fubftance", whether we can
by art make it perfectly fo or not, (p. 5.)
it is all that my hypothefis requires.

By matter attracting, or not attracting,
I could only mean, either that, in certain
circumftances, attraction and repulfion may
be fo balanced, as that no effect would be
apparent, or that leaving out the confideration of attraction of cohefion, there
might be no foreign body to be attracted.
Take away all attraction of cohefion, and
let any perfon fay whether any thing will
be left to correfpond to our common definition of matter, which is my ground for
faying that, in that cafe, it will *ceafe to be*.
There would, in that cafe, be an actual
divifion *in infinitum*. Attraction and repulfion may be, and probably are, in reality,
the fame power; and fome philofophers
are

are inclined to think it to be the one, and some the other.

As to the queſtion to which Dr. Price requires a direct anſwer, viz. " How mat-" ter can *know* when and where to act," I reply, that the anſwer will be the very ſame as to this queſtion : How do the rays of light, or the bodies to which they approach, know at what diſtance they are to begin to recede from each other ? Whatever ſhall be deemed a ſufficient cauſe in this caſe, I ſhall admit to be ſufficient in the other. In my hypotheſis I only mean to combine known *facts*, without entering into the doctrine of *cauſes*.

Dr. Price ſays, that beſides extenſion, ſpirit is poſſeſſed of *conſciouſneſs*, *perception*, &c. I anſwer, that beſides extenſion body poſſeſſes a power of attraction, &c. He ſays, take away attraction, and what is *body* but mere extenſion ; I alſo ſay, take away conſciouſneſs, perception, &c. and what is *ſpirit* but mere extenſion ?

THE

---

### THE THIRD COMMUNICATION.

OF THE NATURE OF MATTER, *contain-ing Remarks by Dr.* Price *on Dr.* Prieft-ley's *Replies in the* Second Commu-nication, (p. 27 and 36.) *with Dr.* Prieftley's *third Replies.*

MATTER that is not folid is the fame with *pore:* it cannot therefore poffefs what natural philofophers mean by the *momentum,* a *force of bodies,* which is always in proportion to the quantity of matter in bodies, void of pore. *Momentum* is the caufe of refiftance, and not *vice verfa.*

I muft here repeat (fee p. 36, 37, &c.) the following propofitions, which I think have been demonftrated; that matter has not the power of attracting and repelling—That this power is the power of fome foreign

C 4                              caufe,

caufe, acting upon matter according to ftated laws—and that, confequently, attraction and repulfion, not being actions, much lefs inherent qualities of matter, it ought not to be defined by them.

## Answer.

I by no means allow, that though matter have not the property called *folidity*, or *impenetrability*, it muft be all *pore*, *i. e.* have no properties at all, or be nothing but empty fpace. If fo, it would follow that *no fubftance* deftitute of folidity can be any thing at all. Even every thing that has been called *fpirit* would be a non-entity.

If what Dr. Price calls fpirit, a fubftance without folidity, and confequently without *momentum*, can neverthelefs act upon bodies; *e. g.* the brain, furely the fubftances that I term material, though they be not impenetrable, may have the fame power with refpect to each other.

Article

Article II.  Every thing that exifts muft be defined by its properties, or to fpeak more exactly, by the circumftances refpecting it.  Thus if I defcribe a magnet, I muft mention, as peculiar and *belonging* to it, the kinds of attraction and repulfion that take place when it is introduced, whether thofe attractions and repulfions, ftrictly fpeaking, neceffarily accompany it, or be caufed by the Deity, or fome intermediate unknown agent.

THE

---

THE FOURTH COMMUNICATION.

OF THE NATURE OF MATTER, *by Dr.*
Price, *with Dr.* Prieftley's *Anfwer.*

IT is, in my opinion, particularly in-
cumbent on Dr. Prieftley, to give a
more explicit anfwer than he has yet given
to the queftion, " What the true idea of
" matter is ?" or " what inherent and ef-
" fential property it poffeffes that diftin-
" guifhes it from mere fpace ?"—I muft
repeat here what I have faid in my firft
remarks, and infift upon it as of particular
importance, that no anfwer is given to this
queftion, by faying, that matter is SOME-
THING which is attracted and repelled; or,
in other words, that it is *fomething* which
is continually acted upon by a foreign force
——What is it that is fo acted upon ?——
Not

Not mere fpace. That is abfurd——Not
a *folid* fubftance. There is no fuch thing
according to Dr. Prieftley——Not the fubject of confcioufnefs and thought. That
would imply there is nothing but fpirit in
nature——The attractions and repulfions
which take place between different bodies
are only *external circumftances* which diftinguifh one parcel of matter from another (a
magnet, for inftance, from other fubftances)
but they enter not into the idea of matter
*as* matter. There are circumftances in
which matter neither attracts nor repels;
as, particularly in the limit between the
fphere of attraction and repulfion.

But this leads me to the chief obfervation
I intended to make——If I underftand
Dr. Prieftley, all bodies at a fmall diftance
repel one another, fo as to make contact
between them impracticable. Within the
fphere of repulfion, the *attraction of cohefion* takes place; and this is the power
which, according to Dr. Prieftley, *unites*
the parts of matter, and gives it exiftence.
But, fince matter is penetrable, will not
this

this attraction drive all the parts of it into
one another, and caufe them to coalefce into
nothing?——This effect muſt follow, unlefs there exiſts, beyond the fphere of attraction and nearer to matter, a fecond
fphere of repulſion, which again prevents
contact.   The argument which Dr. Prieſtley draws from the effect of cold in contract-
ing bodies, and of heat in fwelling them,
makes it probable that this is his opinion.
And, if true, the elementary parts of matter poſſefs juſt the contrary principle to that
which he aſſerts to be neceſſary to preſerve
their exiſtence.

In ſhort, fince we cannot go on aſſigning
a fphere of repulſion beyond a fphere of attraction, and a fphere of attraction beyond
a fphere of repulſion *in infinitum*; either no
power at all acts on the elements of matter,
or, if a power does act, it muſt be either a
power of attraction, or a power of repulſion.
Dr. Prieſtley aſſerts, that if no power at all
acts to keep matter together, it muſt *crum-
ble* into *nothing*.   And it appears evident
to me, that if a power of attracting acts,
it muſt *contract* itſelf into nothing; and
that

that if a power of repulfion acts, it muft *diffipate* itfelf into nothing.

What can be done in this dilemma? The truth feems to be, that there is an abfurdity in fuppofing the elements of matter to confift of parts actually diftinct and feparable, which require a foreign agency to unite them. For the fame reafon that thefe elements muft confift of fuch parts, the elements of thofe elements muft confift of fuch parts, and fo on for ever. I have obferved in my firft remarks, that we muft terminate in parts, each of which is a folid *continuum* incapable of divifion.—Indeed, every real exiftence or fubftance muft be a *monad*. We are fure this is true of the beings we are beft acquainted with; I mean, *our-felves*, and all confcious and fentient beings. And if it be not true of matter, I know not what it is.

### A N S W.E R.

With refpect to the *definition of matter*, I really am not able to be more explicit than I have been. A definition of any particular *thing*, *fubftance*, or *being* (call it what you will) cannot be any thing more
than

than an enumeration of its known *properties*, and in all cafes whatever, as with refpect to *matter, fpirit*, &c. &c. if we take away all the known properties, nothing will be left, of which we can poffibly have any idea at all ; every thing elfe being merely *hypothe-tical*, and the terms *fubftance, thing, ef-fence*, &c. being, as I have obferved, nothing more than a help to expreffion ; it being a convenience in fpeech to have certain words of this univerfal application.

Solid *atoms,* or *monads of matter,* can only be hypothetical things ; and till we can either touch them, or come at them, forne way or other, by actual experiment, I cannot be obliged to admit their exiftence. Admitting the exiftence of thefe folid atoms, they do not help us, in the leaft, to explain any of the known properties of matter. All the *effects* are reducible to attractions or repulfions. Now what connection is there between *folidity*, and *attraction,* or even repulfion at a diftance from the furface of a body ; and though refiftance at the point of contact might be explained by it,

no

no fuch thing as *real contact* can be *proved*; and moft of the known repulfions in nature, do certainly take place in *other circumftances,* and therefore muft have fome *other caufe.*

In reply to Dr. Price, I muft obferve, that the limit between a fphere of attraction and another of repulfion, cannot be a place where neither of thefe powers are exerted, but where they balance each other. It does not follow that becaufe a beam is in equilibrio, there are no weights in the fcales.

That there are fpheres of attraction and repulfion within each other is evident from fact, as in electricity, magnetifm, &c. nor can the cohefion of bodies, the parts of which (as is demonftrable from the phenomena of cold) do not actually touch each other, be explained without it. The parts of bodies muft therefore attract each other at one diftance, and repel at another; and in the limit between both they muft remain; and by this means bodies retain their form and texture.

PART

# PART II.

*Of the Nature of* MIND *or* SPIRIT.

THE FIRST COMMUNICATION,

*By Dr.* Price, *with Dr.* Prieftley's *Anfwers.*

IN anfwer to the feveral arguments in the *Difquifitions,* Sect. III. and IV. it feems enough to fay, that a *connection* and *dependence* by no means prove *famenefs.* We are confcious of the contrary in the prefent cafe. Seeing depends on our eyes, but *we* are not our eyes, any more than the eye it-felf is the telefcope through which it looks, or the artift is the tool which he ufes.

### ANSWER.

This is by no means a juft ftate of the argument. I infer that the bufinefs of thinking is wholly carried on *in,* and *by*

D                              the

the brain itfelf, becaufe all the effects from
which we infer the faculty of thinking,
can be traced to the brain, and *no farther*.
I conclude that the ultimate perceptive
power relating to objects of fight is not in
the eye, becaufe, though the eye be neceffary to acquire ideas of fight, they remain
*fomewhere* when the eye is deftroyed. But
I have no reafon whatever to refer this
perceptive power to any thing beyond the
brain, becaufe when the brain is deftroyed,
there is, to all appearance, an end of all
fenfation and thought. To fuppofe that
when the brain is deftroyed the ideas remain in *fomething elfe*, is a mere hypothefis,
unfupported by any fact whatever.

A philofopher fuppofes no more *caufes*
than are neceffary to explain *effects*. He
finds the bufinefs of thinking to be dependent upon the brain, and therefore he
concludes that the brain itfelf is competent
to this bufinefs, whatever it be. To fuppofe any thing farther is mere hypothefis,
and utterly unphilofophical. What I maintain then is, that, according to the eftablifhed

blifhed rules of philofophizing, we are not authorized to fuppofe any thing *within the brain* to be the feat of thought. If we do, we may juft as well fuppofe it to refide in fomething within that, and in fomething again within that, and fo on without end ; and juft as the Indians are faid to place the earth upon an elephant, the elephant upon a tortoife, and the tortoife on they knew not what.

### Dr. Price.

In the *Difquifitions,* page 37 and 102, it is afferted, that ideas are certainly divifible. This feems to me very abfurd. It would be as proper to affert ideas to be hard or round. The idea of an object is the apprehenfion, view, or notion of it ; and how can this be divifible ?——Perception is a fingle and indivifible act. The object perceived may be divifible ; but the *perception* of it by the mind cannot be fo.

### Answer.

What appears to Dr. Price to be *very abfurd,* I cannot help thinking, after the

moft

moſt deliberate review, to be very certain,
and very clear. What correſpondence can
there be between an idea and its archetype,
if the archetype conſiſt of parts, and the
idea have no parts. He ſeems to have been
miſled, by not diſtinguiſhing between the
*power*, or rather the *act* of perception, and
the thing (*i. e.* the *idea*) perceived. The
object of perception, he acknowledges to
be diviſible, but *the perception of it by the
mind* cannot be ſo. True, becauſe perception is either a faculty, or an act of a
faculty, to which diviſibility is not applicable ; but the thing about which the
perceptive power is employed (which is
not the object itſelf, but the idea, or repreſentation of it in the mind) muſt be as
diviſible as the archetype of that idea. If
the mind be a ſimple and indiviſible ſubſtance, it cannot be poſſeſſed of more than
a ſingle idea, and that the idea of ſomething to which diviſion is not applicable.
However, I do not ſee why Dr. Price
ſhould object to a *repoſitory of diviſible ideas*
in a mind which he ſuppoſes to be actually
extended,

extended, and confequently to have room enough for that purpofe.

## DR. PRICE.

*Difquifitions,* page 44, &c. 74, &c. Mr, *Baxter,* and other ingenious men, have undoubtedly faid a great deal that is very groundlefs about the union of the body to the foul; its being a clog; its leaving the foul more capable of exerting its powers when feparated from it, &c. Were all that has been faid on thefe fubjects true, there would be no occafion for a refurrection. Nay, it would be a calamity, not a benefit. A falfe philofophy has, in this inftance, contradicted nature and experience, as well as revelation. Thus far I agree entirely with Dr. Prieftley; but fome of the objections in Sect. V. have little weight with me, and cannot eafily be anfwered on any hypothefis. If it muft be taken for granted that brutes, or the fentient principles in brutes, are annihilated at death, as feems to be hinted fometimes by Dr. Prieftley, I am afraid it will not eafily be

D 3                                believed

believed that the fame is not true of men. And if true, there will be a complete end of us : a refurrection will be a contra-diction—But it will come in my way to fay more to this purpofe.

### Answer.

My only reafon for not fuppofing that *brutes* will not furvive the grave, is, that there is no hint of it in revelation, where only it is that we are informed that *men* will rife again. It may, however, be true, though we have not been informed of it, and the analogy between men and other animals, makes it not very improbable.

### Dr. Price.

*Difquifitions,* p. 54. Dr. Prieftley here, and throughout a great part of this work, argues on the fuppofition, that, according to the ideas of modern metaphyficians, fpirit can have no relation to place, and is incapable of being prefent any where. This feems to me a miftake. I do not know what modern metaphyficians Dr.

Prieftley

Prieftley means, except the Cartefians. I am certain Dr. Clarke, and fome others of the beft modern writers, did not entertain thefe ideas of fpirit. It is a maxim that cannot be difputed, that *time* and *place* are neceffary to the exiftence of all things. Dr. Clarke has made ufe of this maxim, to prove that infinite fpace and duration are the effential properties of the Deity ; and I think he was right. Sir Ifaac Newton thought in the fame way, as appears from fome paffages at the end of his *Principia*, and in the queries at the end of his *Opticks*. As far, therefore, as Dr. Prieftley combats a notion of fpirit that implies it has no relation to fpace, and exifts no where, he combats an abfurdity and contradiction which deferves no regard ——What the nature is of the relation of fpirit to place, or in what *manner* it is prefent in fpace, I am utterly ignorant. But I can be fure that, if it exifts at all, it muft exift *fomewhere*, as well as in *fome time*.

Dr. Clarke was not for excluding expan-fion from the idea of immaterial thinking

D 4                    fubftances.

fubftances. See his *firft defence of an argument to prove the Immateriality and Natural Immortality of the Soul,* in anfwer to *Collins.* ——Has Dr. Prieftley read this controverfy ? or has he read the chapter on a Future State, with which *Butler's* Analogy begins?——If he had, I fancy he would have writ differently in fome parts of this book. Dr. Clarke is, without all doubt, the beft and ableft of all writers, on the fubjects of the Immateriality and Natural Immortality of the Soul, and alfo on *Liberty* and *Neceffity.* What he fays on thefe fubjects in his *Demonftration of the Being and Attributes of God,* is but inconfiderable, compared with what he has faid in his *Anfwer to Dodwell,* his *Controverfies with Collins,* and the *Letters* between *him and Leibnitz.*

I think it of little confequence, whether it *can,* or *cannot,* be determined, whether the fubject of confcioufnefs and thought in man is matter, if by matter is meant not folid extenfion, but an unknown fomething, that has a relation to place ; and it was hardly worth while to write a book to prove this.

Matter

Matter is incapable of confcioufnefs and thought, not becaufe it is *extended*, but becaufe it is *folid*, and as fuch inert and capable of being divided without being annihilated.

*Solid extenfion*; and *perception, thought, volition*, &c. are totally different things; and it is juft as clear that the latter cannot be the figure, motion, and arrangement of the parts of the former, as that any one thing cannot *be* another ; that a fquare, for inftance, cannot *be*, or be *made to be*, found, or colour. Our ideas of *figured, extended, folid fubftances*, and of *confcious, perceiving, thinking fubftances*, are, according to Mr. Locke's obfervation, equally clear and diftinct. It feems, therefore, very unreafonable to confound them, or to talk of fuperadding one of them to the other.

Dr. Clarke makes ufe of the inftance of *fpace*, to prove that there is no neceffary connection between extenfion and difcerptibility. *Moveantur partes fpatii de locis fuis & movebuntur de feipfis. Newton's Princip. Lib.* I. *Schol. Defin.* 8.

ANSWER.

### ANSWER.

I confider Mr. Baxter as having been one of the moft confiftent of all the Immaterialifts. That fuch a fcheme as his is the only confiftent one, is, I think, fufficiently proved by Dr. Watts. Some of his arguments I have referred to p. 221, and other reafons for this opinion I have fuggefted, p. 55, &c.

If, as Dr. Clarke fuppofes, fpirits have real extenfion, they muft be of fome fhape, and therefore their relation to fpace cannot be a thing of which we are *utterly ignorant*. We may not know *where* they are, or *how much fpace* they occupy, (whether, for inftance, *more*, or *lefs* than the bodies they belong to) but they muft occupy *fome fpace*, as well as bodies.

I will farther obferve, that if, according to Dr. Clarke, the Divine Being has infinite extenfion, and finite fpirits a limited one, they muft mutually penetrate each other; and thefe fpiritual fubftances being

of

of *the same nature*, the difficulty attending
it muſt be juſt as great as that which at-
tends the mutual penetration of material
ſubſtances.

I have carefully read all Dr. Clarke's me-
taphyſical works, but thought it ſufficient
to quote his *Demonſtration*, as the *beſt known*
of all his writings, and containing a ſum-
mary of his ſtrongeſt arguments on all the
topics that I have had occaſion to diſcuſs.
I have alſo read *Butler's Analogy*, but this
work does not ſtand ſo high with me as it
does with Dr. Price. I did not think that,
with reſpect to any thing that I have
written, it was at all neceſſary to conſider
any paſſages of Dr. Clarke's writings, or
any of Butler's; but if Dr. Price thinks
otherwiſe, I will give particular attention
to any thing, in either of them, that he
ſhall be pleaſed to point out to me.

Dr. Price admits, that if matter be not
ſolid and impenetrable, it may be capable
of thought, but wonders that I ſhould have
written a book to prove this. My book
was

was not written to prove this, but to prove that, whatever matter be, *thinking* is the refult of a modification of it, or that this faculty does not belong to an invifible fubftance, different from the body, which I apprehend to have been the fource of the greateft corruptions of the fyftem of revelation. Effectually to explode this notion, originally borrowed from heathenifm, and thereby to difcharge from Chriftianity many enormous errors, that now disfigure it, and make it appear abfurd in the prefent enlightened age of philofophy, appears to me to be rendering it the moft important of all fervices. Whether I have in any meafure *fucceeded*, fuch, if I know my own heart, have been my views in writing both the *Difquifitions* themfelves, and this defence of them.

I wifh Dr. Price would inform me what is the connection between *a capacity of confcioufnefs*, and *being indivifible without being annihilated*. Alfo, if fpirits be extended, and fomething more than fpace, whether they may not be divifible, and difcerptible, as well as matter.

Dr.

Dr. Hartley has fhewn that all the faculties of the human mind may be the
refult of vibration, except that of *fimple
perception*; but this, though *different* from
the other known properties of matter, may
not be *incompatible* with them. The facts
alledged in Sect. III. do, I apprehend,
prove, that according to the eftablifhed
rules of philofophizing, it is a property
that muft *in fact* belong to the brain, whether we ever be able to conceive *how* it
refults from the ftructure of the brain, or
not. In my opinion there is juft the fame
reafon to conclude that the brain *thinks*, as
that it is *white*, and *foft*.

Though Mr. Locke was of opinion that
our ideas of thinking fubftances are as
diftinct as thofe of folid ones, he was likewife of opinion, that, for any thing that
we know to the contrary, thinking *may*
be the mere property of a folid fubftance.

Dr. Clarke fhould have fhewn not only
that *extenfion*, but that *a capacity of motion
from place to place* is not neceffarily connected

nested with difcerptibility. It appears to
me very clear, that, if fpirit be a thing
that is extended and moveable, one part of
it may be conceived to be moved, and the
other part left behind, whether the property of *confcioufnefs* would be deftroyed in
confequence of it, or not.

## DR. PRICE.

In *Difquifitions*, p. 72, Dr. Prieftley fays,
that " it is demonftrable that matter is in-
" finitely divifible"—Can he fay that the
being he calls *himfelf* is likewife infinitely divifible. What would be the refult of fuch a
di-vifion ? Would it not be an infinite number of *other* beings? But does not this imply
a contradiction ? Can there be fuch a thing
as *half* a felf?—Or can the being I call
*myfelf* be fplit into two *others ?* Impoffible !
This would not be to *divide,* but to *annihilate* me—And the truth is, that in this
cafe divifion cannot be imagined without
annihilation—In another place Dr. Prieftley intimates, that matter confifts of *indivifible points,* p. 23. How then can it be
infinitely divifible ?

ANSWER.

## ANSWER.

The matter of which I confift may be divifible, though the *actual* divifion of it might fo difarrange the parts of it, that the property of thinking (which is the refult of a particular modification of them) would be deftroyed. A whole brain may think, but half a brain may be incapable of it. I fee no fort of difficulty in this cafe. Alfo, may not an extended fpirit be conceived to be divided without annihilation, as well as an extended folid fubftance? To the imagination it is equally eafy.

## DR. PRICE.

*Difquifitions*, p. 92. *The percipient power may as well belong to one fyftem as to one atom.* —See likewife the anfwer to the fourth Objection in p. 88. *I am one perfon, but it does not follow that I cannot be divided: A fphere is one thing, but it does not follow that it confifts of indivifible materials*——But if matter confifts of *indivifible points* (as is faid in p. 23.) and the foul is matter, then the

foul

foul confifts of indivifible materials. But
not to infift on this. Can any one believe
of *himfelf* that he is one thinking being
only as a great number of bodies forming
a fphere are one fphere? If this is true, he
muft be either the parts themfelves that
compofe the fphere; and if fo, he is a
*multitude* of beings; or he muft be their
*fphericity*; and if fo, he is nothing but an
*order* or *relation* of parts, and can never remain the fame any longer than that order
is preferved. As any change in the furface of a fphere would deftroy the fphericity, and convert it into fome other
figure, fo would any change in that *order*
of parts which conftitutes *myfelf*, deftroy
*me*, and convert me into fome *other perfon.*

### Answer.

If I fay that matter confifts of indivifible
points, I ufe a common expreffion, though
perhaps not a correct one. But as every
fenfible part of matter confifts of an *infinity*
of fuch points, it is plain that the fubftance
can never be exhaufted by any divifion.
To

To infer from this, that the foul (confifting of matter) confifts of an indivifible fubftance, feems to me to be a play upon words.

If a thinking being be a material fubftance of a particular texture and form, as I define it, it cannot follow, as is here afferted, that it is *a mere order or relation of parts*: A difarrangement of this texture would deftroy all *power of thought*, but would not make *another perfon.*

## Dr. Price.

*Difquifitions,* p. 89. " *It is impoffible to* " *fay a priori, whether a fingle particle, or a* " *fyftem of matter, be the feat of perception,* " *but fact proves the latter.*" If a fyftem of matter is the feat of perception, then the fyftem is the percipient being. But the percipient being is *one.* A fyftem confifts of *many* beings.

It is inconceivable to me how any perfon can think that many fubftances united can be one fubftance or that all

E         the

the parts of a fyftem can perceive, and yet no fingle part be a percipient being.

### ANSWER.

A fyftem, though confifting of many beings or things, is neverthelefs but *one fyftem*. A brain, though confifting of many parts, is but one brain; and where can be the difficulty of conceiving that no fingle part of a brain fhould be a whole brain, or have the properties of a whole brain?

### DR. PRICE.

*Difquifitions*, Sect. IX. It feems evident that Dr. Prieftley's principles go to prove, that the Deity is material, as well as all inferior beings. He would otherwife have no common property with matter, by which it would be poffible for him to act upon it—But at the fame time would there not be fomething fhocking in faying of the Deity, that he is nothing but a power of attraction and repulfion?

ANSWER.

## ANSWER.

By what conftruction am I made to affert that the divine effence is *material*, that is, of *the fame kind of fubftance* with what we generally term *matter*, when I fuppofe it to have quite *different properties*, on account of which I exprefsly fay, that it ought to have a quite *different name*, and not receive its denomination from the mere negation of the properties of matter, which is, in fact, no definition at all? Let all beings, and all things, be defined by their *known properties*, and no miftake can poffibly arife; for then our knowledge and our language will always correfpond to one another. It would certainly be fomething fhocking to fay that "the Deity is nothing but a "power of attraction and repulfion," but it would be faying what is directly contrary to the doctrine of my treatife, as muft, I think, be obvious to the moft fuperficial attention.

## DR. PRICE.

*Difquifitions*, p. 103. I am furprized Dr. Prieftley fhould here fay, that it is almoft

univerfally

univerſally acknowledged that, according to the Scriptures, the Deity *is incapable of local preſence*, when it is ſo well known that ſome of the firſt Chriſtian writers have believed *infinite ſpace* to be an attribute of the Deity.

### Answer.

What I maintain, is, that according to the only conſiſtent ſcheme of immaterialiſm, the Divine Being, as well as other immaterial ſubſtances, have no *local preſence*, and it is the opinion that till lately I held myſelf. That the Divine Being has a proper omnipreſence, and conſequently a proper extenſion, I now admit, but ſhould not chuſe to ſay with any perſon, though ever ſo juſtly called the *firſt Chriſtian writer in other reſpects*, that ſpace is merely *an attribute of the Deity*; becauſe, ſuppoſing that there was no Deity, ſpace would ſtill remain. It cannot be annihilated even in idea.

Dr.

## DR. PRICE.

*Difquifitions,* p. 102, &c. *But till we know fomething pofitive concerning this fup-pofed immaterial fubftance, &c.* ——What is fimilar to this may be more properly faid of matter, according to Dr. Prieft-ley's account of it—Whatever the foul is, it muft, if it is to exift for ever, be fomewhat fo fubftantial as to have no tendency to decay, or wear out. But this cannot be true of any thing com-pounded.

### ANSWER.

If, as Dr. Price fuppofes, a fpiritual fub-ftance be extended, it muft confift of an aggregation of parts, and therefore may be as liable to be diffolved as a homogeneous corporeal fubftance.

## DR. PRICE.

When it is afferted that the foul is *na-turally immortal,* the meaning is, that being

E 3 a *fub-*

a *fubftance* and not a *mode*, it will go on to exift, till by fome pofitive act of the Creator it is annihilated. In the fame fenfe it may be faid of the *atoms*, or *elements* that compofe our bodies, that they are naturally immortal: for it is, I think, a general truth, that only the power that brought any fubftance into being can put it out of being. Does Dr. Prieftley deny the natural immortality of the foul in this fenfe? If he does, and if he really means when he fays, "that the whole man be-" comes extinct at death," that death deftroys, or annihilates the thinking fubftance; and if alfo this is the dictate of nature and reafon, then the doctrine of a refurrection is contradictory to nature and reafon; and Dr. Prieftley, by maintaining the natural mortality of the foul, injures revelation. But it is certain he means the contrary. He muft, therefore, acknowledge, that death does not naturally deftroy the foul; or, in other words, that it preferves its exiftence at death; and that what then happens to it, can be no more than a fufpenfion.

suspension of the exercise of its faculties, or an *incapacitation* from which it will, by the power of Christ, be delivered at the resurrection. If he acknowledge this, he and I, and many other zealous immaterialists, are agreed. If he does not mean this, the resurrection will be, not a *resurrection*, but a *creation* of a new set of beings. If death annihilates us, there can be no future state. This is self-evident. A being who has lost his existence cannot be recovered. It is very improper here to mention the renewal of the flame of a candle after extinction; for the substance of the candle is not affected by the extinction of the flame, just as the substance of the soul is not affected by the suspension of its powers at death. It should be considered also, that the flame of a candle, being nothing but a current of hot and shining vapour, that is constantly passing away, like the water of a river, it never continues a moment the same; and that, consequently, the *renewed* flame is properly a *new* and *different* flame.

E 4          ANSWER.

## Answer.

I am furprifed at thefe conjectures concerning my meaning, which is, I think,
always expreffed with fufficient clearnefs,
viz. that the faculty of thinking is the
refult of a certain arrangement of the parts
of matter ; fo that the difarrangement of
them by death is neither the *extinction*, nor
the *annihilation* of them, and the re-arrangement of them after death, is (if any thing can
be fo called) a proper *refurrection*. It is as
much fo, as that of a feed fown in the ground,
the *germ* of which does not perifh, but
rifes again in the form of a new plant,
though the greateft part of the bulk of the
feed (being merely nutritious, and *extra-*
*neous matter*) does not properly rife again.

## Dr. Price.

If I underftand what is faid in the beginning of Sect. XIII. on *Perfonal Identity*, the
drift of it is to fhew that a being may be the
fame with a *former* being, though their *fub-*
*ftances*, and confequently all their *properties*,

are

are different.—It is likewife implied, that the
men who are to be raifed from death, will be
the fame with the men who have exifted in
this world, *only* as a river is called the
fame, becaufe the water, though different,
has followed other water in the fame chan-
nel ; or as a foreft is called the fame, becaufe the prefent trees, though new, have
been planted and grown up on the fame
fpot, in the room of other trees which had
been cut down and confumed—Did I believe this to be all the identity of man hereafter, I could not confider myfelf as having
any concern in a future ftate.

The affertion that the man or the agent
may be the fame, though his fubftance, or
every component part of him, is different,
appears to me very extraordinary indeed. I
am a different perfon from my neighbour,
though organized in the fame manner, becaufe the organized matter is different—If,
therefore, man after the refurrection will
be, not only a different fyftem of matter,
but alfo a fyftem of matter differently organized, and placed in a different world,
what

what will there be to make him the same
with man in this world?——I think, therefore, that Dr. Prieftley fhould, by all
means, keep to what he advances towards
the conclufion of this 13th Section.  It is
effential to his fcheme to maintain the refurrection of the *fame body*, or that the very
matter that compofes man at death, will
be collected at the refurrection, and compofe him again in another world, and for
ever.

But what am I faying?  Man a compofition of fubftances!  It is utterly impoffible.  The thinking fubftance would then
be not *one being*, but a *multitude*; nor is
it poffible to evade this confequence, without denying that the foul is a fubftance, or
any thing more than a modification of a
fubftance, or an arrangement and order of
the parts of fubftances.  Can this be true?
Is the fubject of thought and perception;
is what every one calls *himfelf*; not *a being*,
and *one being*; but a mere refult from the
figure, motion, and order of a fyftem of
material beings?——In fhort, if the foul

is

is material, it muſt certainly be one of the primary atoms of matter. No where elſe in the corporeal world can we find any thing like that unity and ſubſtantiality which belong to the ſoul of man ; and if it is an atom, it muſt have exiſted from the firſt creation of matter, unleſs there are new atoms created every time an animal is ge- nerated.

## Answer.

In Sect. XIII. I profeſſedly ſpeculate upon principles that are not my own. It is in- tended to prove, that there may be ſuch an *identity of perſon*, as will be a foundation for future *expectation, obligation*, &c. though every particle of the man ſhould be changed. The reaſoning in this ſection I muſt take the liberty to ſay, I do not think to be in- validated by Dr. Price's remarks, though to him it appears ſo very extraordinary.

The remainder of this remark has been obviated again and again, in the courſe of my work, and alſo in the preceding parts of this. What I call *myſelf* is an organized

ſyſtem

fyftem of matter. It is not, therefore, myfelf, but my *power of thought*, that is properly termed the refult of figure, motion, &c.

## DR. PRICE.

*Difquifitions*, p. 160, &c. " *What is there* " *in the matter that compofes my body, that* " *fhould attach me to it more than to the matter* " *that compofes the table on which I write?*" This is a furprizing queftion from Dr. Prieftley. If the matter which compofes my body is myfelf, I certainly have as much reafon to prefer it to the matter of a table, as I have to prefer *myfelf* to a *table*. To affert, as Dr. Prieftley does, that the matter of the body is the foul, and at the fame time to fuppofe, as he does, in this 13th Section, that the foul may remain the fame, though the whole matter of the body is changed, appears to me indeed fo apparently inconfiftent, that I cannot help fufpecting I muft greatly mifunderftand him. Should he fay, that the foul is not ftrictly the *matter* of the body, but the *organization* of that matter ; this, as I have already obferved

more

more than once, is making the foul a modification, an order and juxta-pofition and
connection of parts, and not a *being*, or
*fubftance.* But is it poffible to conceive of
any thing more fubftantial than the foul?
Can there be a *being* in nature, if the fentient principle, the fubject that feels pleafure and pain, that thinks and reafons, and
loves and hates, is not a *being?* Suppofe it,
however, if you can, to be merely the organization of the body; would not a change
in the matter of the body make *another*
body? And would not *another* body make
*another* foul, though the fame organization
fhould be preferved? If not, then may not
I and Dr. Prieftley be the fame man, fince
the organization of our bodies is the fame,
and only the matter different? Would not,
in fhort, any number of living bodies be
one foul, one fentient principle, fuppofing
their organization the fame?

## Answer.

The beginning of this remark relates to
the fpeculation abovementioned, which goes
upon other principles than my own. To
the

the queftion at the end of the remark, viz.
" Would not any number of living bodies
" be one foul, one fentient principle, fup-
" pofing their organization the fame," I
anfwer, that different fyftems of matter,
organized exactly alike, muft make different beings, who would feel and think
exactly alike in the fame circumftances.
Their minds, therefore, would be exactly
*fimilar*, but *numerically different.*

### DR. PRICE.

*Difquifitions*, p. 123. It feems to be hinted
here, that the foul, after death, is as little of
a fubftance (that is, as truly nothing) as
matter would be without extenfion.—It is
added, *if together with the ceffation of thought
they will maintain the real exiftence of the
foul after death, it muft be for the fake of
hypothefis only, and for no real ufe whatever.*
Does Dr. Prieftley then really mean that
the foul lofes its exiftence at death?

How can it be faid to be of no ufe to
maintain the exiftence of the foul after death,
when without this, a refurrection muft be
impoffible?

ANSWER.

## ANSWER.

I fay, that they who maintain the ceffation of thought after death, cannot maintain the feparate exiftence of the foul, except for the fake of an hypothefis, and for
no real *ufe* whatever, for this plain reafon ;
that, during this entire ceffation of thought,
the foul is, in fact, of no ufe, no phenomena indicating that any fuch thing exifts.
Had not the perfons who maintain fuch an
infenfible ftate of the foul, believed a refurrection of the body, they would naturally have concluded that the foul, or
the thinking part of man, *ceafed to be*, becaufe its exiftence would never more be
manifefted by any *effect*.

How is it true, that there can be no
refurrection, unlefs there be a foul diftinct
from the body ? If the foul be the fame
thing with the body, or a part of the body,
may not the body, or this part of it, rife
again without the aid of *another fubftance ?*
On the contrary, I think that a refurrection, properly fo called (becaufe this

can

can be only a refurrection of fomething that
*had been dead*, viz. the body) is manifeftly
ufelefs, upon the fuppofition of there being
a foul diftinct from the body; it being
upon this hypothefis, the foul, and not the
body, that is the feat of all perception,
and the fource of all action.

## Dr. Price.

*Difquifitions*, p. 224. *It was unqueftionably
the opinion of the Apoftles, that the thinking
powers ceafed at death.*

If, indeed, the Apoftles (as is here afferted too pofitively) thought that the powers
of fenfation were deftroyed at death, or as
Dr. Prieftley fpeaks in p. 248, that death
is the utter extinction of all our percipient
and intellectual powers; if, I fay, the
Apoftles thought thus, they believed a contradiction in believing a refurrection. If
thefe powers are not deftroyed, they muft
remain, and it can be only the *exercife* of
them that ceafes at death. Certainly Dr.
Prieftley fhould have guarded better his
language on this fubject, which is often
fuch as implies that the foul lofes its
exiftence

exiftence at death. Indeed, I never knew before that any believer in a future ftate could affert, not only that *thought* and *perception* ceafe at death, but that there is then a total extinction of the very *powers* themfelves. In fhort, Dr. Prieftley fhould be explicit in faying which it is he believes, the *fleep*, or the *non-exiftence* of the foul after death. There is no lefs than an infinite difference between thefe two things. The former may be the truth, and it implies the natural immortality of the foul; but if the latter is true, there is an end of all our hopes. Talking of the reftoration of man after death, will be talking of the reftoration of a non-entity. Dr. Prieftley calls this,(in*Difquifitions*, p.125.) an *extraordinary affertion*; but it appears to me felf-evidently true. Of what ufe, Dr. Prieftley afks, is an exiftence after death, without thought and perception? I have given a plain anfwer to this queftion. It is of infinite ufe, by making a future ftate, or a reftoration of man, poffible. Would it not be ftrange to fay of a man who is fallen

F into

into a fwoon, that fince he is infenfible it makes no difference whether he is in a fwoon or dead?—Would it not be proper to fay in anfwer, that if he is only in a fwoon he may recover, but if he is dead he will never recover.—Juft fo; if a man at death is only *difabled*, he may be reftored. But if his exiftence is gone, he never can be reftored.

### A n s w e r.

I cannot help expreffing my furprife at this remark. As far as I fee, my language upon this fubject is always uniform, and ftrictly proper. I fuppofe that the powers of thought are not merely fufpended, but are *extinct*, or *ceafe to be*, at death. To make my meaning, if poffible, better underftood, I will ufe the following comparifon. The power of *cutting*, in a razor, depends upon a certain cohefion, and arrangement of the parts of which it confifts. If we fuppofe this razor to be wholly diffolved in any acid liquor, its power of

cutting

cutting will certainly be *loft*, or *ceafe to be*, though no particle of the metal that con- ftituted the razor be annihilated by the procefs; and its former *fhape*, and *power of cutting*, &c. may be reftored to it after the metal has been precipitated. Thus when the body is diffolved by putrefaction, its power of thinking entirely ceafes; but, no particle of the man being *loft*, as many of them as were effential to him, will, I doubt not, be collected, and revivified, at the refurrection, when the power of think- ing will return of courfe. I do not, there- fore, think that any thing that I have advanced implies that *the foul*, that is, *the man* lofes his *exiftence* at death, in any other fenfe than that the man lofes his *power of thinking*.

I really do not know how I can be more explicit than I have been through the whole of my treatife on this fubject, with refpect to which Dr. *Price* complains that I am not explicit enough. The latter part of this remark I have replied to before.

F 2                DR.

### DR. PRICE.

*Difquifitions,* p. 96. *All the exertions of the foul are as much produced by fenfations and ideas as any one effect in nature can be produced by its proper caufe. They have a proper impelling force. They are moving powers.* p. 97.———An idea, therefore, is an *agent,* and the foul is paffive under its action in the fame manner a ball is paffive when impelled by another.———But what is an idea? Nothing but a *perception,* or *judgment* of the mind ; that is, of the being that acts. How can this impel? What can it be more than the *occafion* of action?

There muft be fomewhere a *felf-moving power.* For one thing cannot move another, and that another *in infinitum*—And if there is one felf-moving power in nature, why may there not be many?

### ANSWER.

Dr. *Price* fhould diftinguifh between a *perception,* or *judgment,* which is an *act* of *the mind,* and the *idea* perceived and judged

of

of by the mind, which muſt be different from the *mind itſelf*, or any of its *acts*. I maintain that ideas, whatever they be, have a proper *impelling power*, becauſe men are invariably impelled to action in conſequence of them; but as to a *ſelf-motive power*, I deny that man has any ſuch thing, for the reaſons that are alledged in the *Treatiſe on Neceſſity*.

## DR. PRICE.

Upon the whole, it may perhaps be poſſible to convince me that there is no ſuch thing as *matter*, and Dr. *Prieſtley* has contributed a little to it; but I cannot be convinced that there is no ſuch thing as *ſpirit*, meaning by ſpirit ſuch a thinking intelligent nature as I feel myſelf to be. I am indeed full of darkneſs about myſelf; but in the midſt of this darkneſs I am taught the following particulars by an irreſiſtible conſciouſneſs, which will not ſuffer me to doubt, 1ſt. That I am a *being*, or a *ſubſtance*, and not a *property*, or a mere *configuration of parts.*

F 3 2dly,

2dly, That I am *one being*, and not *many beings*, or a *fyftem*.

3dly, That I am a *voluntary agent*, poffeffed of powers of *felf-motion*, and not a paffive inftrument.

4thly, That my fenfes and limbs, my eyes, hands, &c. are *inftruments* by which I act, and receive information; and not *myfelf*; or *mine*, and not *me*.

### ANSWER.

If, by *fpirit*, Dr. *Price* means nothing more than a thinking and an intelligent fubftance, I have the fame confcioufnefs of it that he has. I alfo believe with him that I am a *being*, or *fubftance*; alfo that I am a *fingle being*, and a *voluntary agent*, though not poffeffed of a felf-motive power; and that my limbs and fenfes are inftruments by which I act, and not *myfelf*, or *me*. So that, if thefe be all the effential articles of Dr. *Price*'s faith, and he feems to enumerate them as fuch, we are very nearly agreed, though in *words* we have differed fo widely.

QUERIES

## QUERIES *by* DR. PRICE.

1. Is not the *foul*, or what I call *myfelf* a being, or fubftance, and not merely a mode, or accident.

2. Does the foul lofe its exiftence at death, or am I, the fubject of thought, reafon, confcioufnefs, &c. to be annihilated?

3. If I am to lofe my exiftence at death, will not my refurrection be the refurrection of a non-entity, and therefore a contradiction?

4. If I am not to lofe my exiftence at death, may it not be properly faid that I am *naturally immortal?*

### ANSWER.

I confider myfelf as a being confifting of what is called matter, difpofed in a certain manner. At death the parts of this material fubftance are fo difarranged, that the powers of perception and thought, which

F 4                    depended

depended upon that arrangement, ceafe. At the refurrection they will be re-arranged, in the fame, or a fimilar manner, as before, and confequently the powers of perception and thought will be reftored. But this will require a miraculous interpofition of divine power, and therefore it cannot be faid that thinking beings are *naturally* immortal, (*i. e.* as thinking beings) though the parts that compofe them are fo.

THE

THE SECOND COMMUNICATION,

*Containing Dr.* Price's *Obfervations on the Replies to the Firft Communication, with Dr.* Prieftley's *fecond Replies.*

*Of the Nature of* MIND *or* SPIRIT.

*ObfervationsonDr.*Prieftley's*Reply,* p.49,&c.

WHEN the eye is deftroyed we cannot fee. So likewife when the brain is deftroyed we cannot reafon. If from hence it follows that it is the brain that reafons, why fhould it not alfo follow that it is the eye that fees? From the dependence of actual fenfations and thought on the brain, we have, I think, no more reafon to conclude that the brain is the mind, than a favage who had never heard the mufic of a harpfichord, and did not fee the hand that played upon it, would have to conclude, that it played on itfelf, and was *the* mufician; becaufe he could trace all the founds to the inftrument, and found that when the ftrings
were

were out of order, the mufic was difturbed
or deftroyed.

What experience teaches us, is, that the
*exercife* of the mental powers *depends* on
the brain and the nerves; not that the
mind *is* the brain and the nerves. Common fenfe exclaims againft fuch a conclufion as much as againft concluding that
there is pain in the point of a fword. We
are fure the mind cannot be the brain, becaufe the brain is an affemblage of beings.
The mind is *one* being. Nothing feems
to me more unphilofophical in this cafe
than to reft our ideas in the organ, and to
confound it with the being whofe organ it
is. This, I have faid, is like thinking
that a mufical inftrument plays on itfelf.
But to go higher. It is not unlike refting
our ideas in this vifible world, and fuppofing it the fame with that Deity who
made, and actuates, and governs it. The
laws of nature feem to terminate in matter.
But is it philofophical, in order to avoid
multiplying caufes, to conclude they have
no other caufe than matter itfelf; and,
with

with the French philofophers, to make *nature* the only Deity? In fhort, I am fully of opinion, that if that *mafs of flefh and blood* which we call the *brain*, (no one part of which, or part of any part, touches another) may be that fentient and intelligent being we call the *mind*; then that mafs of corporeal fubftances which we call the *world*, may be *God*; and it muft be unphilofophical to fearch farther than *itfelf* for its caufe. Dr. Prieftley, I know, is far from being fenfible of this: But fuch indeed is the tendency of his principles, and manner of reafoning. The very foundation of this atheiftical conclufion, is totally fubverted by the demonftration which, I think, I have given, that the laws which govern matter, or its attractions and repulfions, are not the actions or properties of matter itfelf, but effects of the conftant operation of a higher caufe.

## Answer, *by Dr.* Prieftley.

I cannot help expreffing fome furprize that my reafoning on this fubject fhould not feem to be underftood, and that fuch ftrange conclufions conclusions should be drawn from it. If, upon examination, nothing could be *found*, or *reasonably conjectured*, to move the strings of the harpsichord, it would be philosophical to conclude, that the cause of the music that came from it was *within itself*. But when we open it, and see the strings to be moved in such a manner as similar strings are never known to be moved but by *human means*, there is reason to conclude, from analogy, that these strings also are moved, though we do not see *how*, by the same, or a similar cause.

In like manner, when we see the parts of which the universe consists, to be arranged in such a manner, as, from analogy, we have reason to believe, that no other than an intelligent being could arrange them, we conclude that an intelligent being, visible or invisible, *has* arranged them.

I conclude, that there is nothing within the brain itself that is the cause of perception, because, for any thing that I know, perception may be the property
of

of that material, as well as of any fuppofed immaterial fubftance; the relation
of *perception* to *material* or *immaterial* fubftances being equally unknown. If the
faculty of *playing could* be fuppofed to
belong to the harpfichord, it would be unphilofophical to inquire for any *concealed
mufician*; fo alfo if the power of arranging
and moving the component parts of the
univerfe *could* belong to themfelves, it
would be unphilofophical to inquire for a
fuperintending mind, or God. But it is
denied that the laws of nature do *feem*
to terminate in the vifible parts of the
univerfe.

For the fame reafon that perception is
afcribed to fome immaterial fubftance within
the brain, it feems to me that attraction
ought to be afcribed to fome immaterial
fubftance within the earth, the fun, &c.
becaufe, according to Dr. Price, *attraction*
is a power quite foreign to the nature of
matter, as well as *perception*

DR.

## Dr. Price.

*Observations on Dr.* Prieſtley's *Reply,* p. 51, 52.

I had ſaid that it is very abſurd to ima‑
gine that ideas are diviſible. Dr. Prieſtley
here ſays, that after the moſt deliberate
review, the contrary is very clear to him.
Others muſt judge. What is the *idea* of an
objeЄt ? Is it not the *notion* or *conception* of
the objeЄt ? A line is infinitely diviſible.
Is the mind's *idea,* or *conception* of a line
alſo infinitely diviſible ? But I find Dr.
*Prieſtley* thinks ideas to be the bodies them‑
ſelves in miniature, which they repreſent,
or models and delineations of external ob‑
jeЄts, diſtinЄt from the mind, but con‑
tained in it, like maps and globes in a
chamber. And I ſuppoſe he will go ſo far
as to aſcribe all the properties of bodies to
them, and particularly attraЄtion and re‑
pulſion ; and maintain, that in volition
they aЄt upon and impel the mind con‑
taining them, as one body aЄts upon and
impels another. The bare repreſentation
of ſuch an opinion ſeems ſufficient to con‑

fute

fute it. But if not, it muft be in vain to argue about it.

## ANSWER.

If ideas be nothing diftinct from the mind, or modifications of the mind, varying as their architypes vary, a mind *with ideas*, and a mind without *ideas*, would be the fame thing; and if the ideas of compound objects be not compounded things, and confift of as many parts as the objects of which they are the ideas, I am unable to conceive any thing about ideas. That motions, or volitions of the mind, do depend upon ideas, or, in other words, that the mind is *influenced*, or *acted upon* by them, is a certain *fact*, whether the reprefentation confute itfelf or not. No perfon acquainted with the principles of *Hartley's theory*, can be at a lofs to know what I fuppofe ideas to be, and in what manner they operate.

## DR. PRICE.

*Obfervations on Dr.*Prieftley's *Reply*, p.58,&c.

I have already faid, that I know nothing of the extenfion of fpirit. I only wifh to diftinguifh

diftinguifh on this fubjeĉt between what is certain, and what is uncertain. I think it *certain,* that whatever the fubjeĉt of confcioufnefs may be in other refpeĉts, it is incapable of being divided without being annihilated.

I do not expeĉt that the chapter in *Butler's Analogy,* on a future State, which I have wifhed to recommend to Dr. Prieftley's attention, can appear to him as weighty as it does to me. *Butler* and *Clarke* are with me two of the firft of all writers. In p. 222 of the *Difquifitions, &c.* to which Dr. Prieftley refers me, the contradiĉtory account of fpiritual beings, which makes them to exift no where, or to have no relation to place, is faid to be " *the only* " *confiftent* fyftem of immaterialifm, held " by Mr. *Baxter,* and *all the moft approved* " *modern* writers on the fubjeĉt." Can it be right to fay this, when there are fuch men as Dr. Clarke and Newton who have entertained different ideas, and extended them even to the fupreme Spirit ? I do not believe

believe that even Mr. Baxter entertained any fuch notion. It is, however, the notion of Spirit which is combated through the greateft part of Dr. Prieftley's work.

Dr. Prieftley's view in writing, was, to prove that there is no diftinction between matter and fpirit, or between the foul and body: and thus to explode what he calls the heathenifh fyftem of chriftianity, by exploding the doctrines of Chrift's præ-exiftence, and an intermediate ftate. But if in doing this, it comes out that his account of matter does not anfwer to the common ideas of matter; or that it is not *folid* extenfion, but fomething *not folid* that exifts in fpace; it agrees fo far with fpirit: And if fuch matter is, as he afferts, the only matter poffible, what he has proved will be, not that we have no *fouls* diftinct from our *bodies*, but that we have no *bodies* diftinct from our *fouls*. Matter which poffeffes folidity, or impenetrability and inertnefs, is certainly the only matter that is the object of natural philofophy. This, *Newton* has faid, in a paffage I have quoted from

G        him

him.   If fuch matter is impoffible, it will
follow that all in nature is Spirit.

Dr. Prieftley, in this reply, p. 60, mentions his *views*.   They are, I doubt not,
the pureft and beft poffible.   There is no
one of whofe heart I have a higher opinion.
But at the fame time my fixed apprehenfion
is, that he is one of thofe great and good
men who have puſhed on too eagerly in the
purfuit of truth, and who, in endeavouring
to ferve the beft of all caufes, have run upon
bad ground, and, without knowing it,
employed means of the moft dangerous
tendency.

## ANSWER.

To this I have nothing particular to fay.
My quotations from various writers prove,
that befides the profeffed Cartefians, many
other philofophers and metaphyficians have
fuppofed that *fpirit bears no relation to fpace.*
Dr. Watts, without having ever been re-
futed that I know of, has fhewn that this
is the only confiftent idea of an immaterial
being.   I have added fome additional arguments

guments to prove the fame thing, and this was my own idea while I held the doctrine of immaterialifm. This idea, therefore, I have *chiefly* combated ; but not this only, but alfo every other idea of immaterialifm that I have met with, that appeared to me to deferve particular notice.

### DR. PRICE.

*Obfervations on the Replies*, p. 65 and 66.

A thinking being, Dr. Prieftley fays, is a material fubftance of a particular texture ; not a mere order or relation of parts. Does it not then follow, that the deftruction of the order or texture of the parts ; that is, their dif-arrangement, cannot be the deftruction of the thinking being ?

" A fyftem," it is farther faid, " though " confifting of many *beings*, is but one " *fyftem:* and a brain, though confifting " of many *parts*, is but one *brain* ; no " fingle part of which can be the whole." But it is felf-evident, that a fyftem, con- fifting of many beings, though *one as a*

*fyftem,*

*syftem*, in the fame fenfe that an army
is one as an army, muft be a *multitude*
of beings ; and can no more be one being
than an army can be one man.   In like
manner, though a brain confifting of many
material fubftances, not one of which,
according to Dr. Prieftley, is in contact
with another ; though I fay fuch a brain
may be one as a *brain*, it cannot certainly
be one *fubftance*.   But the foul is one *fubftance*, one being.   This Dr. Prieftley
grants at the end of thefe replies, and it is
impoffible he fhould deny it.   He cannot,
therefore, think the brain to be the foul.
All that he can believe, is, that the foul's
*thinking* depends on the order and texture
of the brain.   Experience proves this ;
and it is indeed, as I have before faid, all
that experience teaches us.

### Answer.

I cannot fee any thing in this remark
that is not merely verbal.   A man, in my
idea, is *one thinking being*, and not two
thinking beings, let this thinking being
confift

confift of as many fubftances, or *unthinking beings* as any perfon pleafes.

## DR. PRICE,

*Obfervations on the Reply*, p. 67.

" By what conftruction am I made to
" affert, that the Divine Effence is ma-
" terial ; that is, of the fame kind of fub-
" ftance with what we generally term
" matter, when I fuppofe it to have *quite*
" *different properties*, &c. ?"

I have mentioned this only as an inference from Dr. Prieftley's principles ;
and particularly from a principle which he
has argued upon as a maxim, namely,
" that nothing can act upon another with-
" out having *common properties* with it."
If this is true, the Deity muft have *common properties* with matter ; and matter
being a power of attraction and repulfion
united to extenfion, the Deity muft be the
fame. If, in order to avoid this confequence, Dr. Prieftley fhould acknowledge

this maxim not to be univerfally true, it
will follow that Spirit may act upon matter
without having any other common property with it than being locally prefent to
it ; and one of his chief arguments for the
materiality of the foul will be given up.

Indeed, I cannot imagine how it is poffible for him to maintain this maxim
without afferting the impoffibility of the
*creation* of the world out of nothing : For
what common property can the Creator
have with *nothing ?* It would not fatisfy
me to be told here, that the Divine Nature
poffeffing peculiar properties, we can draw
no argument from it.    The contrary is
true in many cafes : Particularly in the
following. — The Deity acts on matter,
without having any common property with
it ; therefore fuch action is poffible.—The
Deity is an immaterial being; therefore immaterial beings are poffible : And the negation of matter is not the fame with the
negation of all exiftence.—In like manner,
the Deity is an intelligent being; therefore
intelligent beings are poffible.—He poffeffes

fefses the powers of felf-determination;
therefore fuch powers are poffible.—He is
an agent; therefore there may be other
agents.—All thefe conclufions appear to
me to be juft.

I have by no means defigned to charge
Dr. Prieftley with maintaining that the
Deity is nothing but a power of attraction
and repulfion. I only mean to fay, that
if the Deity be a material being, and matter (as Dr. Prieftley contends) is nothing
but fuch a power, then the Deity muft
alfo be nothing but fuch a power. I know
that Dr. Prieftley afferts the immateriality
of the Deity. I only doubt about the
confiftence of this with the other parts of
his theory.

Dr. Prieftley fays, p. 68, that he does
not chufe to call fpace an *attribute of the
Deity*; becaufe, fuppofing there was no
Deity, " fpace would ftill remain; it
" being impoffible to be annihilated even
" in idea."

According

According to Dr. Clarke, the impoffibility of annihilating even in idea, *fpace*
and *time,* is the fame with the *neceffary*
*exiftence* of the Deity, whofe attributes they
are. Inftead therefore of faying, " was
" there no Deity fpace would ftill remain,"
we fhould fay " fpace will ftill remain ;
" and therefore the Deity will ftill remain,
" and his non-exiftence cannot be ima-
" gined without a contradiction." It appears to me, that whatever cannot be annihilated, even in idea, muft be an attribute of the Deity. This may be applied not only to *fpace* and *time,* but
to *truth, poffibles,* &c. as I have done
in my *Treatife on Morals. Eternity, im-*
*menfity, infinite truth,* &c. cannot be *con-*
*ceived* not to exift. All exiftence pre-
fuppofes *their* exiftence. That is, there
exifts neceffarily an eternal and omniprefent
intelligence, the parent of all things.—I
am afraid Dr. Prieftley will not like this ;
but I am as much fatisfied with it as he is
with any part of Dr. Hartley's Theory.

ANSWER,

## Answer.

What is attraction or repulfion but a power of moving matter in a certain direction? If, therefore, the Deity *does* thus act upon matter, he muft have that power, and therefore *one* property in common with matter, though he be poffeffed of ever fo many *other* powers of which matter is incapable.

Dr. Price's argument, that becaufe God is *a felf-determined being*, there may be other felf-determined beings, and becaufe God is an *agent* there may be other agents, &c. &c. may, I am afraid, carry us too far. For may it not be faid alfo, that becaufe God is a *felf-exiftent being*, there may be other felf-exiftent beings, and becaufe God can *create out of nothing*, &c. &c. other beings may have the fame powers?

I cannot, I own, fee any thing conclufive in Dr. Price's argument for the being of a God, *a priori.* I do not fee

why

why it fhould be taken for granted, that " whatever cannot be annihilated, even in " idea, muft be an attribute of the Deity." This appears to me to be quite an arbitrary fuppofition. That *fpace, duration, truth, poffibles,* &c. fhould be denominated *attributes,* founds very harfh to me. If the infinite fpace occupied by the Deity be an attribute of his, I fhould think that the finite fpace, occupied by finite minds and things, fhould be called *their* attributes, and alfo the portions of duration to which they are co-exiftent, another of their attributes, &c. fo that the fame individual portions of fpace and time, muft be attributes both of the Deity and of created beings. Alfo mere attributes of things cannot, in idea, be feparated from them; whereas nothing is eafier than to form the idea of *mere fpace,* without any thing to occupy it. But this is not my fubjeƐt.

### Dr. Price.

*Obfervations on Reply,* p. 69.

I muft repeat here what I have already faid, that I know no more of the extenfion

of

of spirit, than that it possesses local presence, and is at the same time indiscerptible. Let any one reflect on himself, or on the immensity of the Divine Nature, and deny the possibility of this if he can.

Space has parts, but they are only *assignable* parts. A separation of them from one another implies a contradiction.

## ANSWER.

If a finite spirit occupy a finite portion of space, one part of that spirit may be *conceived* to be removed from another, as well as one part of solid matter from another; though this is not true of the Deity, who necessarily fills *all space*.

## DR. PRICE.

*Observations on Reply,* p. 75.

Dr. Priestley here says, that he intended in Sect. XIII. to prove, " that there may " be such an identity of person as will be " a foundation

" a foundation for future *expectation*, ob-
" *ligation*, &c. though every particle of
" the man fhould be changed." In anfwer
to this I have obferved, that if every particle that conftitutes the man is to be different at the refurrection, the *man* muft be
different; and that, confequently, the men
who exift in this world can have no fuch
concern in what is to happen to the men
who are to exift hereafter, as lays a foundation for expectation, obligation, &c.
becaufe thofe men will not be *them,* but
*other* men. In anfwer to this, Dr. Prieftley muft fay, either that a man may be the
fame, though every particle that conftitutes
him is different; or he muft fay, that men
in this life are obliged to act with a view
to *their own* exiftence in another life,
though there is to be no fuch exiftence.

I am fenfible that in this fection he reafons
on the opinions of *others*; but, if in reafoning on thefe opinions, he attempts to
prove what is plainly impoffible, the reafoning muft be fo far wrong.

ANSWER,

## ANSWER.

I ftill fay that I have nothing to add on this fubjeƈt. I profeſſedly argue on an hypothefis that is not my own, and fubmit the force of the argument to the judgment of the reader.

### DR. PRICE.

*Obfervations on Reply,* p. 79.

It is here faid, that " if the ceffation of " thought at death is allowed, it can be of " no ufe whatever to maintain the feparate " exiftence of the foul." I have given what appears to me a full anfwer to this obfervation, by faying, that if the foul does not *exiſt* after death, there can be no *reftoration* of it : And that, confequently, it muft be of the utmoft ufe to maintain that it does fo exift, though perhaps in an *incapacitated* ftate. There is an infinite difference between the *annihilation* of the foul at death, and its *incapacitation.* One who believed the former could not poffibly entertain the hope of a future ftate, but one who

who believes the latter, might reasonably
entertain fuch an hope. He might think
that a period would come when it fhould
be reftored. He might even think of men,
as Dr. Prieftley (*Difquifitions*, p. 239) feems
to think of brutes, that their refurrection
may be a part of the courfe of nature.

Dr. Prieftley here adds, that " a refur-
" rection is manifeftly ufelefs, if there is a
" foul diftinct from the body." He well
knows, that according to Mr. Locke, and
many others, the future refurrection taught
in the Scriptures, is to be the refurrection
not of the *body*, but of the *foul*. It is to
be the reftoration of the *man* (incapacitated
by the deftruction of the organization by
which he here acted, and received information) to the exercife of all his powers,
in a new ftate of being, by furnifhing him
with another, and (if virtuous) a more durable and perfect organization. All then
that can be faid with any propriety, is, that
a refurrection of the *fame body* is ufelefs, if
there is a foul diftinct from the body; and,
in faying this, fome of the moft zealous
Chriftians

Chriftians and immaterialifts will agree with him.

## ANSWER.

What I fay of the refurrection being manifeftly ufelefs, if there be a foul diftinct from the body, is upon the common hypothefis; according to which the foul is the only fource of action, and the body is fo far from being neceffary to its exertions as to be a *hindrance* to them. This is the original and genuine hypothefis of *a foul*, as a fubftance diftinct from the body, though the phenomena have at length compelled thofe who cannot yet perfuade themfelves to give up the notion of a foul altogether, to acknowledge its neceffary dependance upon the body, unaccountable as the mutual connection and dependance of fubftances fo very different in their nature muft appear. It has been in confequence of finding more and more of the phenomena of the mind to depend upon the body, that myfelf and others conclude, that *every thing* belonging to man is corporeal. And I cannot help thinking that the general

perfuafion

perfuafion of the foul being incapable of
any perception or action without the body,
and therefore that all its faculties are in a
perfectly dormant state from death to the
refurrection, muft gradually abate men's
zeal in the defence of the doctrine of a
foul, and prepare the way for the general
belief, that the hypothefis is altogether
unneceffary.

## DR. PRICE.

*Obfervations on Reply,* p. 82, *and the following.*

In p. 75, at the top, Dr. Prieftley fays,
" What I call myfelf, is, *an organized*
" *fyftem of matter.*" Is not every atom of
the matter that compofes a *fyftem,* a diftinct
*fubftance,* or being? Does not, therefore,
Dr. Prieftley, here call himfelf a *fyftem*
of beings?—But waving this, becaufe perhaps it has been too often repeated, I
will here beg leave to ftate, as briefly
as I can, the whole queftion relating to
the nature of the human foul and its
mortality, according to my ideas. Should
I be

I be wrong in any inftance, Dr. Prieftley will, I hope, be fo good as to fet me right.

The foul, that is, the being that thinks and acts, muft, if an organized fyftem of matter, be either the material fubftances themfelves which compofe that fyftem ; or it muft be their organization, their texture, motion, arrangement, &c.

If the latter is true, it will follow :

*Firft,* That man is not a fubftance or a *being,* but a *mode.* For texture, motion, and arrangement of parts, are not fub-ftances, but modes of fubftances.

*Secondly,* It muft follow, that any num-ber of men, having the fame organization, have the fame foul, or are the fame man ; juft as points having the fame arrangement round a center, make the fame figure.

*Thirdly,* It muft follow, that the fame fyftems of matter organized differently, will make different fouls, or new men; juft as the fame points, arranged differently round a center, will make different figures.

H                    Now

Now it fhould be remembered, that at the refurrection, man being to live in a new ftate, the organization of his body muft be new : And this, if man be that organization, muft make a new man.

But I need not urge thefe confequences; becaufe Dr. Prieftley has allowed, that the man is the matter itfelf which conftitutes the man, and not its form or arrangement: And two fyftems of matter organized alike, he exprefsly fays, would make two men thinking, indeed, alike, but *numerically different*. The former, therefore, of the two accounts I have mentioned, muft be his account of the foul of man, and it will follow from it.

*Firft*, That the man will always remain while the matter which conftitutes him remains ; however different its organization, or arrangement may be.

*Secondly*, That fince death does not deftroy the matter which conftitutes man, it does not deftroy the man : And that, confequently,

fequently, he goes on to exift after death; or is naturally immortal.

*Thirdly,* That in order to the refurrection of the fame man, the fame matter muft arife; and that for this reafon, if the contrary is intended to be proved in *Difqui-fitions* Sect. XIII. it cannot be right.

*Fourthly,* That it is no lefs poffible for man to have exifted *before* his *birth,* than it is that he fhould *exift* after his *death:* And that, confequently, all the fupport to the Socinian fcheme, which Dr. Prieftley derives from his fentiments of materialifm, falls to the ground. Indeed, man muft have exifted, according to this account, before his birth, if the matter that conftitutes him exifted before his birth: And his birth, or rather his conception, could have been nothing but putting that matter together, or new arranging it after it had been dif-arranged in fome former ftate.

But this leads me to the main inference from this account of the foul; namely, that the organization of the matter which

conftitutes

conftitutes man, fince it is not the being that
thinks, can only conftitute actual thinking;
and, confequently, that it is only *actual
thinking*, or the *exercife* of our powers, that
depends on the bodily organization, and
which can ceafe at death. Even his own
fimile in p. 82, implies that he means no
more. For matter formed into a razor,
would not lofe its *exiftence*, but its *cutting
power* only, by being dif-arranged. And,
though, fuppofing the fame matter formed
into a *bullet*, we fhould fay the *razor* was
deftroyed, yet we fhould mean no more
than that the matter which conftituted it
had affumed another fhape, and could no
longer cut. To this iffue I wifhed to
bring this difpute. Dr. Prieftley agrees
with me in believing that the foul does
not lofe its exiftence at death, p. 83.
He, therefore, believes what I mean by
the natural immortality of the foul: And I
fancy he will go even farther with me,
and allow that the being which thinks,
cannot *then* ceafe to exift, without a pofitive act of the Creator to deftroy it, like
that which firft brought it into exiftence.

In

In return, I am ready to concede to Dr. Prieftley, what he feems in p. 88, to give as the whole of his meaning, that "as "thinking beings we are not immortal;" that is, "that fometimes we fall into an "unthinking ftate." Sound fleep may be fuch a ftate. Death, being the deftruction of the whole machinery that connects us with this world, may be a more remedilefs ftate of the fame kind; and the chief difference between thefe two ftates may be, that whereas there are natural and ordinary means by which we are recovered from the one, there may be no fuch means by which we can be recovered from the other. Dr. Prieftley, indeed, feems to be doubtful about this. But does it not deferve his confideration, whether he has not, by expreffing fuch a doubt, contradicted a fentiment on which he has laid great ftrefs, namely, that "fince man becomes extinct "at death, our only hope of furviving the "grave is derived from revelation?" For if the refurrection may be, as he fays, (Difquifitions, p. 239) within the proper courfe of nature: that is, if there may be natural

H 3       means

means by which the dead may be hereafter reftored, why may there not be arguments from reafon which make it probable that it is fact? He has mentioned, in the paffage to which I have juft referred, one argument which he thinks may lead to fuch a hope with refpect to *brutes.* Why may there not be likewife arguments which, independent of revelation, may reafonably produce the fame hope with refpect to *men?*

I am of opinion, however, that all appearances are againft the exiftence of any fuch *natural* and *ordinary* means; and I will take this opportunity to add, that the fcripture doctrine feems to be, that death is a diftrefs in which our fpecies has been involved by *extraordinary* caufes; and from which we have obtained the hope of being faved by the moft *extraordinary* means; I mean, by the interpofition of *Jefus Chrift;* who by taking upon him our nature, and *bumbling himfelf to death,* has acquired the power of *deftroying death;* and is on this account ftyled *the Saviour of the World.*

*Reply,*

*Reply*, p. 84. *Dr. Price should distinguish*, &c.

With refpect to what is here faid by Dr. Prieftley, I muft refer to what I have faid in p. 51, 84, 94; and what will be faid on the fubject of the Doctrine of Neceffity at the end of this correfpondence.

### A N S W E R.

Admitting, as I do, that a man is a material fyftem, fo organized as to perceive and think, I muft believe that the *materials* of which he is made had a pre-exiftence, and, confequently, thofe of *the man Jefus*. But this is certainly a very different *kind* of pre-exiftence from that of thofe who make Chrift, or rather the principal part of him, to have pre-exifted in an active ftate, and to have afterwards entered into the embryo of the child of Mary. The belief that Chrift was the maker of all things, the doctrine of a purgatory, and the worfhip of the dead, could never have arifen from my hypothefis; but thefe, and many other

H 4 corruptions

corruptions of the chriftian fyftem, arofe but too eafily from the other. As a chriftian, (though it is not every body that, like Dr. Price, has the candour to allow me to be one) I think I have the greateft reafon to be jealous of this kind of pre-exiftence, but none at all of the mere pre-exiftence of the parts of which, men, animals, and even plants are com-pofed.

I am happy to concur with Dr. Price in the bulk of what he fays under this head. My idea of the ftate of man be-tween death and the refurrection, is, in fact, no way materially different from his. It is a ftate of *inaction* and *infenfibility*, from which we fhall not recover till the refurrection ; which, whether it will be brought about in a manner that may be faid to be *within the laws of nature ex-tenfively confidered,* or not, I cannot tell, and I am fometimes inclined to one opinion, and fometimes to the other. But though I fhould decide for the former, the *evidence* for it is not fo ftrong ; but that I think myfelf

felf juftified in faying, " that our only hope
" furviving the grave is derived from re-
" velation." For *hope* implies a *preponderance* of the arguments in favour of a
defirable event, which preponderance of
evidence *nature* does not appear to me to
furnifh. What the amount of that evidence, in my opinion, is, I have ftated in
my *Inftitutes of Natural and Revealed Religion*, Vol. I.

THE

# PART II.

## THE THIRD COMMUNICATION.

*Containing Remarks by Dr.* Price *on Dr.*
Prieftley's *Replies to the* fecond *Communication with Dr.* Prieftley's third *Replies.*

*Obfervations on Dr.* Prieftley's *Reply,* p. 91.

MOST certainly the attraction of the
earth, the fun, the planets, &c. (See
page 93.) not being the action of the
*matter itfelf* that is faid to attract, ought
to be afcribed to the action of fome other
fubftance *within* the earth, the fun and
planets—Does not Dr. Prieftley himfelf
acknowledge this?—And does he not, by
maintaining God to be the fource of all the
motions in the world, allow a *foul* to the
*world,* though he will not to *men*?

### ANSWER.

My argument goes to prove, that for
the fame reafon that *man* has been fuppofed

to

to have a foul, every *particular fubftance* to which any powers or properties are afcribed, may have *a feparate foul* alfo.

## Dr. Price.

*Ibid.* It is here faid, that *perception is the property of the brain.* I muft again repeat, that the being that perceives is *one.* The brain confifts of *many* fubftances. It is not, therefore, the brain that perceives. —In p. 100, it is faid, *that though man is one thinking being, he may confift of many un-thinking beings*——Nothing can be more incomprehenfible to me than this. Is it not the fame with faying, that *many* beings who want reafon, may make *one* being who has reafon? Or that a perfection may exift in the whole which does not exift in any of the parts? If this can be true, why may not the component parts of this material world, though all of them feparately un-intelligent, make one fupreme intelligent being?

## Answer.

### ANSWER.

I find no difficulty in conceiving that
*compound fubftances* may have properties
which their *component parts* cannot have.
But it does not, therefore, follow, that all
the conjoined parts of any *particular whole,*
*e. g. the univerfe,* can have the peculiar attributes of the being that we call *God;*
though they may have various properties
that cannot be affirmed of any of the parts
feparately taken.

### DR. PRICE.

If I underftand Dr. Prieftley, he fays in
page 105, that the Deity has a common
property with matter, becaufe, like matter, he has the power of attracting and
repelling.   But I have all along denied
that matter has this power.   According
to Dr. Prieftley himfelf, no being in nature *acts* but the Deity.

### ANSWER.

If the fuppofed immaterial principle in
man can really act upon the brain, it muft
necessarily

neceffarily be in the manner that we term attraction or repulfion : becaufe thefe comprife all the poffible affections of body; and what may be predicated of a finite mind, in this refpect, may alfo be predicated of the infinite mind.

### Dr. Price.

Does not Dr. Prieftley's manner of arguing in p. 92, imply, that it is *poffible* for a harpfichord to play on itfelf, and that there are circumftances in which it would be philofophical to draw this conclufion ?

### Answer.

My argument only proves, that, in certain *given,* but *impoffible circumftances,* there could be no *apparent ground* to conclude that the mufic came from any thing but the harpfichord itfelf.
*What can we reafon but from what we know?*

### Dr. Price.

It is faid, in p. 95, that *if ideas are not things diftinct from the mind, a mind with ideas,*

*ideas, and a mind without ideas, would be the same*——I maintain, that ideas are not diſtinct from the mind, but its conceptions; or not themſelves *things,* but *notions* of things. How does it follow from hence, that a mind with or without ideas, is the ſame? It would ſeem that this follows much more from the contrary aſſertion.

### Answer.

By a *thing* I mean whatever has properties. Now ideas have many properties, and a mind may have ideas, or be without them. According to Dr. Hartley's Theory, how-ever, ideas are only *vibrations in the brain,* which correſponds to what Dr. Price might call *modifications of the mind;* ſo that on this ſubject our opinions are not materially, if at all, different.

PART

# P A R T  III.

## Of the Doctrine of NECESSITY.

### THE FIRST COMMUNICATION.

#### QUERIES, by Dr. Price.

1. DO we not neceffarily afcribe our volitions and actions to ourfelves?

2. Do we not determine ourfelves?

3. If we do not determine ourfelves, are we not deceived when we afcribe our actions to ourfelves, and for that reafon reckon ourfelves accountable for them?

#### ANSWER.

By the principle of affociation we do afcribe our volitions and actions to ourfelves,

felves, and therefore we *neceffarily* do fo;
but not in fuch a manner as to exclude
*motives* from being neceffary to every determination; and if we fuppofe that our
volitions and actions have no caufe foreign
to themfelves, that is, to our wills, we
deceive ourfelves, as in various other wrong
judgments.

By being *liable to punifhment* for our
actions, and *accountable* for them, I mean
its being wife and good in the Divine
Being to appoint that certain fufferings
fhould follow certain actions, provided they
be *voluntary*, though *neceffary* ones; fuch
a connection of voluntary actions and fufferings being calculated to produce the
greateft ultimate good.

## Dr. Price.

*Query* 4. Does it follow from its being
certain that we fhall determine ourfelves in
a particular way, that we do not in that
inftance determine ourfelves at all?

Answer.

## Answer.

I confider all *felf-determination*, properly fo called, as an impoffibility, implying, that fuch a determination has, in fact, *no caufe at all.* If the determination be *certain*, it muft have a *certain or neceffary caufe*, arifing from views of things prefent to the mind. For the illuftration of this argument, I refer to my *Treatife of Neceffity*, Sect. II. and to the *Letter to Dr. Horfeley.*

---

## THE SECOND COMMUNICATION,

*On the Doctrine of* NECESSITY.

*Observations on Dr.* Prieftley's *Anfwers to the* Queries *in* p. 127 and 128, *by*

## DR. PRICE.

IN order to bring the difpute between me and Dr. Prieftley as much to a point as poffible, and to difcover how far we *agreed* and *differed*, I fent to him, after my firft communication, on the nature of matter and fpirit, and the immortality of the foul, the following Queries:

1. Can any thing act on another without being *prefent* to it?

2. Can, therefore, matter act on other matter without contact and impulfe?

3. Is

3. Is not the *foul*, or what I call *myfelf*, a *being*, or *fubftance*; and not merely a *mode* or *property*?

4. Does the foul lofe its exiftence at death? Or am I, the fubject of thought, reafon, confcioufnefs, &c. to be then annihilated?

5. If I am to lofe my exiftence at death, will not my refurrection be the refurrection of a non-entity; and therefore impoffible?

6. If I am not to lofe my exiftence at death, may it not be properly faid that I am naturally immortal?

7. Do we not neceffarily afcribe our volitions or actions to ourfelves?

8. Do we not determine ourfelves?

9. If we do not determine ourfelves, are we not deceived when we afcribe our actions to ourfelves; and, for that reafon, reckon ourfelves accountable for them?

10. Does

10. Does it follow from its being certain, in any inftance, that we fhall determine ourfelves in a particular way, that we do not, in that inftance, determine ourfelves at all?

In anfwer to thefe queries, I wifhed for no more than a fimple affirmation, or negation; thinking it would be a matter of fome curiofity, fhould it appear that our minds were fo differently framed, as that one of us would write an *yes* where the other would write a *no*. But I find that we are more nearly agreed than I expected. To the two firft queries, Dr. Prieftley has given no direct anfwer; but what he has faid in different places, feems to imply that he would agree with me in anfwering them in the negative. The 3d query he has in p. 86 and 87, anfwered, as I fhould, in the affirmative; and the 4th and 6th in the negative. It appears, however, I think, that I had fome reafon for expecting that he would not grant the foul to be a *fub-ftance*; much lefs *one fingle fubftance*. For the obvious inference from hence, is, that the

the foul cannot be, either any fyftem of
fubftances, or the *organization* of any
fyftem; and, therefore, not fuch an affemblage of fubftances as the brain, or the
organization of the brain.

To the 7th query it appears alfo, (fee p. 127)
that he anfwers in the affirmative, and yet that
to the 8th he anfwers in the negative. In
other words, he acknowledges that we neceffarily afcribe our determinations to ourfelves, but denies that we do *really* determine ourfelves; afferting in anfwer to
the 9th query, that we are deceived when
we imagine that our volitions are not produced by a caufe foreign to our wills, and
*on that account* believe ourfelves refponfible
for them; all felf-determination being impoffible; and *accountablenefs* or liablenefs
to punifhment, being only the connexion
which divine wifdom, in order to produce
the greateft ultimate good, has eftablifhed
between certain *voluntary* though *neceffary*
actions, and certain fufferings.

In feveral paffages in my *Review of
Morals* (p. 301 to 304, and p. 349 to 352,

I 3                              *fecond*

*second edit.*) I have stated, in the beft manner I am able, the queftion concerning Liberty and Neceffity. Dr. Prieftley, in his fecond volume (Sect. 5th and 6th) has replied to what I have faid in moft of thofe paffages, with *candour* and *ability:* But I cannot fay that I think he has done it with *fuccefs.* He feems to mifunderftand me, and, therefore, I will endeavour to give a more diftinct account of my ideas on this fubject. If they are wrong, I fhall rejoice to fee them proved to be fo. If they are right, it will be eafy to form a judgment of all Dr. Prieftley's arguments in his fecond volume, and to determine how far we *agree,* and *differ.*

After Dr. Clarke, I define Liberty to be " a power to act", or " a power of *felf-* " *motion,* or felf-determination." On this definition I would make the following obfervations.

1. That liberty is common to all *animals,* as well as to all *reafonable beings;* every animal, as fuch, poffeffing powers of *felf-motion,* or *fpontaneity.*

2. There

2. There are no *degrees* of liberty, be-caufe there is no medium between *acting*, and *not acting*; or between poffeffing felf-motive powers, and not poffeffing them.

3. The liberty now defined is poffible. One thing cannot move another, and that another *in infinitum*. Some where or other there muft exift a power of beginning motion, that is, of *felf-motion*. This is no lefs certain than that fince one thing cannot produce another, and that another *in in-finitum*, there muft be a *firft* caufe.

This argument feems to me decifive, not only for the *poffibility*, but the *actual exiftence* of liberty. But farther. We are confcious of it in ourfelves. I can fay nothing to convince a perfon who will de-clare that he believes *his* determinations do not originate *with himfelf*, or that he has no power of moving or determining himfelf. It is another queftion, whether he moves himfelf *with* or *without* a regard to *motives*. Afferting felf-determination with a regard to motives, (and no one ever yet afferted the contrary) is afferting *felf-*

*determination,*

*determination,* and, therefore, it is the fame with afferting liberty. Dr. Prieftley often fays, that felf-determination implies an effect without a caufe. But this cannotbe juftly faid. Does it follow that becaufe I am *myfelf* the caufe, there is no caufe?

4. This definition implies, that in our volitions, or determinations, we are not *acted upon. Acting,* and being *acted upon,* are incompatible with one another. In whatever inftances, therefore, it is truly faid of us that we *act,* in thofe inftances we cannot be *acted upon.* A being in receiving a change of its ftate, from the exertion of an adequate force, is not an *agent.* Man therefore would not be an *agent,* were all his volitions derived from any force, or the effects of any mechanical caufes. In this cafe it would be no more true that he ever acts, than it is true of a ball that it *acts* when *ftruck* by another ball. But the main obfervation I would make is the following.

5. " The liberty now defined is confiftent with acting with a regard to motives." This has been already intimated;
**but**

but it is neceffary it fhould be particularly attended to and explained.

Suppofing a power of felf-determination to exift, it is by no means neceffary that it fhould be exerted without a regard to any end or rule. On the contrary, it can never be exerted without fome view or defign. Whoever acts, means to do fomewhat. This is true of the loweft reptile, as well as of the wifeft man. The power of determining ourfelves, by the very nature of it, wants an *end* and *rule* to guide it; and no probability, or certainty, of its being exerted agreeably to a rule, can have the leaft tendency to infringe or diminifh it. All that fhould be avoided here, is, the intolerable abfurdity of making our reafons and ends in acting the phyfical *caufes* or *efficients* of action. This is the fame with afcribing the action of walking, not to the feet (or the power which moves the feet) but to the eye, which only *fees the way*. The perception of a reafon for acting, or the judgment of the underftanding, is no more than feeing the way. It is the eye of the

mind,

mind, which informs and directs; and whatever *certainty* there may be that a particular
determination will follow, such determination will be the *self-determination* of the
mind; and not any change of its state stamped
upon it, over which it has no power, and in
receiving which, instead of being an *agent*,
it is merely a *paſſive ſubject* of agency.

In a word, There is a distinction here
of the last importance, which must never
be overlooked. I mean the distinction so
much insisted on by Dr. Clarke, between
the *operation* of *phyſical cauſes*, and the *influence* of *moral reaſons*. The views or ideas
of beings may be the *account* or *occaſions* of
their acting; but it is a contradiction to
make them the *mechanical efficients* of their
actions. And yet I suspect that Dr. Prieſtley will avow this to be his opinion. Ideas
he makes to be divisible and extended. He
ascribes an impulsive force to them: And
asserts that they act by mechanical laws on
the mind, as one material ſubſtance acts
upon another. See his *Replies*, p. 52, 85,
95; and the *Diſquiſitions*, p. 38.

In

In order better to explain the diſtinction I have mentioned, I will beg leave to give an account of the following particulars, in which it appears to me that *phyſical* and *moral* cauſes differ.

1. The one are *beings*; the others are only the *views* of beings.

2. The one always *do*, and the other *may* produce a certainty of event. But the certainties in theſe two caſes differ eſſentially. It is, for inſtance, *certain* that a man dragged along like a piece of timber, will follow the ſuperior force that acts upon him. It may be alſo *certain*, that a man invited by the hope of a reward, will follow a guide. But who ſees not that theſe certainties, having different foundations, are of a totally different nature ? In both caſes the man might in common ſpeech be ſaid to *follow*; but his following in the one caſe, however certain in event, would be *his own* agency : In the other caſe, it would be the agency of *another*. In the one caſe, he would really *follow*: But in the other caſe, being dragged, he could not properly be

ſaid .

faid to *follow*. In the one cafe, fuperior power moves him : In the other, he moves himfelf. In fhort; to afcribe a neceffary and phyfical efficiency to motives, is (as Dr. Clarke has obferved) the fame with faying, that *an abftract notion can ftrike a ball*.

3. The certainty of event arifing from the operation of *phyfical* caufes is always equal and invariable, but the certainty of event arifing from *moral* caufes, that is, from the views and perceptions of beings, admits of an infinite variety of degrees; and fometimes paffes into *probability* and *contingency*.

Suppofing contrary reafons equally balanced in the mind, it may be *uncertain* how a being will act. If, for inftance, a temptation to an act of wickednefs comes in the way of a man whofe love of virtue is nearly equal to the ftrength of his paffions, it may be doubtful which way he will determine. If his love of virtue exceeds the influence of paffion, there will be a *probability* of his acting virtuoufly, proportioned

portioned to the degree in which the love
of virtue prevails within him : And it may
be fo prevalent as to make it *certain* that
he will always follow his perceptions of
virtue.

4. In the operation of phyfical caufes, it
is always implied that there is not in any
fenfe a power to produce, or a poffibility
of producing any other effect than that
which is produced; but the contrary is
true of effects dependent on the wills,
and occafioned by the views of free agents.
A benevolent man will *certainly* relieve mi-
fery when it falls in his way; but he has
the *power* of not relieving it. On the contrary, a ftone thrown from the hand *muft*
move. There is no fenfe in which it can
be faid, that it poffeffes the power of not
moving in the precife direction in which it
is thrown. The reafon of this is, that the
benevolent man *acts :* The ftone only *fuffers.*
Were the determination to give relief in
the former cafe, and the motions of the
ftone in the latter, both alike *fufferances,*
(if I may fo fpeak) or both effects of a
force which could not be refifted, they
would

would be both alike void of all merit A man at the bottom of St. Paul's *will* not jump *up:* A man at the top *will* not jump *down.* Both events may be *certain.* But a man at the bottom *cannot* jump up: A man at the top *can* jump down. And if in common fpeech we fhould fay in the latter cafe, that a man at the top *cannot* jump down, we fhould fpeak figuratively and improperly; meaning only that he certainly *will* not. Who can deny, even with refpect to the Supreme Deity, that, however certain it may be that he will not make his creation miferable, he has the power to do it? It is, indeed, on this power that all our notions of moral excellence in the actions of beings depend. Were the beneficence of a being no more *his* action, or *felf-determination,* than the falling of rain is the action, or felf-determination, of rain, it would not be the object of moral approbation; or the ground of efteem and gratitude. (See *Review of Morals,* p. 410 to p. 415. *fecond edit.*) This leads me to obferve, laftly,

6. That

6. That the *cafuality* implied in the views and difpofitions of beings is entirely confiftent with moral obligation, and refponfibility: But that all effects brought about by mechanical laws are inconfiftent with them. This appears fufficiently from the preceding obfervations.

Upon the whole. The queftion concerning Liberty is not, " Whether the " views or ideas of beings *influence* their " actions," but " what the *nature* of that " *influence* is." That it is not any kind of *mechanical* or *phyfical* efficiency, appears to me palpably evident. But if I am miftaken in this opinion; and if indeed, as Dr. Prieftley maintains, man has no other liberty in following motives than water has in running down hill, or than the arms of a fcale preft by weights, have in rifing and falling: If, I fay, this is the truth, man never *acts*. It is folly to applaud or reproach ourfelves for our conduct; and there is an end of all moral obligation and accountablenefs—Dr. Prieftley does not acknowledge thefe confequences. I think them clear to fuch a degree

degree as not to admit of proper proof. The beſt that can be done in this caſe is to ſtate the queſtion diſtinctly and intelligibly, and leave the deciſion to common ſenſe.

In reviewing theſe papers I have found, that my deſire to explain myſelf fully has led me to a redundancy of expreſſion and many repetitions. Dr. Prieſtley will, I hope, excuſe this. I refer myſelf to his candour, and chuſe now to withdraw from this controverſy——His firſt volume concludes with ſome obſervations in defence of the *Socinian* ſcheme of chriſtianity. I will not enter into any debate with him on this ſubject. My opinion is, that the Socinian ſcheme degrades chriſtianity, and is by no means reconcileable to the Scriptures. But I know that ſome of the beſt men and wiſeſt chriſtians have adopted it. Among theſe I reckon Dr. *Prieſtley*, Mr. *Lindſey*, and Dr. *Jebb*; and ſhould it, contrary to my apprehenſions, be the true chriſtian doctrine, I wiſh them all poſſible ſucceſs in propagating it.

ANSWER.

## Answer.

On the fubject of *Neceffity* I have nothing
material to add to what is contained in the
fecond volume of my work, and I cannot
help thinking, that if what I have there
advanced be attended to, it will be fufficient to obviate the objections here urged
by Dr. Price. But as he has been fo obliging as to give his ideas with great franknefs, and diftinctnefs, on the fubject, and
I conceive this to be the only difference of
real confequence between us, I fhall fo far
repeat the fubftance of what I have faid
before, as may be neceffary to reply with
equal explicitnefs to what he has here obferved.

If *felf-motion*, or *felf-determination*, properly fo called, be effential to liberty, I
muft deny that man is poffeffed of it ; and
if this, and nothing elfe, muft be called
*agency*, I muft deny that, *in this fenfe*,
man is an agent ; becaufe every human volition is invariably directed by the circumftances in which a man is, and what we

K                              call

call *motives*. It appears to me that we have no more reafon, *from fact and obfervation*, to conclude that a man can *move himfelf*, that is, that he can *will without motives*, than that a ftone can move itfelf. And if the will is as invariably influenced by motives as the ftone is influenced by gravity, it may juft as well be faid that the ftone moves itfelf, though always according to the laws of gravity, as that the will, or the mind, moves itfelf, though always according to the motives; and whether thefe motives be called the *moral* or the *phyfical* caufes of our volitions, is of no fort of fignification; becaufe they are the *only* and the *neceffary* caufes, juft as much as gravity is the only and neceffary caufe of the motion of the ftone. Let the mind act contrary to motives, or the ftone move contrary to the laws of gravity, and I fhall then, but not before, believe that they are *not* the only and neceffary caufes.

"The perception of reafons or motives
" Dr. Price calls the eye of the mind,
" which informs and directs;" but if the
determination

determination of the mind, which follows upon it, be invariably *according to* that perception, I muft conclude that the nature of the mind is fuch, as that it *could not* act otherwife, and therefore that it has no felf-determination properly fo called. A power manifefted by no effects, muft be confidered as merely imaginary, it being from *effects* alone that we arrive at the knowledge of *caufes*.

Judging from facts, I muft conclude that a proper *felf-motion* can no more belong to man than *felf-exiftence*. Indeed, we have no more idea of the nature of felf-motion than we have of felf-exiftence. Motion and exiftence cannot be eternally derived, and *actual exiftence* and *actual motion*, necef-farily lead us to fome *felf-exifting*, and confequently *felf-moving being*. Though the idea be ever fo incomprehenfible, and confounding to our faculties, we muft acquiefce in it; for to ftop *fhort* of this, or go *beyond* it, is equally impoffible.

The difference that Dr. Price and others make between *moral* and *phyfical* caufes and

K 2                                                   effects,

effects, appears to me to be that which subsists between *voluntary* and *involuntary* causes and effects; and this is indeed a most important difference. Where involuntary motions are concerned, as in the case of a man dragged by force, it is absurd to use any reasoning or expostulation, or to apply rewards or punishments, because they can have *no effect*; but where voluntary motions are concerned, as in the case of a man who is at liberty to go where he pleases, and chuse what company he pleases, &c. reasoning and expostulation, rewards and punishments, have the greatest *propriety*, because the greatest *effect*; for they are applied to, and influence or move the will, as much as external force moves the body.

It is on this circumstance, viz. *the influence of motives on the will*, that the whole of *moral discipline* depends; so that if the will of man were so formed, as that motives should have no influence upon it, he could not be the subject of moral government; because the hope of reward, and the fear of punishment, operate in no other manner than

than as *motives applied to the will*. And
fince the whole of moral government depends upon the diftribution of rewards and
punifhments, what has been called *liberty*,
or a power of acting independently of
motives, is fo far from being the only foundation of moral government, that it is abfolutely inconfiftent with it, as I have
fhewn at large in my fecond volume.

The ideas belonging to the terms *accountablenefs, praife and blame, merit and
demerit*, all relate to the bufinefs of moral
difcipline, and therefore neceffarily imply
that men are influenced by motives, and
act from *fixed principles*, and *character ;*
though, on account of our not comprehending the doctrine of *caufes*, and ftop-
ping where we ought not, we are generally
under fome miftake and mifconception with
refpect to them.    Therefore, to guard
againft all miftake, it may be more ad-
vifable that, in treating the fubject philofophically, thofe words be difufed.    Every
thing that really correfponds to them may
be clearly expreffed in different language,

K 3                              and

and all the *rules of difcipline,* every thing in practice, on the part both of the *governor* and the *governed,* will ftand juft as before. To make my meaning intelligible, and fhow that I do not advance this at random, I fhall here endeavour to exprefs in a ftrict and philofophical manner the full import of all the terms abovementioned.

In common fpeech we fay that we are *accountable creatures,* and *juftly liable to rewards and punifhments* for our conduct. The philofopher fays, that *juftice* ought to be called *propriety* or *ufefulnefs,* or a rule of conduct adapted to anfwer a good purpofe, which in this cafe is the good of thofe who are the fubjects of government or difcipline; and therefore, inftead of faying, We are *juftly liable to rewards or punifhments,* he fays, We are beings of fuch a conftitution, that to make us happy upon our obfervance of certain laws, and to make us fuffer in confequence of our tranfgrefling thofe laws, will have a good effect with refpect both to our own future conduct and that of others; *i. e.* tending to our own melioration,

melioration, and operating to the melioration of others.

In common language we say a man is *praise-worthy*, and has *merit*. The philosopher says, that the man has acted from, or been influenced by good principles, or such principles as will make a man happy in himself, and useful to others; that he is therefore a proper object of complacency, and fit to be made happy; that is, the *general happiness* will be promoted by making him happy.

So also when, in common language, a man is said to be *blame-worthy* and to have *demerit*, the philosopher says, that he has acted from, or been influenced by bad principles, or such as will make a man unhappy in himself, and hurtful to others; that he is therefore a proper subject of aversion, and is fit to be made unhappy; that is, the making him unhappy will tend to promote the general happiness.

Upon the whole, therefore, though the vulgar and philosophers use different language,

guage, they would fee reafon to *act* in the fame manner. The governors will rule voluntary agents by means of rewards and punifhments, and the governed, being voluntary agents, will be influenced by the apprehenfion of them. It is confequently a matter of indifference in whatever language we defcribe actions and characters. If the common language be in fome refpects inconfiftent with the doctrine of neceffity, it is ftill more inconfiftent with the doctrine of liberty, or the notion of our being capable of determining without regard to motives.

For the *effect* of the more exalted views of the philofophical neceffarian, (as unfpeakably fuperior to the more imperfect views of the vulgar) I refer to what I have faid upon that fubject in my fecond volume. We are not, however, to expect that neceffarians fhould univerfally, and to the eye of the world, be better than other men. Even chriftianity does not univerfally appear to this advantage in the lives of its profeffors. But of this I am perfuaded, that

OF THE DOCTRINE OF NECESSITY.

that if any man had ftrength of mind fully to comprehend the doctrine of ne- ceffity, and to keep his mind at all times under the influence of it, he would be much fuperior to the *mere chriftian*, though not perhaps as much fo as the chriftian may be to the *mere virtuous heathen*.

Before I conclude this fubject, I cannot help noticing what appears to me to be an inconfiftency in Dr. Price's account of his view of it. He fays, p. 137, " The " power of felf-determination can never " be exerted without fome view, or de- " fign," *i. e.* the will cannot be deter- mined without motives, and " The power " of determining ourfelves, by the very na- " ture of it, wants an end, and rule, to " guide it." From this I fhould infer, that the end and rule by which the will was guided being given, the determination would be certain and invariable ; whereas, in another place, p. 139, he fays, that " moral caufes only *may* produce a cer- " tainty ; and even that the certainty of " an event arifing from moral caufes, that is,

" from

" from the views and perceptions of things,
" admits of an infinite variety of degrees,
" and fometimes paffes into probability
" and contingence," p. 140. Alfo that " in
" the operation of moral caufes there is a
" poffibility of producing any other ef-
" fect than that which is produced."

Now that the will fhould, by the very
nature of it, want an end and rule to
guide it, and yet be capable of determining not only *without*, but *contrary* to that
rule, is, I think, inconfiftent; and yet
upon this it is that the whole controverfy
hinges. If the will be always determined
according to motives (whether it be alledged to be *by itself*, or *by the motives*)
the determination is certain and invariable,
which is all that I mean by *neceffary*;
whereas if it may determine *contrary to
motives*, it is *contingent*, and uncertain;
which I maintain to be a thing as impoffible as that, in any cafe whatever, an effect fhould arife without a caufe; and alfo
to be a thing that is, in its nature, incapable of being the object of *fore-knowledge*.

*ledge.* And yet, if there be any truth in the scriptures, the Divine Being certainly forefees every determination of the mind of man.

THE

---

## THE THIRD COMMUNICATION.

## *Of the Doctrine of* NECESSITY.

### DR. PRICE,

ON the fubject of neceffity I will only fay farther, that notwithftanding what Dr. Prieftley has faid in his laft reply, p. 145, &c. I remain of opinion that " *Self*-deter-
" mination and certainty of determination
" are perfectly confiftent."—" That a felf-
" determining power which is under no
" influence from motives, or which de-
" ftroys the ufe of difcipline and the fu-
" perintendency of providence, has never
" been contended for, or meant by any
" advocates for liberty."—And, that I am
by no means fenfible of any inconfiftency
between

between afferting that every being who
acts at all muſt act for ſome end, and with
ſome view; and afferting, that a being may
have the power of determining his choice
to any one of different ends, and that
when a regard to different ends is equal,
*contingency* of event takes place.——The
controverſy, however, does not according
to my views of it, hinge on the conſideration laſt mentioned; but merely on this,
whether man is a proper agent, or has a
ſelf-determining power, or not. Beings
may have a ſelf-determining power, as, according to Dr. Prieſtley's conceſſion, the
deity has; and yet they may be always
guided, as the deity certainly is, by a rule or
end.—I know Dr. Prieſtley will not allow
me to argue thus from the deity to inferior
beings. But this method of arguing appears
to me fair; and, in the preſent caſe, it ſeems
deciſive. It is only the *manner* in which God
poſſeſſes his attributes that is incommuni-
cable. We may juſtly ſay, God poſſeſſes
power. Therefore, he may *give* power.
But we cannot, without a contradiction,
ſay, God is ſelf-exiſtent: Therefore, he
may

may give felf-exiftence; for this would be to fay, that he can make a *derived* being, *underived*.——Nor can we fay, God pof-feffes infinite power; therefore, he can communicate *infinite* power; for this would be to fay, that he can make a being, who, as a creature, muft be finite and dependent, infinite and independent.——It might be fhewn, that creation out of nothing im-plies infinite power, and therefore cannot be communicated.

Dr. Prieftley will, I hope, allow me to add the following queries.

Is is not more honourable to the deity to conceive of him, as the parent, guide, governor, and judge of free beings formed after his own image, with powers of rea-fon and felf-determination, than to con-ceive of him, as the former and conductor of a fyftem of confcious machinery, or the mover and controuler of an univerfe of puppets?

Can Dr. Prieftley believe eafily, that in all thofe crimes which men charge
*themfelves*

*themſelves* with, and reproach *themſelves* for, God is the agent; and that (ſpeaking philoſophically) *they*, in ſuch inſtances, are no more *agents*, than a *ſword* is an agent when employed to commit murder?

Is it ſurpriſing that few poſſeſs ſtrength of mind enough to avoid ſtarting at ſuch concluſions?—I am, however, ready to own the weight of ſome of the obſervations Dr. Prieſtley has made to explain and ſoften them. And though I think, that were they commonly received, they would be dreadfully abuſed; yet I doubt not, but Dr. Prieſtley may be, as he ſays he is, a better man for believing them.

But I muſt not go on. Were I to write all that offers itſelf, I ſhould fall into numberleſs tautologies; and there would be no end of this controverſy.

### Answer.

I know very well that Dr. Price, and other advocates for what is called philoſophical free-will, do not *think* that a ſelf-determining

determining power deftroys the ufe of difcipline, and but I contend that it neceffarily does fo, I alfo deny that, ftrictly
fpeaking, there can be any fuch thing as
*contingency*, it always implying that there is
*an effect without a caufe*; and therefore that
a determination of the mind in circumftances in which a regard to different objects is
equal, is an impoffibility. This muft be
univerfal, and confequently refpect the fupreme mind as well as others. Thofe who
fpeak with the greateft reverence of the
Divine Being, always fuppofe that he never
acts but for fome *end*, and that the beft,
*i. e.* he acts according to fome invariable
*rule*. But we foon lofe ourfelves in fpeculation concerning the *firft caufe*.

In anfwer to the *Queries*, I reply, in general, that I cannot conceive any thing
honourable to the deity, becaufe the thing
is *not poffible in itfelf*, and if poffible, not
at all *beneficial to man*, in the fuppofition
of his having endued us with what is
called *felf-determination*. And though the
doctrine of neceffity may, like every thing
the

the moft true and fublime, be exhibited in a ridiculous light, it is the only fyftem that is even *poffible*; and in my opinion it is in the higheft degree *honourable*, both to the univerfal parent, and his offspring; the juft contemplation of it being eminently improving to the mind, and leading to the practice of every thing great and excellent, as I think I have fhewn in my fecond volume.

It certainly founds harfh to vulgar ears, to fay that " in all thofe crimes that men " charge themfelves with, and reproach " themfelves for, God is the agent; and " that, in fuch cafes, they are in reality " no more *agents*, than a fword is an agent " when employed to commit a murder." It does require *ftrength of mind* not to ftartle at fuch a conclufion; but then it requires nothing but ftrength of mind; *i. e.* fuch a view of things as fhall carry us beyond *firft* and *fallacious appearances*. And it requires, I think, but a fmall degree of fagacity to perceive that, whatever there is fhocking in thefe conclufions, it is actually

L                              found,

found, and under a very flight cover, in Dr. Price's own principles; since, I believe, he admits that God forefees all the crimes that men would commit, and yet made man; that he still has it in his power, in various ways, to prevent the commiffion of crimes, and yet does not chufe to do it. If Dr. Price will anfwer a queftion that is frequently put by children, viz. " Papa, Why does not God " kill the Devil?" I will undertake to tell him why God *made* the Devil. Let him tell me why God *permits* vice, and I will tell him why he *appoints* it.

However, the very language that Dr. Price ufes to make the doctrine of neceffity appear horrid and frightful, is the very language of the fcriptures, in which wicked men are exprefsly called *God's fword*, and are faid, in a great variety of phrafes, to do *all his pleafure*; though, in a different fenfe, the very contrary expreffions occur. The reply that Paul makes to what might be objected to his faying, *God has mercy on whom he will have mercy, and whom he*

*will*

*will he hardeneth,* Rom. 9, &c. viz. *Thou
wilt say then unto me, Why doth he yet find
fault, for who has resisted his will,* favours
more of the ideas of a neceffarian, than
I fufpect, the abettors of the contrary
doctrine can well bear; *Nay but? O man,
who art thou that repliest against God?
Shall the thing formed say unto him that
formed it, why haft thou made me thus?
Hath not the potter power over the clay,
of the same lump to make one veffel unto honour, and another unto dishonour?*

I do not fay it is impoffible to explain
this paffage of fcripture in a manner confiftent with Dr. Price's opinions; but I
will fay that, with lefs latitude of interpretation, I will undertake to explain every
text that can be produced in favour of the
Arian hypothefis, in a manner ,confiftent·
with Socinianifm.

Since, upon all fchemes, it is a fact, that
vice, as well other evils, *does* and *muft* exift,
at leaft for a time; is it not more honourable to the univerfal creator, and fupreme

L 2          ruler,

ruler, to fuppofe that he *intended* it, as an
inftrument of virtue and happinefs, rather
than that, though he by no means chofe it
(as a thing that neceffarily thwarted his
views) it was not in his power to forefee
or prevent it; but that he is content to
make the beft he can of it when it does
happen, interpofing from time to time to
*palliate* matters, as *unforefeen emergencies* require. This, if it be poffible in itfelf, is
what we muft acquiefce in, if we rejeƈt
the doƈtrine of neceffity. There is no
other alternative.

I think it hardly poffible that a perfon
who believes in *contingencies* can have a
fteady faith in the doƈtrine of *divine pre-
fcience*; and to diveft the Divine Being of
this attribute, which in the fcriptures he
claims as his diftinguifhing prerogative, is
fuch a *leffening* and a *degradation* of God,
refpeƈting him too in his moft important
capacity, or that in which we are moft
concerned, viz. as *governor of the univerfe*,
that every thing that Dr. Price can reprefent

fent as the confequence of the doctrine of neceffity appears to me as nothing in comparifon with it.

But, as Dr. Price is fully fenfible, we fee things in very different lights; and it is happy for us that, in general, every light in which we view *our own principles* is more or lefs favourable to virtue. The Papift, I doubt not, thinks his mind powerfully and advantageoufly impreffed with the idea of the facramental elements being *the real body and blood of Chrift*; the Trinitarian with the notion of *the fupreme God being incarnate*, and the Arian with his opinion, that it was the *maker and governor of the world that died upon the crofs*; and numbers will fay that chriftianity is of no value, and with Mr. Venn, that they would *burn their bibles*, if thefe ftrange doctrines be not contained in them.

Dr. Price, however, does not *feel* that chriftianity is degraded *in his apprebenfion*, by confidering thefe opinions as abfurd, or ill founded, though he

L 3                                    does

does think it degraded by the Socinian hypothefis. Neither do I think chriftianity degraded, but, on the contrary, I think its effect upon the mind is much improved, and the wifdom and power of God more confpicuous, on the fcheme which fuppofes that our Saviour was a *mere man, in all things like unto his brethren*; and that as by a *mere man came death,* fo *by a mere man,* alfo, *comes the refurrection of the dead.* I chearfully conclude with Dr. Price in faying, in his *letter* fubjoined to the *Introduction,* " that our agreement in " expecting this awful period, makes it " of little confequence in what we dif- " fer."

## QUERIES *addreffed to* DR. PRICE.

### *Of the penetrability of matter.*

1. Is it not a fact, that *refiftance* is often occafioned not by the contact of folid matter, but by a *power of repulfion* acting at a diftance from the fuppofed fubftance, as in electricity, magnetifm, optics, &c. ?

2. What

2. What is the effect of fuppofed *contact*, but another refiftance?

3. Is it not even certain, that this fuppofed contact cannot be *real contact*, fince the particles that compofe the moft compact bodies, being capable of being brought nearer together by cold, appear not actually to touch one another?

4. Since, therefore, there cannot be any evidence of impenetrability, but what refults from the confideration of *contact*, and there is no *evidence* of any real contact, does not the doctrine of impenetrability ftand altogether unfupported by any *fact*; and therefore muft it not be unphilofophical to admit that it is any property of matter?

### Of the SOUL.

1. If matter be not impenetrable, Dr. Price feems (if I may judge from what he fays in page 56,) not unwilling to admit that it may be endued with the properties of perception and thought. Since, therefore, *the uniform compofition of the*

*whole*

*whole man* will be gained by the preceding hypotheſis, is it not a conſideration in favour of it? It can only be a ſuppoſed *neceſſity* that could lead any perſon to adopt the hypotheſis of *two ſubſtances* in the compoſition of *one being*, eſpecially two ſubſtances ſo exceedingly heterogeneous as *matter* and *ſpirit* are defined to be.

2. Admitting matter to have the property of impenetrability, is there any reaſon to believe that the powers of perception and thought may not be ſuperadded to it, but that we cannot *conceive* any connection between the different properties of impenetrability and thought, or any relation they can bear to each other?

3. Have we, in reality, any idea of a connection between the property of perception, and extended ſubſtance, that is *not impenetrable*?

4. If not, is it not more philoſophical to ſuppoſe that the property of perception *may* be imparted to ſuch a ſubſtance as the body; it being certainly unphiloſophical to ſuppoſe

suppose that man consists of *two kinds of subftance,* when all the known properties and powers of man *may* belong to *one fubftance.*

5. If the foul of man be an extended fubftance, it is certainly in idea, and why may it not *in fact,* be as difcerptible as matter. If fo, are all the parts into which it may be divided, thinking and confcious beings? If not, why may not a material being, poffeffed of thought, confift of material fubftances, not poffeffed of thought, as well as a fpiritual one?

6. Whether is it more probable that God can endue organized matter with a capacity of thinking, or that an immaterial fubftance, poffeffed of that property, can be fo dependent upon the body, as not to be capable of having a perception without it, fo that even its peculiar power of *felfmotion* cannot be exerted but in conjunction with the body?

7. If there can be any fuch thing as a proper connection between material and

imma-

immaterial fubftances, muft not the former neceffarily, according to the common
hypothefis, impede the motions of the
latter ?

8. Is there, therefore, any proper medium between the hypothefis which makes
man *wholly material*, and that which makes
the body a clog upon the foul, and confequently the death of the body the freedom
of the foul ?

9. They who maintain the Arian hypothefis, believe that an immaterial fpirit,
fimilar to the human foul, is capable of
the greateft exertions in a ftate independent of any connection with body, at leaft
fuch bodies as ours. They alfo fuppofe
that between the death and the refurrection
of our Lord, he poffeffed, and exerted, his
original powers. Is it not then inconfo-
nant to this fyftem, to fuppofe that the
human foul, which to all appearance is
influenced by bodily affections exactly like
the embodied foul of Chrift, fhould be incapable of all fenfation or action during
the fleep or death of the body ?

10. Con-

10. Confequently, does not every argument that proves the dependence of the foul on the body favour the Socinian hypothefis, by making it probable, that the foul of Chrift was equally dependent upon his body, and therefore was incapable of exertion *before* as well as *after* its union to it? In other words, that Chrift had no proper exiftence before his birth?

## *Of the Doctrine of* NECESSITY.

1. If any mental determination, or volition, be preceded by nothing, either within the mind itfelf, or external to it, but what might have exifted without being followed by that determination, in what does that determination differ from *an effect without a caufe*?

2. Admitting the poffibility of fuch a determination, or a determination without any previous motive, with what propriety can it be the fubject of praife or blame, there being no *principle*, or *defign* (which would come under the denomination of *motive*) from which the determination proceeded?

ceeded ? How then can such a power of self determination make us *accountable creatures,* or the proper objects of rewards and punishments ?

3. If certain definite determinations of mind be always preceded by certain definite motives, or situations of mind, and the same definite motives be always followed by the same determinations, may not the determinations be properly called *necessary;* necessity signifying nothing more than the *cause of constancy* ?

4. If certain determinations always follow certain states of mind, will it not follow, whether these determinations be called necessary, or not, that no determination could have been *intended,* or *expected,* by the author of all things, to have been otherwise than it *has been, is,* or *is to be* ? Since, in this case, they could not have been otherwise without a miracle.

5. If any event be properly *contingent,* *i. e.* if the determination does not depend upon the previous state of mind, is it possible that the most perfect knowledge of
that

that mind, and of all the ftates of it, can enable a perfon to tell what the determination will be? In other words, is a contingent event the object of fore-knowledge, even to the deity himfelf?

## Dr. Price.

In anfwer to Dr. Prieftley's 4th query, (page 172,) and alfo to what he fays in page 161, 162, &c. I readily admit that all events are fuch as the power of God (acting under the direction of infinite wifdom and goodnefs) either *caufes* them to be, or *permits* them to be. I rejoice in this as the moft agreeable and important of all truths: But I by no means think with Dr. Prieftley, that there is no difference between it, and God's *producing* all events. I fcarcely think he would conclude thus in other cafes. Are there not many inftances in which Dr. Prieftley would think it hard to be charged with *doing* what he only forefees, and for the beft reafons, thinks fit not to *hinder*?

Active and felf-directing powers are the foundation of all morality; all dignity of
nature

nature and character; and the greateft poffible happinefs. It was, therefore, neceffary fuch powers fhould be communicated;
and being communicated, it was equally
neceffary that fcope, within certain limits,
fhould be allowed for the exercife of them.
Is God's *permitting* beings, in the ufe of
fuch powers, to act wickedly, the fame
with being himfelf the agent in their wickednefs? Or can it be reafonable to fay,
that he *appoints* what cannot be done without breaking his laws, contradicting his
will, and *abufing* the powers he has given?

Were I to be afked fuch a queftion as that
which Dr. Prieftley (in page 162,) puts into
the mouth of a child—" Why God made
the Devil?" or, " Why God does not con-
" fine or kill the Devil?" I fhould probably anfwer, that God made the Devil
good, but that he made himfelf a Devil;
and that a period is near when the Devil
and all wicked beings will be deftroyed;
but that, in the mean time, the mifchief
they do is not prevented by confining
them, or taking away their power, for
the

the fame reafon that a wife government does not prevent crimes by fhutting men up in their houfes, or that a parent does not prevent his children from doing wrong by tying up their hands and feet.——— I would, in fhort, lead the child to under-ftand if poffible, that to prevent wicked-nefs by denying a fphere of agency to be-ings, would be to prevent one evil by pro-ducing a greater.

The anfwer I would give to moft of Dr. Prieftley's other queries, may be eafily col-lected from my former replies.

With refpect to the laft of them in par-ticular, I cannot help obferving, that it implies what I can by no means admit, that free agency is inconfiftent with a depen-dence of our determinations on the ftate of our minds, and with a certainty of event. I think I have proved that our determinations may be *felf*-determinations, and yet this be true of them.

The fore-knowledge of a *contingent* event carrying the appearance of a contradiction,

is

is indeed a difficulty; and I do not pretend to be capable of removing it.

## ANSWER.

I ſtill cannot ſee any difference, with re-ſpect to *criminality*, between *doing*, and *per-mitting* what may be prevented, even with reſpect to men, and much leſs with reſpect to the deity; and I ſhould *not* think it hard to be charged with what I thought proper not to hinder. If I had, as Dr. Price ſays, *the beſt reaſons for it*, they would ſufficiently juſtify me, and in both caſes alike.

But men have only an imperfect con-trol upon each other, and the exertion of it is often difficult, or at leaſt inconve-nient. We, therefore, make an allowance with reſpect to men, for which there is no reaſon with reſpect to God. He diſtinctly foreſees every action of a man's life, and all the *actual conſequences* of it. If, there-fore, he did not think any particular man, and his conduct, proper for his plan of creation and providence, he certainly would

**not**

not have introduced him into being at all.

All that Dr. Price obferves with refpect to what he calls *active* and *felf directing powers*, I entirely approve; but I think the fame conclufions will follow on the fuppofition of man and fuperior beings, having what we call mere *voluntary powers*, liable to be influenced by the motives to which they will be expofed, in the circumftances in which the Divine Being thinks proper to place them. It is this that I call *the foundation of morality*; and not to have given this power, or, by miraculous interpofition, to controul it, would either be, as Dr. Price fays, *to prevent fmaller evils by producing greater*, or not to produce the greateft poffible good. His reply to the child is the fame that I make, but the queftion has a meaning to which the capacity of a child does not extend.

If Dr. Price admits, as, in this, place, he feems to do, that our determinations *certainly* depend upon the ftate of our minds,

M                                           I

I shall have no objection to his calling us *free agents*. I believe we are so, in the popular sense of the words, and I think it perfectly consistent with all the *necessity* that I ascribe to man. When men say that they are *free*, they have no idea of any thing farther than a freedom from the control of others, or what may be called *external force*, or causes of action not arising within themselves. *Internal causes* are never so much as thought of, and much less expressly excluded, when they speak of this most perfect liberty.

LETTERS

# LETTERS

TO

DR. KENRICK,

MR. JOHN WHITEHEAD,

AND

DR. HORSELEY.

## To *Dr.* KENRICK.

SIR,

YOU and I differ fo very little with refpect to any thing of importance in my *Difquifitions*, &c. that notwithftanding the obligation I have laid myfelf under, I fhould hardly have thought it neceffary to addrefs you on the fubject; and I freely acknowledge, that it is rather your importunity, than any thing elfe, that has induced me to do it.

We equally maintain that matter is not that impenetrable ftuff that it has been imagined to be, that man is an homogeneous being, the fentient principle not refiding in a fubftance diftinct from . the body, but being the refult of organization; and, as far as I can perceive, you likewife

M 3                                    agree

agree with me in holding the doctrine of philofophical neceffity.

Of what then is it that you complain; It feems to be, principally, that I do not acknowledge to have learned my doctrine in your fchool, and that the manner in which I explain it is not perfectly confiftent, or juft. You fay, *Review* for 1778, p. 48, " I cannot eafily abfolve you from the cen- " fure of unpardonable neglect, in being ig- " norant of what has fo recently, and re- " peatedly been advanced on the fundamental " fubject of your *Difquifitions*. Twenty years " are now nearly elapfed fince I firft took " up the fubject, on occafion of the late " Cadwallader Colden's treatife of the *prin-* " *ciple of action in matter*, a fubject on which " I have frequently defcanted, in various " publications, as occafion offered." In the fame page you fay, " that this neg- " lect of mine is not fo much *real* as *af-* " *fected*."

Now, Sir, whatever be the degree of *blame* that I have juftly brought upon my-felf, I do affure you that my ignorance of

your

your having maintained what I contend for is not affected, but *real*; and indeed my not having learned *more* of you, and my not holding your doctrine with perfect confiftency, may be allowed to weigh fomething in anfwer to a charge of *plagiarifm*. Befides, whatever injury I have done you, I reap no advantage from it; becaufe I do not advance the doctrine as my own difcovery, but profefs to have learned the fyftem from F. Bofcovich, and Mr. Michell.

I am but an occafional reader of *Reviews*, and I have not the leaft recollection either of Mr. Colden's treatife, or of any thing that was ever faid about it; and yet I am far from thinking difrefpectfully either of *anonymous*, or of *periodical* publications, of which, without the leaft reafon, you frequently charge me : but certainly there is lefs chance of an anonymous publication being generally known, and efpecially of its being afcribed to its right author.

You fay, p. 402, that you find I do not think you much my *friend*, becaufe I faid fo of the author of the *Effay* in your

M 4                              Review

Review for September 1775; but I had not
the moſt diſtant ſuſpicion of your being
the writer of that Eſſay. It is there called
*a Letter to the Reviewers*, and was announced by yourſelf, as a piece ſuppoſed to
be written either by *myſelf*, or *ſome of my
able friends*; and, in conſequence, probably, of that manner of announcing it, it
has, with many perſons, paſſed for mine.
You muſt not blame me for not knowing
it to be yours, when yourſelf announced it
as mine.

As you ſeem not to have any recollection
of this circumſtance, which has led myſelf and others into a miſtake, I ſhall take
the liberty to recite the whole paragraph,
which is in a note of your Review for
Auguſt 1775, p. 175, " For the rea-
" ſons alledged in our account of Dr.
" Prieſtley's Eſſays, we beg leave to be
" excuſed for the preſent from entering
" into this intereſting diſpute, and that
" ſtill the more earneſtly, as we have had
" ſent us a long and laboured defence of
" the paſſage that appeared ſo exception-
" able

" able to Mr. Seton, intended to have been
" printed in a pamphlet by itſelf, had not
" the author (either the Dr. himſelf, or
" ſome able friend) juſtly conceived ſo
" good an opinion of our candour, as to
" think we ſhould afford a place for it
" in our Review, which we purpoſe to do
" in our next number." Accordingly in
the very next number (September 1775,)
appeared this Eſſay, which you now call
your own.

There are ſeveral other things in your
letters to me that are almoſt as unaccountable as this. I am very far from having
a mean opinion of your underſtanding,
and men of ſenſe are generally candid; at leaſt they are able to perceive
the real meaning of a writer who wiſhes
to be underſtood, and they are above little
cavils. And yet, p. 64, you aſcribe to
me what I am profeſſedly refuting, and
only ſuppoſe for the ſake of that refutation,
viz. the ſolidity of the atoms, or the ultimate conſtituent parts of bodies. You
write variouſly, and perhaps not very con-
ſiſtently

fiftently with refpect to me; but, in general, you feem to think that I write with tolerable *perfpicuity*, as well as readinefs; you fhould therefore have reconfidered the paffages which you except againft. I fee little, if any thing, that I can amend in them; and yet you fay that, " with the " beft difpofition in the world to compre- " hend me, you cannot poffibly conceive " what I am about.

Your cavil, p. 65, appears to me to be equally ill founded: for by the *fmalleft parts* of bodies, I evidently mean thofe that are *fuppofed to be* the fmalleft, or the folid indifcerptible atoms of other philofo- phers; which I maintain to be refolvable into ftill fmaller parts. I do not wonder to find this wretched cavil in fuch a writer as Mr. Whitehead, but it is altogether unworthy of a perfon who has any degree of reputation, as a writer, or a man of fenfe, and candour.

You ridicule what you call my *pompous lift* of authors prefixed to the *Difquifitions,*
when

when I barely mention thofe of which
there are *different editions,* that, as I quote
the *pages,* thofe who had different editions
of the fame book might be apprized of it.
What could the moft modeft writer, yourfelf for inftance, who wifhed to be underftood, do lefs ? Had I meant to fwell the
lift, I fhould have inferted in it *all* that I
have quoted; which, however, is a very
common practice, and not at all exceptionable. On many occafions you charge me
with *vanity* and *conceit* ; and once, in imi-
tation, I fuppofe, of the ftyle of Dr. John-
fon, you term it *an exuberance of felf-exal-
tation:* but this charge is founded upon
nothing but the moft forced and uncandid
conftruction of my expreffions. This I
confider as an unworthy artifice. Had I
affected an unufual degree of *modefty,* inconfiftent with writing fo much as I do,
(as it certainly implies that I think myfelf
capable of inftructing, at leaft, fome part of
mankind) there would have been more reafon for your conduct.

As to the work which you promife the
public, I fhall expect it with fome impa-
tience,

tience, and fhall certainly read it with the
greateft attention; and as you fay that
" the *theory of phyfics,* or the fyftematical
" principles of natural philofophy, the fci-
" ence which Lord Bacon reprefents as the
" bafis and foundation of all human know-
" ledge is the department of your pecu-
" liar profeffion," I do hope that you will
throw fome light upon it, and I have every
reafon to wifh you fuccefs. If you can
prove, as you fay, page 277, that *all mat-*
*ter is poffeffed of fome degree of perception,*
you will effectually remove the only difficulty under which my fcheme labours;
which is *how* a fentient principle is the
refult of organization. The *fact* I think
indifputable, and muft be admitted on the
received rules of philofophizing; but that
it *muft be fo,* from the nature of things, I
own I do not yet fee, any more than I am
yet fatisfied that " the form and magnitude
" of bodies are to be confidered as gene-
" rated by motion," p. 161, or that
" every natural phenomenon, or diftinct
" object of fenfe, is a compound of active
" and paffive phyfical powers," notwithftanding

standing the very ingenious obfervations that you have advanced with refpect to them.

You frequently hint that, the reafon why I have generally appeared to advantage in controverfy, is that I have always pitched upon *weak antagonists*. I can only fay, that, if this has been the cafe, it has been becaufe I have not had the good fortune to meet with any better; and in general they have not been weak either in their own eyes, or in thofe of the public. This character, however, can by no means apply to Dr. Brown, Dr. Balguy, Dr. Blackftone, Dr. Reid, or Dr. Beattie, whatever you may fay of Dr. Ofwald, on whofe work you will find the higheft encomiums in the Reviews of the day; and it was in fact, held in very great and general admiration.

You will alfo find the fame to be, in a great meafure, true of the *Letters on Materialifm*. Befides the ftating of *objections actually made*, and anfwering them, has a much better effect than propofing them in
other

other words; as it may be fufpected, that, by this means, the anfwerer gives himfelf an unfair advantage; and when I replied to him, no other anfwer had appeared. For as to your *Mr. Seton*, who, it feems, notwithftanding the incredulity of fome, did really *live*, and is now actually *dead*, I could not, though I endeavoured to do it, perfuade myfelf to take any notice of him; he appeared to know fo very little of the very rudiments of theological know-ledge. Many other opponents I have neg-lected to notice becaufe I thought them infignificant, though they are not without their admirers, and boaft, as you do, that I make no reply, becaufe I am not able to do it. As to yourfelf, pretend what you will, I cannot confider you in the light of an adverfary.

You afk me repeatedly, why, fince I deny all folidity or impenetrability, I fhould chufe to make ufe of fo obnoxious a term as *matter*, when the lefs exceptionable one of *fpirit* would anfwer my purpofe full as well. I anfwer, that the caufe of truth is
beft

beſt anſwered by calling every thing by its *uſual name*, and I think it a mean ſubterfuge to impoſe upon mankind by the uſe of words.

Man, I believe, was wholly made of *the duſt of the ground*, or of the ſame ſubſtance with the earth itſelf. Now by what term has the earth, and all the ſubſtances that belong to it, been diſtinguiſhed, but that of *matter*? I ſuppoſe the ſentient principle in man to be the brain itſelf, and not any *inviſible ſubſtance* reſiding in the brain, and capable of ſubſiſting when the brain is deſtroyed. Now of what has the brain been always ſaid to conſiſt, but *matter*, another ſpecies indeed from that of the duſt of the ground, but ſtill compriſed under the ſame common appellation of matter? In what other manner than that which I have choſen, is it poſſible to rectify the miſtakes of men? To call matter by the name of *ſpirit* might tend to give them an idea that my opinions were, in fact, the ſame with theirs, though expreſſed in different words; and by this means, I might ſcreen myſelf from their cenſure, cenfure; but I fhould only *deceive*, and fhould not *inftruct* them at all.

In this manner too many chriftian preachers, and writers, adopting the phrafeology of the Athanafian fyftem, pafs for orthodox, without, as they think, any violation of truth. But what accrues from this conduct? No advantage to the *caufe of truth*; nothing but the mere *fafety of the preacher, or writer*;

This, Sir, is not my object. I have hitherto purfued a different plan, and have feen no reafon to repent of it. Upon this general principle, I have chofen to fay that *man is wholly material*, rather than *wholly fpiritual*, though both the terms were in my option.

You muft give me leave to clofe this letter with fome notice of a paffage of yours to me, which is in the fame ftrain with many others, and of which we have but too many examples in fuch writers as Voltaire and Mr. Hume. You fay, p. 489, " As to your concern for the con-
" verfion

" verfion of infidels, I look upon it as
" the cant of a philofophical crufader, and
" am forry I cannot coincide with you in
" your projected conciliation of the *ra-*
" *tional truths* of philofophy, with the
" *myfterious truths* of chriftianity. I am
" apprehenfive that it is impoffible, with-
" out endangering the caufe of both, to
" bring them into too clofe a contact."
In a note, (*ib.*) you add, " It is a moot
" point with me, whether the really think-
" ing and intelligent philofophers, whom
" Dr. Prieftley wifhes to convert, are great-
" er infidels, in their prefent ftate of un-
" belief, than they would be be, if con-
" verted by him into rational chriftians."

Now I muft take it for granted, that a
man of much lefs difcernment than you,
cannot but be fenfible, that no propofition
can be *true* and *falfe* at the fame time, or
true with refpect to philofophy, and falfe
with refpect to theology, or *vice verfa*; fo
that if what is called a *myftery in chriftianity*,
be really a *falfehood in philofophy*, i. e. reducible to a contradiction, the belief of it

muft

muſt be abandoned altogether, at any hazard; and the ſcheme of religion that neceſſarily ſuppoſes it to be true muſt be confeſſed to be ill founded, and an impoſition on mankind.

If, for example, *bread and wine*, philoſophically, *i. e.* ſtrictly and juſtly conſidered, cannot be *fleſh and blood*, the popiſh doctrine of *tranſubſtantiation* cannot be true. So alſo if *one* cannot be *three*, or *three*, *one*, mathematically conſidered, neither can the Athanaſian doctrine of the *Trinity* be true. It certainly, therefore, behoves every rational chriſtian to prove the conſiſtency of the articles of his faith with true philoſophy and the nature of things. This is the only method of effectually ſilencing ſuch unbelievers as, with the low view of impoſing on the weakeſt chriſtians, pretend to believe chriſtianity, at the ſame time that they maintain it is *not founded on argument*; thinking to loſe no character with men of ſenſe, like themſelves, who will eaſily perceive the deſign with which ſuch abſurd profeſſions are made, and will be ready to

join

join in the laugh at the credulity of thofe who are taken with them. If I were really an unbeliever, I think I fhould not fcruple to avow it, rather than debafe my mind by fuch paltry evafions. But it muft be owned, that an unbeliever has not the fame caufe for *a ftrict attachment to truth,* that a chriftian has.

I am, Sir,

Your very humble fervant,

J. PRIESTLEY.

Calne, June 1778.

N 2

## To *Mr.* WHITEHEAD.

SIR,

AN attack from a perfon of your religious perfuafion is a thing that is
new to me; and as I have frequently mentioned your people with refpect, and have
always had very agreeable connections with
individuals of your body, it would have
been a real fatisfaction to me to have found
that, even in their *oppofition* to me, they
were refpectable; and therefore to have had
it in my power to fpeak as handfomely of
you *all*, as I have hitherto done. However,
though an individual has fhewn that want
of civility and candour, which I had thought
infeparable from all Quakers, and, alfo too
little acquaintance with his fubject, I fhall
by no means impute thefe faults to the
whole body to which you belong; many
of whom I know to be equally diftinguifhed
for their candour and knowledge.

You

You know, Sir, I prefume, that I profefs to believe in a *God,* a *providence,* and a
*future ftate,* in the *divine miffion of Chrift,*
and the *authority of the fcriptures.* I have
written not a little in the direct defence of
thefe principles, and I hope my general
character and conduct does not give the lie
to my profeffion. Why then fhould you
fuppofe me not to be *fincere,* and to be *fe-
cretly undermining* thefe great principles of
of religion? Might not I, if I were fo
difpofed, retort the fame furmifes and
calumnies refpecting you? You are certainly at liberty to urge me with what
you apprehend to be the real confequences
of my doctrine, but this you might do
without intimating, as you frequently do,
that I was *apprized* of the immoral and
dangerous confequences of my principles,
and wifhed to propagate them *on that account.*

" Materialifm," you fay, p. 163, " muft
" terminate in Atheifm ;" and p. 90,
" The doctrine of materialifm muft be at-
" tended with the moft deftructive and
" fatal

" fatal confequences. It fuppofes that this
" life is our only place of exiftence, and
" by this means takes away all confidence
" in God, all hope of future rewards, and
" fear of punifhment. It tears up all
" religion by the very roots, and renders
" all our moral powers and faculties wholly
" ufelefs, or fuppofes them to be mere
" creatures of education and human policy.
" In fhort, its language is, *let us eat and*
" *drink, for to-morrow we die.*" You are
pleafed to add, " I do not fay that Dr.
" Prieftley will *directly* defend thefe prin-
" ciples, or that he *altogether* believes
" them to be the confequences of his doc-
" trine." This however, is an infinuation,
that, though not *altogether,* I do *in part* believe them to be the confequences of my
doctrine ; and other paffages in your work
fufficiently fhew, that you think me capable of advancing and fupporting thefe principles, even though I fhould be altogether
perfuaded of their horrid confequences.

" It muft be owned," you fay, p. 108,
" that our author fhews no great delicacy

N 4            " refpect-

" refpecting the character of the facred
" penmen. He very freely, though in-
" directly, befpatters them with dirt; from
" whence one might naturally fufpect, that
" he owes them no very good will. Pro-
" feffions of this kind," you fay, p. 110,
" from one who profeffes to believe the
" gofpel, looks fo much like a *feigned*
" *friendfhip*, in order to deliver it more fe-
" curely into the hands of the deifts, that
" it will not fail to recall to memory the
" treatment of our Lord by one of his
" profeffed difciples, to which, with re-
" fpect to the gofpel revelation, it bears a
" ftriking refemblance. There," you fay,
p. 112, " is an end of all fcripture au-
" thority at once, which perhaps would
" not be very difagreeable to this writer."
Laftly you fcruple not to fay, page 106,
" I fhould not wonder to hear this learned
" gentleman, armed cap-a-pee, with logic
" and philofophy, reprefent his Lord and
" Saviour as a greater deceiver than Ma-
" homet. To fuch miferable and profane
" fhifts, may rafh reafoning bring an un-
" guarded man."

For

For the honour of the chriftian name, and of the particular profeffion to which you belong, I hope that, on reflection, yourfelf, or at leaft your friends, will blufh for thefe things. In the preceding quotation, I hope, Sir, you will be thought to have given a very unfair account of my *moral principles* and *views*; let us now fee whether you be any better acquainted with the *profeffed defign* of my work, and the *nature of the argument*.

" The great object in view," you fay, p. 171, " it feems, in contriving and mo-" delling thefe enquiries into matter and " fpirit, was to lay a foundation for the " better fupport of *Arianifm*." Now, Sir, fo much are you miftaken, that the great object in view was the very reverfe of what you fuppofe, viz. the radical overturning of the fyftem of Arianifm, by proving the abfurdity, and explaining the origin, of the doctrines of a *foul*, and of *pre-exiftence*, which are neceffarily fuppofed in the Arian fyftem; and a very great part of my work is, not indirectly, but *openly*, and both *really*,

and

and *by name,* an attack upon Arianiſm, and both what is called the *high* and the *low* *Arian hypotheſis,* which I conſider ſeparately.

Let us now ſee the light in which my account of *the opinions of the chriſtian Fathers* has happened to ſtrike you; and in this you are no leſs unfortunate. " The thing " he propoſes to prove," you ſay, p. 140, " is that the chriſtian Fathers believed that " the ſoul can have no exiſtence ſeparate " from the body, that thought and con- " ſciouſneſs may be the reſult of an orga- " nized ſyſtem of matter. Conſequently," you ſay, p. 149, " our author's grand boaſt, " that the apoſtles and primitive fathers " thought with him, that the ſoul is ma- " terial and mortal, vaniſhes into air; " where, perhaps, this experimental phi- " loſopher may be able to make more of " it than we can do in theſe lower re- " gions."

Again, p. 148, after reciting the opinion of Cl. Mamertus, who ſays of the ſoul, that it is neither *extended,* nor *in place,*
you

you fay, " Thefe feem to me moft ex-
" traordinary affertions, to prove that the
" foul is material, and dies with the body.
" It requires more fkill in Logic than I
" am mafter of to find this conclufion in
" either of the premifes."

A very extraordinary conclufion indeed,
but, if that had been my idea, it would
not have been more extraordinary than your
miftake of the whole drift of my argument
in this bufinefs. I had afferted that the
idea of *refined fpirituality*, maintained, I find,
by yourfelf, was unknown to all antiquity;
and therefore I have fhown, that though,
according to the notion of the heathen
philofophers, the foul was confidered as a
fubftance diftinct from the body, being a
detached part of the great foul of the univerfe, it had the property of *extenfion*, and
was, in reality, what we fhould now call
*a more refined kind of matter*; and that true
*fpiritualifm* was introduced gradually; but,
if any more diftinct æra can be fixed on,
it was that of this very Mamertus.

I

I farther prove, that, according to the
true fyftem of revelation, though the fentient and thinking principle may be fpoken
of as diftinct from the other functions of
the man, it was always fuppofed to refide
in fome part of his body, and to be infeparable from it. For the facred writers never
fpeak of the foul as in one place, and the
body in another; and it was not till the introduction of the heathen philofophy into
chriftianity, that it was imagined that the
foul retained its perceptivity and activity
while the body was in the grave. Of this,
I prefume, I have given fufficient proof.

You are pleafed, indeed, to alledge, page
144, as a proof that the early chriftians
thought differently, a paffage in the epiftle
of Polycarp, who fays that " Paul, and
" the reft of the apoftles, are in the place
" appointed for them, παρα τω κυριω, with the
" Lord." But if you had attended to the
Greek, you would have perceived that
this is not the *neceffary* fenfe of the paffage,
and Archbifhop Wake renders it " the place
" that was due to them, from the Lord."
Indeed,

Indeed, had you been sufficiently conver-
sant with *ecclesiastical history*, you would
have known, that it was not till many
centuries after the time of Polycarp, that
any christian thought that the separate soul,
whether sentient or not, was in any other
place than that which is distinguished by
the term *hades*. It was universally thought
that good men were not *with God and
Christ* till after the resurrection, which is
clearly the scripture doctrine.

In John xvi. 3. our Lord says, *I will
come again, and receive you unto myself, that
where I am, ye may be also.* Here is a plain
limitation of the time when the disciples
of our Lord, and even the apostles themselves, were to be admitted to his presence,
and live with him, viz. at his return to
raise the dead, and not before.

What you say on the subject of the
state of the soul between death and the resurrection, is too trifling to deserve a particular notice. As you seem not to have
given sufficient attention to this subject, I
would take the liberty to recommend to
your

your careful perufal, what the excellent
Bifhop of Carlifle has written on it, Arch-
deacon Blackburne's *Hiftorical View of this
Controverfy*; the Differtation prefixed to
*Alexander's Commentary on* 1 *Cor.* xv. and
a fummary of the principal arguments in
the third volume of my *Inftitutes of Natural
and Revealed Religion.*

It is upon this fubject that you note,
with great triumph, that I have quoted
as one, two fimilar paffages in the book
of *Revelation.* Another perfon would have
fuppofed this to have happened through
*inadvertency,* and not, as you will have it,
*with defign.* It muft have been infatuation
to have done this in a work fo inviting of
criticifm as mine is. A new edition of
the work will fhew you that my argument
lofes nothing by the rectification of that
miftake.

I fhall mention one more miftake of my
meaning, though in a thing of no great
confequence. " It is a great miftake,"
you fay, p. 10, " to fuppofe with Dr.
" Prieftley, and fome other philofophers,
                                    " that

" that there is fome unknown fubftance
" in material nature, diftinct from the pro-
" perties of folidity and extenfion." Now
what I have faid, and repeated many times,
is, that when all the properties of fubftance are taken away, the fubftance itfelf
is gone; and that the terms *fubftance, effence*, &c. &c. are merely a convenience in
fpeech.

You triumph exceedingly in my fpeaking of the *fmalleft particles of matter* being
refolved into others ftill *fmaller*. For an
explanation of this, I refer you to my letter to Dr, Kenrick,

Your ftrictures on the fubject of *perfonal
identity* I freely leave to have their full effect
on the minds of our readers, without any
apprehenfion of the confequence.

Before I clofe this letter, I fhall briefly
mention a few particulars, which fhow
that you are not fufficiently acquainted
with the *ftate of opinions* for a controverfial
writer on fuch fubjects as thofe of the
*Difquifitions*.

" Nor

" Nor do I prefume," you fay, p. 25,
" that any philofopher will contend for an
" earlier and earlier exiftence of this world,
" and the creatures in it, *ad infinitum.*"
Now, Sir, many philofophers and divines
maintain the very doctrine that you think
not to exift. It was the opinion of the
Platonifts, it is afferted by Dr. Hartley, it
is what I have given in my Inftitutes, and
I believe it is that of Dr. Price, who is
far from thinking with me on the fubject
of the *Difquifitions.*

" Our learned author," you fay, p. 81,
" indeed, affects to difbelieve the continual
" flux of the particles of the human body;
" but this I prefume no one will ferioufly
" deny, who has a competent knowledge
" of its ftructure and œconomy."

Now many perfons, Sir, and even Dr.
Watts, whom you quote with fo much
refpect, ferioufly believed that there are
parts of the body, fome *ftamina,* that never
change.

There

There is another thing that you take for
granted, in which I believe you are quite
fingular, and it is, indeed, fufficiently curious. You fay, p. 167, that "where body
"is, fpace is neceffarily excluded," and
from this extraordinary fuppofition you
draw many curious inferences, in your reafoning about the nature of fpirit, and of
the deity. Now I have heard of fpace being
*occupied*, but never of its being *excluded*
before.

I muft not quite conclude without acknowledging myfelf obliged to you for
furnifhing me with a proof, which you
will find, by Dr. Price's remarks, was in
fome meafure wanting, of its being the
*real opinion* of any perfon, that *fpirit bears
no relation to fpace*. You do it in the
ampleft manner, and build upon it your
argument againft the materiality of the human foul. According to you Dr. Clarke,
Dr. Price, and others, who maintain the
*locality*, and confequently the *extenfion* of
fpirit, are as much materialifts as myfelf.
I leave them and you to difpute that point;

O                                 and

and you may imagine I fhall not feel un-
pleafantly in the fituation of a *fpectator*.
It will give me fome refpite, and I fhall
expect to derive fome advantage from the
iffue of the conteft, in whofe favour foever
it may be.

" No corporeal fubftance," you fay, p. 63,
" whatever can poffibly be the feat of fen-
" fation; for all of them have extenfion,
" and muft be of fome figure or form.
" On the fame principles," p. 128, " we
" may explain the omniprefence of God
" not by extenfion through all bodies, as
" this writer feems to believe, which is
" an idea fo grofs that it deferves a name
" which, for the fake of the author, I fhall
" not beftow upon it."

Now, as you have not fcrupled to make
ufe of the terms *materialift*, and *atheift* in
this controverfy, I have really a good deal of
curiofity to know what dread name it is, that,
*out of regard to me*, you fupprefs the mention of. If it be too dreadful for the
*public ear*, could you not favour me with
the intimation of it in a private letter? I
fhall

fhall communicate it to my friend Dr. Price, whom it concerns as much as it does myfelf. Dr. Clarke, you will alfo find, and in the opinion of Dr. Price, all the moft diftinguifhed immaterialifts, will fall under this dread cenfure. But, being fo many of us, materialifts and immaterialifts, we fhall bear it the better; for bodies, and large companies of men, we know, are not eafily affected either by *fhame* or *fear*.

I am, Sir,

Your very humble fervant,

J. PRIESTLEY.

Calne, June 1778.

O 2

To *Dr.* HORSELEY.

DEAR SIR,

I THINK myfelf particularly happy that
a perfon of your abilities, and mathematical and philofophical knowledge, has
vouchfafed to allude to my work, though
only in a *fermon,* as it gives me an opportunity of explaining myfelf more fully with
refpect to the ftate of the queftion concerning *liberty* and *neceffity,* and likewife of
fhowing that the *fect* of neceffarians, though
almoft *every where fpoken againft,* is more
numerous and refpectable than is generally
imagined; for that you, Sir, belong to it
as much as I do; with this only difference,
that you chufe to make ufe of one fet of
phrafes, and I of another.

It

It is impoffible for me to exprefs in
ftronger terms than you do, the abfolute
certainty of every determination of the
will of man, as depending upon the circumftances he is in, and the motives prefented to him. " A moral motive and a
" mechanical force," you fay, p. 10, " are
" equally certain caufes, each of its proper
" effect. A moral motive," you fay, " is
" what is more fignificantly called the
" final caufe, and can have no influence
" but with a being that propofes to itfelf
" an end, chufes means, and thus puts it-
" felf in action. It is true that while this
" is my end, and while I conceive thefe
" to be the means, a definite action will
" as certainly follow that definite choice
" and judgement of my mind, provided I
" be free from all external reftraint and im-
" pediment, as a determinate motion will
" be excited in a body by a force applied
" in a given direction. There is, in both
" cafes, an equal certainty of the effect."

Having granted this, it is not poffible
that you and I can have any difference that
is

is not merely *verbal*. Our *ideas* are pre-
cisely the same; nor have I indeed any objection to your *language*, in any sense in
which it can be consistent with the above
assertions.

You are too good a mathematician to require being told, that, if every determination of the mind of man certainly depends
upon preceding causes, whether the causes
be moral, or physical, it is not possible
that any determination, or consequently
that any event, in which men are concerned, could have been otherwise than it
*has been, is,* or *is to be*; or that the Divine
Being, who, as you justly say, " knows
" things by their causes, as being himself
" the first cause, the source of power and
" activity to all other causes," should not
have *intended* every thing to be just as it is.
On this ground only can you affirm, as you
do, that " to him every thing that shall
" ever be is at all times infinitely more
" certain, than any thing, either past or
" present, can be to any man," &c. This,
I say, you need not be told. It is an im-

mediate

mediate and neceſſary inference from your own principle. Indeed, it is little more than repeating the ſame thing in other words.

You even apply theſe principles to a caſe of the greateſt virtue that was ever exerted by man, viz. the voluntary ſufferings and death of Chriſt, and likewiſe to a caſe of the greateſt wickedneſs, viz. that of his enemies in voluntarily inflicting thoſe ſufferings upon him. No perſon can expreſs this with more perſpicuity or energy than you have done,

" Now therefore," you ſay, p. 3, " he be-
" gins to ſhew them" (his diſciples) " that
" he *muſt* go to Jeruſalem, and, after much
" malicious perſecution from the leaders
" of the Jewiſh people, he *muſt* be killed.
" The form of expreſſion here is very re-
" markable in the original, and it is well
" preſerved in our Engliſh tranſlation. He
" *muſt* go, he *muſt* ſuffer, he *muſt* be kil-
" led, he *muſt* be raiſed again on the third
" day. All theſe things were fixed and
" determined——muſt inevitably be——no-
" thing

" thing could prevent them—and yet the
" greater part of them were of a kind that
" might *seem* to depend intirely upon man's
" free-agency. To go, or not to go to
" Jerufalem, was in his own power, and
" the perfecution he met with there,
" arifing from the folly and the malice of
" ignorant and wicked men, furely de-
" pended upon the human will; yet, by the
" form of the fentence, thefe things are
" included under the fame *Neceffity of Event*
" as that which was evidently an immedi-
" ate effect of divine power, without the
" concurrence of any other caufe, the re-
" furrection of Jefus from the dead. The
" words which in the original exprefs the
" *going*, the *fuffering*, the *being killed*, the
" *being raifed again*, are equally fubject to
" the verb which anfwers to the word
" *muft* of our language, and in its proper
" meaning predicates *neceffity*. As he *muft*
" be raifed on the third day, fo he *muft*
" go, he *muft* fuffer, he *muft* be killed.
" Every one of thefe events, his going to
" Jerufalem, his fuffering, and his death
" there, and that thefe fufferings, and that
" death

" death fhould be brought about by the
" malice of the elders and chief priefts
" and fcribes; every one of thefe things
" is plainly announced, as no lefs unal-
" terably fixed, than the refurrection of
" our faviour, or the time of his refur-
" rection, that it was to happen on the
" third day."

If then the virtuous determinations of
Chrift, and the wicked determinations of
his enemies, were equally neceffary (for I
have no other idea to the word *muft be*,
and indeed you yourfelf ufe them as fy-
nonymous) every other act of virtue, or act
of vice, is equally neceffary, or *muft be*, and
nothing but a miracle, or an arbitrary in-
fringement of the laws of nature, can prevent its taking place. Though you do not
chufe to call this a *phyfical*, but a *moral*
neceffity, you allow it to be a *real* neceffity, arifing from the operation of the
eftablifhed laws of nature, implying an impoffibility of the thing being otherwife
than it is, which is all that I wifh you to
grant.

For

For any man to have acted differently from what he did, in any given cafe, he muft have been differently difpofed at the time, or muft have had different views of things prefent to his mind; neither of which, properly fpeaking, depends upon himfelf. For though it does fo *immediately*, it does not do fo *ultimately:* for fince every particular determination depends upon his immediately preceding circumftances, it neceffarily follows that the whole chain of his determinations and actions depends upon his *original make*, and *original circum-ftances.* And who is our maker but God? or who is it that difpofes of us but the fame God?

You could not, dear Sir, have written what you have done, if you had not felt, and enjoyed this moft important truth. Let us do it freely and without referve, let us not fcruple to exprefs it in its proper language, and let us openly acknow-ledge, and chearfully embrace, all the fair confequences of it. I need not with you, Sir, make any encomium on our common

prin-

principles. The doctrine of neceffity, (moral neceffity, if you chufe to call it fo) contains, or implies, all that the heart of man can wifh. It leads us to confider ourfelves, and every thing elfe as at the uncontrolled difpofal of the greateft and beft of beings; that, ftrictly fpeaking, nothing does, or can, go wrong; that all *retrogade motions,* in the moral as well as in the natural world, are only *apparent,* not *real.* Being under this infallible guidance, our final deftination is certain and glorious. In the language of Pope,

All nature is but art, unknown to thee;
All chance, direction, which thou canft not fee;
All difcord, harmony not underftood;
All partial evil, univerfal good :
And, fpite of pride, in erring reafon's fpite,
One truth is clear, *whatever is, is right.*

Let us now confider why it is that you object to the term *phyfical,* as applied to the caufes of human actions. For I am ready to difufe it, if it imply any thing more than we both agree in maintaining. The word itfelf is derived from φυσις *nature,* and therefore, literally rendered, fignifies *agreeable*

*able to nature,* or the *laws of nature.* A physical cause, therefore, is simply that which, according to the established laws of nature, will produce a given effect; and of course respects the laws to which the mind is subject, as well as those by which the external world is governed, both being equally within the compass of *nature.* I therefore apply it to both cases indiscriminately.

If you say the *operations,* and therefore the *laws,* are of a very different nature, I readily acknowledge it. For, with respect to this, it is impossible that we can really differ. The compass of nature is great, and comprizes very various things. *Chemistry,* for instance, and common *mechanics* are very different things; and accordingly we have different *kinds of laws,* or *rules,* by which to express, and explain, their operations; but still they are equally branches of *Physics.* So also though the *phenomena,* and consequently the *laws of the mind,* are different from those of the *body,* that is no sufficient reason why we
should

should not comprize them under the same general term of *physics*. However, if you dislike the word, in the extensive application in which I use it, I am very well content to use it in your more restrained sense, and will call the things that influence the mind *moral*, and not physical causes. Only allow that there *are* laws, and causes, by which the mind is truly and properly *influenced*, producing certain definite effects in definite circumstances, and I shall not quarrel with you for the sake of a term.

You say, p. 10, that I confound moral and physical necessity, or, to use your own words, that " when I represent the influ-
" ence of moral motives, as arising from
" a physical necessity, the very same with
" that which excites and governs the mo-
" tions of the inanimate creation, I con-
" found nature's distinctions, and contra-
" dict the very principles I would seem to
" have established ; and that the source of
" the mistake is, that I imagine a simili-
" tude between things which admit of no
" comparison."

Now,

Now, Sir, I will allow as much difference as you *can* fuppofe between moral and
phyfical caufes. Inanimate matter, as the
pen that I write with, is not capable of
being influenced by *motives*, nor is the
*hand* that holds the pen, but the *mind*
that directs both. I think I diftinguifh
thefe things better by the terms *voluntary*
and *involuntary*; but thefe are mere *words*,
and I make no comparifon between them,
or between moral and phyfical caufes, but
in that very refpect in which you yourfelf
acknowledge that they agree, *i. e.* the
*certainty* with which they produce their
refpective effects. And this is the proper
foundation of all the *neceffity* that I afcribe
to human actions. My conclufion, that
men could not, in any given cafe, act
otherwife than they do, is not at all affected
by the *terms* by which we diftinguifh the
laws and caufes that refpect the mind from
thofe which refpect the external world.
That there are *any laws*, and that there
are *any caufes*, to which the mind is fubject, is all that my argument requires.

Give

Give me the thing, and I will readily give you the name.

Again, you diftinguifh between *efficient* and *final* caufes, and fay that, by means of the latter, a perfon *puts himfelf in motion*. But ftill, if it be true, as you allow, that, notwithftanding this, a definite act will certainly follow a definite choice and judgment of the mind, there is, in no cafe, any more than *one way* in which the mind can put itfelf in motion, or only one direction that it can take, which is all the neceffity that I contend for. I chufe to fay that *motives determine the mind,* whereas you fay that the *mind determines itfelf according to the motives*; but, in both cafes, the determination itfelf is the very fame, and we both agree that it *could not have been different.* Our difference, therefore is merely verbal, and cannot poffibly be any thing more.

Turn over this fubject, Sir, in your own mind as you pleafe, you will find that one who controverts the doctrine of neceffity,

has

has the choice of no more than *two things.*
He muſt either ſay that, in a given ſituation of mind, with reſpeƈt to diſpoſition
and motives, the determination is *definite,*
*i. e.* agreeable to ſome general rule, or that
it is *indefinite, i. e.* ſubjeƈt to no rule at
all. If the former be admitted, which is
what you allow, you are, to all intents and
purpoſes, a neceſſarian. You may (unknown to yourſelf) conceal your principles under the cover of ſome ſpecious and
ambiguous phraſeology, but you certainly
maintain the *thing.* If, on the other hand,
you ſay, that the determination is *indefi-*
*nite,* you are very ſenſible that you ſuppoſe *an effeƈt without a cauſe,* which is
impoſſible. This ſide of the dilemma, therefore, you carefully avoid. In ſhort, Sir,
there is no choice in the caſe, but of the
doƈtrine of neceſſity (diſguiſed, perhaps,
under ſome other name) or abſolute nonſenſe. There is no poſſibility of finding
any medium.

*Incidit in Scyllam qui vult vitare Charybdim.*

P                                   You

You are pleaſed, Sir, to call philoſophical neceſſity the doctrine of the *ſubtle mo-*
*derns*, and that of predeſtination that of
their *more ſimple anceſtors*, ſaying, that we
ſubtle moderns, are *deeply verſed in phyſics*,
*and maintain the regular operation of ſecond*
*cauſes;* and you candidly acknowledge that
we are both actuated by the *ſame humble*
*ſpirit of reſigned devotion.* This, Sir, is
frank and generous, and I hope true.   I
only object to your characterizing us neceſſarians as *ſubtle*, when, in reality, Sir,
our doctrine is the plaineſt thing in the
world, and it requires no ſmall degree of
ſubtlety to believe any thing elſe.

What are your diſtinctions between things
*moral* and *phyſical*, *efficient* and *final*, *cer-*
*tain* and *neceſſary*, theſe relating to *ſelf-*
*determination*, or *ſelf-motion*, &c. &c. &c.
but *ſubtleties*, to which we have no recourſe.
We are content to call all things by their
common names.   With us laws are laws,
and cauſes cauſes.   If the laws are invariable, and the cauſes certain in their operation (and without this they are, in reality

ality, *no laws*, and *no caufes* at all) we fay that all that follows is *neceffary*, or what *could not but be*. What is there, Sir, of *fubtlety* in all this?

As you are a man of undoubted fenfe, and candour, and particularly well verfed in mathematical and philofophical knowledge, I doubt not you will carefully attend to thefe few plain confiderations; and I am confident that, with the honeft mind that I believe you to be poffeffed of, you will henceforth avow yourfelf to be what, without hitherto knowing it, you really are, a believer in " the great and glorious, though " unpopular doctrine of *philofophical necef-* " *fity.*"

I am,

With the greateft refpect,

Dear Sir,

Yours, very fincerely,

J. PRIESTLEY.

Calne, June 1778.

P 2          *P. S.*

*P. S.* I fhall take it as a particular favour, if you will oblige me and the public
with your *fecond thoughts* on this fubject.
I have had, and expect, fo many weak
and hafty anfwers, that, I own, I am eager
to lay hold of a man who is equal to the
difcuffion of the fubject, and efpecially one
who is, at the fame time, truly liberal and
candid. The Doctrine of Neceffity is very
far from being well underftood by the generality of fcholars, and it is certainly of
great confequence to have their attention
drawn to it. I fhall be happy, likewife,
to walk with you over *all* the ground
marked out in the *Difquifitions*, with refpect to which I perceive that you hold a
fyftem very different from mine.

ILLUSTRATIONS

# ILLUSTRATIONS

## OF SOME PARTICULARS IN THE

## DISQUISITIONS on MATTER and SPIRIT.

THAT I might not obtrude upon the public a crude and hasty performance on subjects of so much importance as those which I have ventured to discuss in these *Disquisitions*, I put copies of the work, after it was completely printed off, into the hands of several of my friends, both well and ill affected to my general system, that I might have the benefit of their remarks, and take advantage of them, in an additional sheet of *Illustrations*, if that should appear to be necessary.

Accordingly I have received, and considered, with as much attention as I can,

various

various remarks that have been communicated to me, and have thought it might be of ufe to add fome explanations in confequence of them. I hope they will be the means of obviating fome cavils, and ferve to make my meaning better underftood, whether they make the doctrine itfelf more or lefs acceptable to my readers in general.

### I. *Of Bodies acting where they are not.*

It is objected to the doctrine of thefe papers, which fuppofes that the repulfion, afcribed to bodies, takes place at fome diftance from their real furfaces; that bodies muft then *act where they are not,* which is deemed to be an abfurdity. I acknowledge that there is a confiderable difficulty in this cafe; but it does not in the leaft affect the hypothefis that I have adopted concerning matter, any more than that which is commonly received. According to Sir Ifaac Newton's Obfervations, rays of light begin to be reflected from all bodies at a certain diftance from their furfaces;

faces; and yet he confiders thofe rays as
reflected by thofe bodies, that is, by powers
inhering in and properly belonging to thofe
bodies. So alfo the gravitation of the
earth and of the other planets to the fun,
he confiders as produced by a power of
attraction properly belonging to the fun,
which is at an immenfe diftance from
them.

If Sir Ifaac Newton would fay that the
impulfe, by which light is reflected from
any body, and by which planets are driven
towards the fun, is really occafioned by
other *invifible matter* in actual contact with
thofe bodies which are put in motion, I
alfo am equally at liberty to relieve my
hypothefis by the fame means. But the
exiftence of this invifible fubftance, to the
agency of which that great philofopher
afcribes fo very much, and which he calls
*ether*, has not yet been proved, and is
therefore generally fuppofed not to exift.
And, indeed, if it did exift, I do not fee
how it could produce the effects that are
afcribed to it. For the particles of this

P 4                                  very

very ether could not impel any fubſtance, if they were not themſelves impelled in the ſame direction; and muſt we provide a ſtill more fubtle ether for the purpoſe of impelling the particles of the groſſer ether? If ſo, we muſt do the ſame for this other ether, and ſo on, *ad infinitum*, which is abſurd.

Alſo, if the parts of ſolid bodies, as, for inſtance, of gold (which by its expanſion when hot, and contraction when cold, appear not actually to touch one another) be kept aſunder by a fubtle matter, viz. the ſame ether above-mentioned, the parts of this ether muſt be kept aſunder by a ſtill more fubtle ether as before, and ſo on, till the whole ſpace, occupied by the dimenſions of the piece of gold, be abſolutely ſolid, and have no pores or vacuum whatever, which would be contrary to appearances, and make it impoſſible to contract by cold, or by any other means. I do not ſay that there is no difficulty in this caſe, but it is not a difficulty that affects my ſyſtem more than the common one;
and

and therefore it is no particular bufinefs of mine to difcufs it.

If it be fuppofed that no kind of matter is concerned in producing the above-mentioned effects at a diftance from the furfaces of bodies, but that the Deity himfelf caufes thefe motions, exerting his influence according to certain laws, am not I at liberty to avail myfelf of the fame affiftance? And furely I muft have lefs objection to this refource than thofe who believe that God is not the only proper agent in the univerfe. As a neceffarian, I, in fact, afcribe every thing to God, and, whether mediately or immediately, makes very little difference. But I believe that it is poffible, though we cannot clearly anfwer every objection to it, that God may endue fubftances with powers, which, when communicated, produce effects in a manner different from his own immediate agency.

II. *Whether Matter be any thing, on this Hypothefis.*

It is faid that, according to my definition of matter, it muft be abfolutely *nothing*; becaufe,

becaufe, befides extenfion, it confifts of nothing but the powers of attraction and repulfion, and becaufe I have fometimes faid that it confifts of phyfical points only, poffeffed of thofe powers. In this I may have expreffed myfelf rather incautioufly; but the *idea* that I meant to convey was evidently this, that, whatever other powers matter may be poffeffed of, it has not the property that has been called *impenetrability*, or *folidity*.

From the manner of expreffing our ideas we cannot fpeak of powers or properties, but as powers and properties of fome *thing* or *fubftance*, though we know nothing at all of that thing or fubftance befides the powers that we afcribe to it; and, therefore, when the powers are fuppofed to be withdrawn, all idea of fubftance neceffarily vanifhes with them. I have, therefore, the fame right to fay that matter is a fubftance poffeffed of the properties of attraction and repulfion only, as another has to fay, that it is a fubftance poffeffed of the property of impenetrability together with them, unlefs

it

it can be proved that the property of attraction or repulfion neceffarily implies,
and cannot exift without, that of impenetrability. Whether it be poffeffed of *any*
of thefe properties muft be determined by
experiment only. If, upon my idea of
matter, every thing vanifhes upon taking
away the powers of attraction and repulfion,
in like manner every idea vanifhes from the
mind; if, upon the common hypothefis,
folidity or impenetrability be taken away.
I own that I can fee no difference in this
cafe; *impenetrability* being as much a property as *penetrability,* and its actual exiftence equally to be afcertained by experiment, which, in my opinion, is decifive
in favour of penetrability.

They who fuppofe fpirit to have proper
*extenfion,* and the Divine Being to have a
proper *ubiquity,* muft believe the mutual
penetrability of real fubftance; and by
whatever names they may choofe to call the
fubftances, is of no confequence. If they
fay that, on my hypothefis, there is no fuch
thing as matter, and that every thing is fpirit, I have no objection, provided they
make

make as great a difference in *spirits*, as they have hitherto made in *substances*. The world has been too long amused with mere names.

### III. *Of the laws of Motion.*

It is said, that if there is not what has been termed a *vis inertiæ* in matter, the foundation of the Newtonian Philosphy is overturned: for that the *three laws of motion*, laid down by Sir Isaac Newton, in the beginning of his *Principia*, have no meaning on any other supposition.

I answer, that these laws of motion are founded on certain *facts*, which result just as easily from my hypothesis concerning matter, as from the common one. It is an undoubted fact that every body perseveres in a state of rest or motion, till it be compelled to change that state by some external force, which is the first of the three laws, and the foundation of the other two. But this will follow just as well upon the supposition of that mutual action between two bodies taking place at any given dis-
tance

tance from their furfaces. Newton himfelf fhews, that rays of light are reflected
by a power belonging to other bodies,
without actually impinging upon them, and,
confequently, by a power which takes place
at a certain diftance from their furfaces,
without fuppofing that any of his laws of
motion were violated.

## IV. *Of the Divine Effence.*

It is fufpected that, notwithftanding I
decline the term, it will be thought that
I virtually make the Deity to be a material
being. I anfwer that, fince, according to
my ideas, the divine effence, and other ef-
fences have quite different properties or
powers, they ought, in ftrictnefs, to be
denoted by quite different names; and,
therefore, I can have no other objection to
the term *immaterial*, as applied to the Divine Being, but as it is apt to imply that
the divine effence is incapable of any property whatever in common with other ef-
fences, fuch as even relation to fpace.

I

I will farther obferve, that, notwithftanding I *may* have expreffed myfelf in an un-
guarded manner on this fubject (though I
am not at prefent aware of it) it will be
found, by the candid and attentive, that I
have not, in reality, any idea of the divine
effence that is at all different from that of
thofe philofophers and divines, who maintain the *proper omniprefence*, or *ubiquity* of
the Divine Being, which neceffarily implies
a real extenfion; and that he has a power
of acting upon matter.

I will take this opportunity of faying,
farther, that, upon no fyftem whatever, is
the great Author of Nature more diftinct
from his productions, or his prefence with
them, and agency upon them, more neceffary. In fact, the fyftem now held forth
to the public, taken in its full extent,
makes the Divine Being to be of as much
importance in the fyftem, as the apoftle
makes him, when he fays, *In him we live,
and move, and have our being.* The contemplation of it impreffes the mind with
fentiments of the deepeft reverence and humility,

mility, and it inculcates a degree of de-
votednefs to God, both active and paffive,
that no other philofophical fyftem can in-
fpire. Confequently the obligation to all
thofe virtues that are more immediately derived from that great vital fpring and principle of all virtue, *devotion*, thofe which
give a fuperiority to the world, a fearlefs
integrity, and a noble independence of mind
in the practice of our duty, is more ftrongly
felt, and therefore may be fuppofed to take
a deeper root in the mind, than upon any
other fyftem whatever. In fhort, it is that
philofophy which alone fuits the doctrine
of the *fcriptures*, though the writers of
them were not philofophers, but had an
inftruction infinitely fuperior to that of any
philofophical fchool. Every other fyftem
of philofophy is difcordant with the fcriptures, and, as far as it lays any hold upon
the mind, tends to counteract their influence.

In the laft place, I think it may not be
unufeful to obferve, that a diftinction ought
to be made with refpect to the *relative im-*
*portance*

*portance* and *mutual subordination* of the different positions contended for in this treatise. The principal object is, to prove the uniform composition of man, or that what we call *mind*, or the principle of perception and thought, is not a substance distinct from the body, but the result of corporeal organization; and what I have advanced preliminary to this, concerning the *nature of matter*, though subservient to this argument, is by no means essential to it: for whatever matter be, I think I have sufficiently proved that the human mind is nothing more than a modification of it.

Again, that man is wholly material is eminently subservient to the doctrine of the *proper*, or *mere humanity* of Christ. For, if no man has a soul distinct from his body, Christ, who, in all other respects, appeared as a man, could not have had a soul which had existed before his body; and the whole doctrine of the *pre-existence of souls* (of which the opinion of the preexistence of Christ was a branch) will be effectually overturned. But I apprehend that,

that, fhould I have failed in the proof of
the materiality of man, arguments enow
remain, independent of this, to prove the
non pre-exiftence of Chrift, and of this
doctrine having been introduced into chriftianity from the fyftem of Oriental philofophy.

Laftly, the doctrine of *neceſſity*, maintained in the Appendix, is the immediate
refult of the doctrine of the materiality of
man; for mechanifm is the undoubted confequence of materialifm. But whether man
be wholly material or not, I apprehend
that proof enough is advanced that every
human volition is fubject to certain fixed
laws, and that the pretended *felf-determining power* is altogether imaginary and impoffible.

In fhort, it is my firm perfuafion, that
the three doctrines of *materialifm*, of that
which is commonly called *Socinianifm*, and
of philofophical *neceſſity*, are equally parts
of *one fyſtem*, being equally founded on juft
obfervations of nature, and fair deductions
from the fcriptures; and that whoever fhall

Q                         duly

duly confider their *connection*, and *dependence on one another*, will find no fufficient confiftency in any general fcheme of principles, that does not comprehend them all. At the fame time each of thefe doctrines ftands on its own independent foundation, and is capable of fuch feparate demonftration, as fubjects of a moral nature require, or admit.

I have advanced what has occurred to me in fupport of all the three parts of this fyftem; confident that, in due time, the truth will bear down before it every oppofing prejudice, how inveterate foever, and gain a firm eftablifhment in the minds of all men.

ADDITIONAL

## ADDITIONAL ILLUSTRATIONS.

### I. *Of the Nature of Matter.*

SEVERAL of my friends have proposed to me queries concerning the
*phyfical indivifible points*, of which I have
fometimes fuppofed matter to confift. But
I beg it may be confidered, that the only
mention I have made of fuch *points* is in
the extract from my *Hiftory of Vifion*, &c.
in which I gave an account of the hypothefis of Father Bofcovich and Mr. Michell, adding only a fingle obfervation of
my own; and that, in what properly belongs to the *Difquifitions*, I have not, as
far as I can recollect, encumbered my doctrine with any of the difficulties attending
the confideration of the *internal ftructure
of matter*; concerning which we know, indeed, very little; having few *data* to argue
from.

In

In this *metaphyfical work*, I have confined myfelf to the exclufion of the property of *impenetrability*, which is generally
confidered as effential to all matter, and to
the claim of the property of *attraction* or
*repulfion*, as appearing to me not to be properly what is *imparted* to matter, but what
really *makes is to be what it is*, in fo much
that, without it, it would be nothing at
all; which is giving it the fame rank and
importance that has ufually been affigned
to the property of *folidity* or *impenetrability*.
By this means it is that I leave no room for
the popular objection to the materiality of
man founded on the idea of matter, as *folid*
and *inert*, being incapable of the powers of
fenfation and thought.

This, I fay, is all that my purpofe in the
*Difquifitions* requires; and fo far I fee no
difficulty, that appears to me to be of much
moment, and the argument lies in a very
fmall compafs. I deny that matter is impenetrable to other matter, becaufe I know
no one *fact*, to the explanation of which
that fuppofition is neceffary; all thofe facts
which

which led philofophers to this fuppofition, later, and more accurate obfervations, having fhewn to be owing to, *fomething elfe* than folidity or impenetrability, viz. a *power of repulfion*, which, for that reafon, I would fubftitute in its place. As other philofophers have faid " Take away folidity, and " matter vanifhes:" fo, I fay, " Take " away attraction and repulfion, and mat" ter vanifhes." Alfo, if any perfon afks *what it is* that attracts and repels, or what is left when the powers of attraction and repulfion are taken away, I, in my turn, afk, What is it that is folid, or what is left when the property of folidity is taken away. The immaterialift, whether his immaterial fubftance be extended, or not, cannot, with the leaft reafon, afk fuch a queftion as this. If he do, he muft be effectually filenced by being afked, what will be left of *fpirit*, when the powers of fenfation and thought are taken from it If the immaterial fubftance he contends for be extended, it muft, in that cafe, be reduced to *mere fpace*, and if it be not extended, it muft be reduced to *nothing at all*

Q 3                                    It

It is, moreover, not a little remarkable, that, according to the common hypothefis, fpirit, though deftitute of folidity, has the power of acting upon matter, or in other words, has the fame property of attraction and repulfion with refpect to matter, that I afcribe to unfolid matter; fo that it is with a very ill grace indeed that the abettors of that hypothefis can object to mine, that nothing will remain when the powers of attraction and repulfion are withdrawn.

Farther than this, which I think very clear ground, it does not appear to me that I have any proper call, or bufinefs, to proceed. In what *manner* matter, penetrable or impenetrable, is formed, with what interftices, &c. and how far the powers which we afcribe to it may be faid to *inhere in,* or *belong to* it, or how far they are the effect of a *foreign power,* viz. that of the deity, concerns not my fyftem in particular. And whatever difficulties may be ftarted as refulting from thefe confiderations, the very fame, I think, or greater, may fairly be charged upon the oppofite
fyftem.

fyftem. If I have advanced beyond thefe narrow bounds, it has been inadvertently, and for the fake of anfwering objections. The metaphyfician has no bufinefs to fpeculate any farther, and the natural philofopher will find, I imagine, but few *data* for farther fpeculation.

In fact, what I have advanced above is all that I have afcribed to that excellent and truly cautious philofopher Mr. Michell. See *Difquifitions*, p. 21. I will venture, however, in order to give all the fatisfaction I am able to the inquifitive natural philofopher, to go one ftep farther in this fpeculation, on the idea fuggefted at the conclufion of my account of that hypothefis, p. 33. I am well aware that the generality of my readers will revolt at the ideas I am about to prefent to them; but I beg their patient attention, and I may perhaps convince them, that the common hypothefis, when confidered in connection with *facts*, is no lefs revolting.

Suppofe then that the Divine Being, when he created *matter*, only fixed certain

Q 4 *centers*

*centers of various attractions and repulfions*
extending indefinitely in all directions, the
whole effect of them to be upon each other;
thefe centers approaching to, or receding
from each other, and confequently carrying
their peculiar fpheres of attraction and repulfion along with them, according to certain
definite circumftances. It cannot be denied
that thefe fpheres may be diverfified infinitely, fo as to correfpond to all the kinds
of bodies that we are acquainted with, or
that are poffible. For all effects in which
bodies are concerned, and of which we can
be fenfible by our eyes, touch, &c. may
be refolved into attraction or repulfion.

A compages of thefe centers, placed
within the fphere of each others attraction,
will conftitute a body that we term *compact*; and two of thefe bodies will, on their
approach, meet with a repulfion or refiftance, fufficient to prevent one of them
from occupying the place of the other,
without a much greater force than we are
capable of employing, fo that to us they
will appear perfectly hard.

As

As in the conftitution of all actual bodies that we are acquainted with, thefe
centers are placed fo near to each other,
that, in every divifion that we can make,
we ftill leave parts which contain many of
thefe centers, we, reafoning by analogy, fuppofe that every particle of matter is infinitely divifible; and the *fpace* it occupies
is certainly fo. But, ftrictly fpeaking, as
thefe centers which conftitute any body
are not abfolutely infinite, it muft be naturally poffible to come, by divifion, to one
fingle center, which could not be faid to
be divifible, or even to occupy any portion
of fpace, though its fphere of action fhould
extend ever fo far; and had only *one* fuch
center of attraction, &c. exifted, its exiftence could not have been known, becaufe
there would have been nothing on which
its action could have been exerted; and
there being no *effect*, there could not have
been any ground for fuppofing a *caufe*.

Father Bofcovich fuppofes that no two of
thefe centers can ever coincide, the refiftance at the point itfelf being infinite. But
admitting

admitting their coincidence, they would only form *another center*, with different powers, thofe belonging to one center modifying thofe belonging to the other. Had their powers been *the very fame* before fuch coincidence, at the fame diftances, they would have been juft doubled at thofe diftances. Alfo, though united by one caufe, they might poffibly be feparated by another.

To philofophical people, and I am not now writing for the ufe of any other, I do not need to explain myfelf any farther. They will eafily fee, or F. Bofcovich, in his elaborate work will fhew them, that this hypothefis will account for all the phenomena of nature.

The principal objeƈtion to this hypothefis is, that matter is, by this means, refolved into nothing but the *divine agency*, exerted according to certain rules. But as, upon the common hypothefis, it has been again and again admitted, that, notwithftanding the exiftence of folid matter, every thing is really *done* by the divine power, what material

terial objection can there be to every thing *being* the divine power. There is, at leaft, this advantage in the fcheme, that it fuppofes *nothing to be made in vain*.

Admitting that bodies confift of folid atoms, there is no fort of connection between the idea of them, and that of *attraction*; fo that it is impoffible to conceive that any one atom fhould approach another without a *foreign power*, viz. that of the deity; and therefore bodies confifting of fuch atoms could not hold together, fo as to conftitute *compact fubftances*, without this conftant agency.

There is, again, as little connection between the idea of thefe folid atoms, and that of *repulfion at the leaft diftance from the point of contact*. So that, fince the conftituent particles of no fubftance actually touch one another, as is evident from the effects of cold (which brings them nearer together) their coherence cannot be accounted for without the conftant agency of the fame external power. And though mere *refiftance* (not repulfion) *at the place of contact* might be explained on the principle

ciple of folidity, it is remarkable, that in no *known cafe* of refiftance can it be proved, that real contact is concerned, and in moft cafes of refiftance it is demonftrable that there is no real contact; and therefore there can be no *reafon from fact* to believe that there is any fuch thing as real contact in nature; fo that if there be fuch a thing as folid matter, it is altogether *fuperfluous,* being no way concerned in producing any effect whatever.

If I have bewildered myfelf, and my reader, with this fpeculation, I can only fay that I have been drawn into it, when I would willingly acquiefce in what I have obferved concerning the fimple *penetrability of matter*; confeffing myfelf unable to proceed any farther on tolerably fure ground, and my readinefs to abandon all this hypothefis, whenever a better, that is, one more nearly correfponding to facts, fhall be fuggefted to me: and I own that I fhould much prefer an hypothefis which fhould make provifion for the ufe of created matter without the neceffity of fuch a *par-*
*ticular*

*ticular agency* as the preceding hypothefis requires; though, of the two, I fhall certainly
prefer one which admits of nothing being
made in vain.

Being, however, engaged thus far, I muft
be permitted to advance one ftep farther,
for the fake of obferving, that there is nothing more approaching to *impiety* in my
fcheme than in the common one. On this
hypothefis every thing is the *divine power* :
but ftill, ftrictly fpeaking, every thing is
not *the Deity himfelf*. The centers of attraction, &c. are fixed by him, and all
action is his action; but ftill thefe centers
are no part of *himfelf*, any more than the
folid matter fuppofed to be created by him.
Nor, indeed, is making the deity to *be*,
as well as to *do* every thing, *in this fenfe*,
any thing like the opinion of Spinoza; becaufe I fuppofe a fource of infinite power,
and fuperior intelligence, from which all
inferior beings are derived, that every inferior intelligent being has a confcioufnefs
diftinct from that of the fupreme intelligence, that they will for ever continue diftinct,

tinct, and that their happiness or misery to endless ages will depend upon their conduct in this state of probation and discipline.

On the other hand, the common hypothesis is much less favourable to piety, in that it supposes something to be *independent of the divine power*. Exclude the idea of deity on my hypothesis, and every thing except *space*, necessarily vanishes with it; so that the Divine Being, and his energy, are absolutely necessary to that of every other being. His power is the very *life and soul* of every thing that exists; and, strictly speaking, *without him, we* ARE, as well as, *can* DO *nothing*. But exclude the idea of Deity on the common hypothesis, and the idea of *solid matter* is no more excluded, than that of *space*. It remains a problem, therefore, whether matter be at all dependent upon God, whether it be *in his power* either to *annihilate*, or to *create* it; a difficulty that has staggered many, and on which the doctrine of *two original independent principles* was built. My hypothesis, whatever other defects it may have,

leaves

leaves no foundation for this *fyftem of impiety*; and in this refpect it has, I think, a great and defirable advantage.

I own that, for my part, I feel an inexpreffible fatisfaction in the idea of that moft intimate connection which, on my hypothefis, myfelf, and every thing in which I am concerned, have with the deity. On his will I am entirely dependent for my *being*, and all my *faculties*. My fphere, and degree of influence on other beings and other things, is *his* influence. I am but an inftrument in his hands for effecting a certain part of the greateft and moft glorious of purpofes. I am happy in *feeing* a little of this purpofe, happier in the *belief* that the operations in which I am concerned, are of infinitely greater moment than I am capable of comprehending, and in the perfuafion that, in the continuance of my exiftence, I fhall fee more and more of this great purpofe, and of the relation that myfelf and my fphere of influence bear to it. Let the abettors of the common hypothefis fay more than this

*if*

if they can, or any thing different from this, that fhall give them more fatisfaction.

II. *Of the connection between fenfation and organization:*

I have been afked, whether I confider the powers of fenfation and thought as *necefarily refulting* from the organization of the brain, or as fomething independent of organization, but *fuperadded* and *communicated* to the fyftem afterwards; having exprefled myfelf doubtfully, and perhaps varioufly on the fubject. *

I anfwer, that my idea *now is,* that fenfation and thought do necefarily refult from the organization of the brain, when the powers of mere *life* are given to the fyftem. For I can eafily conceive a perfect man to be formed without life, that is, without refpiration,

* In the *Efay* prefixed to my edition of Hartley, I exprefled myfelf with abfolute uncertainty in this refpect, " I " rather think that the whole man is of fome uniform com- " pofition, and that the property of perception, as well as " the other powers that are termed mental, is the refult " (whether necefary, or not) of fuch an organical ftructure " as that of the brain."

respiration, or the circulation of the blood, or whatever else it be in which life more properly consists, and consequently without every thing necessarily depending upon life; but I cannot imagine that a human body, completely organized, and having life, would want sensation and thought. This I suppose to follow *of course*, as much as the circulation of the blood follows respiration; and if there be any expressions in my work that intimate the contrary, I shall take care to alter them.

As to the *manner* in which the power of perception results from organization and life, I own I have no idea at all; but the *fact* of this connection does not appear to me to be, on that account, the less certain. Sensation and thought do always accompany such an organization; and having never known them to be separated, we have no reason to suppose that they *can* be separated. When, therefore, God had made man of the *dust of the earth*; nothing was wanting to make him all that he is, viz. a *living soul*, but simply the *breath of life*.

R                                 In

In all other cases we deem it sufficient to say that certain circumstances are the causes, and the *necessary causes*, of certain appearances, if the appearances always accompany the circumstances. We are not, for example, in the least able to conceive how it is that a magnet attracts iron; but having observed that it never fails to do it, we conclude that, though we do not see the *proximate cause*, or *how* the attraction is effected, the magnet nevertheless *has* that power, and must cease to be a magnet before it can lose it; so that our reasoning with respect to the result of sensation from organization is exactly similar to our reasoning concerning the attraction of iron by magnetism.

Also, for the very same reason that it is said that it is not the organized body that feels and thinks, but an *immaterial substance* residing in the body, and that will remain when the body is destroyed, we might say that it is not the material magnet that attracts, but a peculiar immaterial substance within

within it, that produces the effect, and that will remain when the material magnet is deftroyed. And, for the fame reafon, we may imagine *diftinct immaterial fubftances* for every operation in nature, the proximate caufe of which we are not able to perceive.

The manner in which the affociation of ideas is formed, or in which motives influence the mind, was equally unknown; but affociation of ideas was neverthelefs known to be a *fact*, and the influence of motives was not, on that account, denied. But now that Dr. Hartlev has fhewn us what ideas probably are, we fee much farther into the *mechanifm of the mind*. We fee *how* one idea is connected with another; and *the manner* in which motives (which are only trains of ideas) produce their effect. Now we are not more (or not much more) ignorant how fenfation refults from organization, than we were how the motion of the hand refults from a volition, or how a volition is produced by a motive, which

R 2                    are

are now no longer fuch very difficult pro-
blems.  It is not impoffible but that in
time we may fee *how* it is that fenfation refults from organization.


III. *A general view of the origin and pro-*
*grefs of opinions relating to the* ESSENCE
OF THE SOUL, *with fome confiderations on*
*the notion of its being an* EXTENDED,
*though an* IMMATERIAL SUBSTANCE.


After the deduction that I have given of
the hiftory of opinions concerning the foul
in the *Difquifitions,* it may be ufeful to give
a fummary view of the whole, that the
feveral fteps in the progrefs, and their natural connection, may more eafily appear.


Man is a being poffeffed of various faculties, or powers.  He can *fee, hear, fmell,*
*feel, walk, think,* and *fpeak.*  He is alfo a
very complex being, confifting of various
diftinct parts, fome of which are evidently
appropriated to fome of thefe powers, and
others to others of them.  Thus it is the
eye only that fees, the ear that hears, the
nofe

nofe that fmells, the feet that walk, and the tongue is of principal ufe in modulating the voice. What it is in man that *thinks* is not fo obvious, and the opinions concerning it have been various. I apprehend, however, that it was always fuppofed to be fomething *within* a man, and not any part that was confpicuous.

The writers of the Old Teftament feem to have conceived of it varioufly, fometimes referring it to the *heart,* perhaps as the moft central part of man, as when the Pfalmift fays, *My heart is inditing a good matter,* &c. but at other times to the *reins,* as *My reins inftruct me in the night feafon.* The *paffions* are generally feated by them in the heart, but the fentiments of pity and commiferation are more frequently affigned to the *bowels,* which are faid to yearn over an object of diftrefs. It is remarkable that the *head,* or *brain,* never feems to have been confidered by them as having any thing to do in the bufinefs of thinking, or in any mental affection whatever. But the reafon of it may be that ftrong mental af-

R 3　　　　　fections

fections were fooner obferved to affect the heart, reins and bowels, than the head.

In antient times the fimple power of *life* was generally thought to be in the *breath*, or animal *heat*, becaufe breathing and warmth are the univerfal concomitants of life. I do not, however, recollect that the latter idea ever occurs in the fcriptures, but there life is fometimes faid to be in the *blood*.

When men reflected a little farther, and began to conceive that poffibly both the property of *life*, and alfo all the powers that we term *mental*, might belong to the fame thing, the breath (the fuppofed principle of life) was imagined to be competent to the whole; and then the idea of a *foul* was completely formed. Confequently, it was firft conceived to be an aerial, or an igneous fubftance, which animates the body during life, and makes its efcape at death; after which it was fuppofed to be either detained near the place where the body was depofited, being held by a kind of of attraction, or an affection to its former companion, or to rise in the atmofphere to a region in which it was counterpoifed by the furrounding elements.

We may fmile at the ignorance of mankind in early ages, in fuppofing that the breath of life could be any thing more than part of the common air, which was firft infpired, and then expired. But though this be a thing well known in the prefent age, I can eafily conceive that, when the nature of air and refpiration were little under- derftood, men might not immediately conceive that the breath, though it mixed with the air, and was invifible, was therefore the very fame thing with it. They might well enough imagine that it was fomething diftinct from it, which was in part drawn in and out during the continuance of life, and wholly difcharged and fet loofe at death. There are other inftances of the ignorance of the antients in matters of philofophy, and even in tolerably enlightened ages, almoft, if not altogether, as grofs as this.

When,

When, at length, it was difcovered that the breath was nothing more than the air, ftill the idea of an *invifible principle of life and thought* being once fixed, would not be immediately exploded, but would be fuppofed to be a fubftance more attenuated, and refined; as being, for inftance, of an *ethereal* or *fiery* nature, &c. ftill invifible, and more active.

Whatever was the invifible fubftance of which the human foul confifted, the *univer-fal foul* of the heathen philofophers, or the *divine effence*, was fuppofed to be the very fame; and all other fouls were fuppofed to have been parts of it, to have been detached from it, and to be finally refumed into it again. In this ftate of opinions, therefore, the foul was fuppofed to be what we fhould now call *an attenuated kind of matter*, capable of divifion, as all other matter is.

This was the notion adopted by the chriftian Fathers from the Oriental and Platonic fyftem of philofophy, and therefore many of thefe Fathers did not fcruple to to affert that the foul, though conceived to be a thing diftinct from the body, was properly *corporeal*, and even *naturally mortal*. The opinion, however, of its being naturally immortal gained ground; and, *matter*, according to the philofophical fyftem, being confidered as a thing that was neceffarily *perifhable*, as well as *impure*, the doctrine of the immateriality as well as of the immortality of the foul was pretty firmly eftablifhed; an immaterial fubftance being, however, ftill confidered as only fomething more refined than grofs matter.

The idea of the foul being immaterial foon led to the idea of its not having any property in common with grofs matter, and in time with matter ftrictly confidered; and being confounded with, and illuftrated by, the idea of the *principle of life*, it was afferted to have no length, breadth, or thicknefs, which are properties peculiar to matter; to be *indivifible* alfo, and finally *not to exift in fpace*. This was the idea that generally prevailed after the time of Mamertus, though various other refinements occur

occur in the writings of the fchoolmen
upon the fubject.

But the doctrine of *pure fpiritualifm*
was not firmly eftablifhed before Defcartes,
who, confidering extenfion as the effence
of matter, made the want of extenfion the
diftinguifhing property of mind or fpirit.
Upon this idea was built the immaterial
fyftem in its ftate of greateft refinement,
when the foul was defined to be *immaterial,
indivifible, indifcerptible, unextended,* and to
have nothing to do with *locality* or *motion,*
but to be a fubftance poffeffed of the fimple powers of thought, and to have nothing
more than an arbitrary connection with an
organized fyftem of matter.

This was the idea of mind or fpirit that
was prevalent about the time of Mr. Locke,
who contributed greatly to lower it, by
contending that whatever exifts muft exift
*fomewhere,* or in *fome place,* and by fhewing
that, for any thing that we know to the
contrary, the power of thought may be fuperadded by the Divine Being to an organized fyftem of mere matter, though at the
                                                      fame

fame time declaring himself in favour of the notion of a feparate foul. From this time, the doctrine of the nature of the foul has been fluctuating and various; fome ftill maintaining that it has no property whatever in common with matter, and bears no relation to fpace, whereas others fay that it exifts in fpace, and occupies a portion of it, fo as to be properly extended, but not to have folidity, which they make to be the property that diftinguifhes it from matter.

The object of my late work is to prove that the doctrine of a foul is altogether unphilofophical, and unfcriptural; for that, judging from the phenomena, all the powers of *the fame being*, viz. *man*, ought to be referred to *one fubftance*, which, therefore, muft neceffarily be *the body*, and that the refined and proper fpiritualifm above defcribed is peculiarly chimerical and abfurd. Abfurd, however, as is the notion of a fubftance which has *no property in common with matter*, which bears *no relation to fpace*, and yet both acts upon body, and is acted upon by it, it is the doctrine that, in the courfe

of

of gradual refinement, philofophers and divines were neceffarily brought to, and is the only confiftent immaterialifm. For every other opinion concerning fpirit makes it to be, in fact, the fame thing with matter; at leaft every other opinion is liable to objections fimilar to thofe which lie againft the notion of a foul properly material. Becaufe, however, I have not been thought to have given fufficient attention to this idea of *extended fpirit*, I fhall here make a few animadverfions upon it.

1. The chief reafon why the principle of thought has been fuppofed to be incompatible with matter, is that there is no *conceivable connection* between *thought* and *folidity*, that the two ideas are altogether different, and *diffimilar*. But is there any more conceivable connection between thought and mere *extenfion*? Are ideas, according to the opinion of the perfons who hold this doctrine, extended things? Is the *judgment* extended, is the will *extended*, or have the *paffions* extenfion? How, then, do they require an extended fubftance in which to inhere?

inhere ? If there be fome unknown reafon why they *do* require an extended *fubftratum,* may not this fubftance have *folidity* added to its extenfion, the idea of folidity not being more foreign to the idea of thought, than that of extenfion, nor more diffimilar to it.

2. The effence of the foul, it is faid, cannot be matter, becaufe it would then be *divifible*; but is not every thing that is extended divifible? It is not the folidity of bodies that makes them capable of divifion fo properly as their extenfion. It is this property that makes divifion poffible; and then all that is neceffary to actual divifion is *difcerptibility*, or the poffible feparation of one part of its fubftance from another. For wherever there is extenfion, there muft be conceivable parts, viz. a half, a third, a fourth, &c. But till the fubftance of which the foul (exclufive of its power of thinking) confifts be more known to us, fo that we can fubject it to a rigorous exami-nation, it is impoffible to fay whether it be more or lefs difcerptible than any fpecies

of

of matter; for all that we know of it is that it is *extended*, and that it *thinks*. The firmnefs of its texture, is a thing of which we have no knowledge at all; and if it be any thing more than *mere fpace*, it muft have that which may be called *texture*, or *confiftence*, folid or fluid, elaftic or non-elaftic, &c. &c. Confequently, it may, for any thing we know, be as corruptible, and perifhable, as the body. The boafted *unity of confcioufnefs*, and *fimplicity of perception and thought*, can be no fecurity againft divifion and diffolution, unlefs they inhere in a fubftance naturally incapable of divifion, and confequently of diffolution.

3. As divifibility may always be predicated of any fubftance that is extended, and not infinite, I wifh the advocates of this doctrine of extended fpirit would confider a little what would be the probable confequence of an actual divifion of it. Suppofing the fubftance of a human foul to be divided into two equal parts (which to divine power muft, at leaft, be poffible) would the power of thinking be neceffarily deftroyed,

deſtroyed, or would the reſult be *two ſpirits,* of inferior powers, as of ſmaller ſize? If ſo, would each of them retain the conſciouſneſs of the whole undivided ſoul, or would the ſtock of ideas be equally divided between them?

4. As every created being muſt *exiſt* before it can *act,* I wiſh the advocates of this doctrine would conſider what idea they can form of the extended ſubſtance of a ſpirit before it has acquired any ideas at all, and conſequently before it has begun to think. In what will it differ from mere ſpace? Whatever this ſtate be, in what does it differ from the ſtate of the ſoul whenever it ceaſes to think, as in a deep ſleep, a ſwoon, or the ſtate between death and the reſurrection!

5. I would alſo ſubmit it to the conſideration of the partiſans of *extended ſpiritualiſm,* what *ſize* or *ſhape* they would give to the human ſoul (for if it be extended, ſize and ſhape it muſt have) and whether ſome inconvenience may not ariſe to their ſyſtem

in

in the difcuffion of the queftion. If nothing can act but where it is, I fhould
think that the foul muft have the fize and
form of the brain, if not of the whole ner-
vous fyftem. For there is no region within
the brain of lefs extent than the medullary
part of it, that can be imagined to be the
*fenforium*, or the immediate feat of fenfation; and as the nerves confift of the fame
fubftance with the medullary part of the
brain, and are properly a production, or
part of it, I do not fee why the foul fhould
be confined to the fize of the brain only,
exclufive of the nerves; and then as the
nerves are in every part of the body, the
foul would, in fact, be of the fame form
and fize with the body to which it belongs,
though with more interftices.

6. It is alfo a matter of fome curiofity
to the fpeculatift to confider whether the
fize and form of thefe extended fouls be
invariable, or whether, as we fuppofe the
body to undergo fome change at the refurrection, in order to adapt it to its new
mode of exiftence, the foul may not undergo

2

a proportionable change, and be transformed together with it.

7. We are apt to impofe upon ourfelves, and to confound our underftandings, by the ufe of *general terms*. To gain clear perceptions of things we muft infpect them more clofely, in order to difcover what particular and more *definite ideas* are neceffarily comprized in the more general ones. Thus while we content ourfelves with faying that man is a compound being, confifting of two fubftances, the one *corporeal* and the other *fpiritual*, the one both extended and folid, and the other extended indeed, but deftitute of folidity; and that an intimate union fubfifts between them, fo that they always *accompany* and *affect* one another (an impreffion upon the body caufing a fenfation in the mind, and a volition of the mind caufing a motion of the body) we are fatisfied. The hypothefis feems to correfpond to the *firft view* of the phenomena; and though we cannot help being ftaggered when we confider this intimate union of two fuch *heterogeneous fubftances*,

S                                    we

we ftill acquiefce in it, as an union effected
by almighty power; and we are likewife
repelled from a rigorous examination of it
by the idea, however ill-founded, that our
profpects of a future life are materially affected by it.

But a future life being fecured to us by
the promifes of the gofpel, upon *other and
better principles*, we need not be afraid to
confider what this fuppofed union of body
and foul really implies, and it appears to
me to imply that the foul, having *locality*,
and *extenfion*, muft have *folidity* alfo.

That the mind fhould move the body,
and at the fame time *move itfelf* along with
the body, we may think a tolerable eafy
fuppofition; but what fhall we fay to the
cafe of the body being moved during fleep,
or a fwoon, to which removal the mind
does not at all contribute. It will hardly
be faid that, in this cafe, the foul is firft
of all left behind, in the place from which
the body was taken, and that it aftewards
*voluntarily* joins its former companion.
And,

And, if not, the motion of the mind muft, in all cafes, *neceffarily* accompany the motion of the living body, or, in other words, the mind muft be *involuntarily dragged* along with it. But can this motion be communicated from *body* to *mind* without real *impulfe*, implying a *vis inertiæ*, and *folidity*, without which, it fhould feem, that the one cannot lay hold of the other?

8. It will alfo, I think, be difficult to account for the feparation of the foul from the body after death, unlefs the fpiritual fubftance be fuppofed to be a proper conftituent part of the *folid mafs*, which, like fixed air in bodies, is fet loofe when the reft of the mafs is diffolved by putrefaction, or otherwife. If putrefaction, or total diffolution, be the phyfical caufe of this feparation, is there not a good foundation for the practice of the Egyptians, who preferved the bodies of their friends as long as they poffibly could, probably with a view of retaining their fouls in them, or near them?

S 2                    If

If the foul be really infeparable from the body, which is probably the opinion of thofe who maintain that, during the death of the body, the foul is in a ftate of infen-fibility until the refurrection, what part of the body does it accompany? If it be in-difcerptible, it muft be wholly in fome one place; and as all the conftitutent parts of every member of the body are completely diffolved and difperfed, it muft, in fact, accompany fome one of the *ultimate parti-cles*, and which of them can that be?

If the extended fpirit does *not* accom-pany any particle of the diffolved body, and all fouls be preferved, during their dor-mant ftate, in fome *general repofitory* (whether in the fun, the earth, or fome part of the intermediate fpace) in what manner will the re-union of the fouls and their refpective bodies be effected at the refurrection? Will it be by any thing like what is called *elective attraction* between them, or will it be ef-fected by a new and exprefs *fiat* of the deity?

Thefe objections do not much, if at all, affect the doctrine of *fpirit bearing no relation*

*to*

*to space,* or any fpeculation concerning the divine effence, which fills all fpace.

9. Many other queries will neceffarily obtrude themfelves on any perfon who fhall begin to fpeculate on the nature of extended fpiritual fubftances, which it will be impoffible to difmifs without fome degree of attention; and it appears to me that, let the advocates for this doctrine anfwer them in whatever manner they pleafe, they muft occafion fome degree of embarraff-ment, fo as to leave a fufpicion of the doctrine from which they arife, as wanting a fufficient foundation in probability and truth; fuch as, What is the origin, or com-mencement, of the extended fpirit? Is every foul a feparate creation, or, are fouls pro-pagated from each other like bodies? Does it grow in fize with the growth of the body and brain? Are thefe extended fpirits mu-tually penetrable to each other? There can be no doubt but that they muft occupy a portion of the fame univerfal fpace that is already occupied by the divine effence. Is the effence of thefe extended fpirits fimilar

S 3

to

to that of the deity, and will no impediment arife from this neceffary mutual penetration?

Many more obfervations might be made on this notion of extended fpirit, which appears to me not to have been fufficiently confidered by thofe who hold it. They have concluded, or rather, have taken it for granted, that there is in man a foul diftinct from his body, but they revolt at the idea of this foul having no extenfion, or relation to fpace, and therefore admit that it has thefe properties; but, being driven by mere neceffity to admit thus much, they are unwilling to confider the fubject any farther, and fhut their eyes on all the concomitants and confequences of their conceffions; though, if they would attend to them, they would find them fuch as would probably make them revolt at the whole fyftem. Their arguments for a feparate foul from the topics of thought being diffimilar to matter, from the unity of confcioufnefs, indifcerptibility, &c. properly belong to the advocates for refined fpiritualifm, and

are

are impertinently and ineffectually alledged by thofe, who, admitting a real extenfion, and confequently real fize and form in the foul, in vain imagine that they are advo-cates for the doctrine of proper immateri-ality. In fact, they are themfelves *femi-materialifts*.

How eafy is it to get rid of all the em-barraffment attending the doctrine of a foul, in every view of it, by admitting, agree-ably to all the phenomena, that the power of thinking belongs to the *brain* of a man, as that of walking to his feet, or that of fpeak-ing to his tongue; that, therefore, man, who is *one being*, is compofed of *one kind of fubftance*, made of *the duft of the earth*; that when he dies, he, of courfe, ceafes to think; but when his *fleeping duft* fhall be reanimated at the refurrection, his power of thinking, and his confcioufnefs, will be re-ftored to him?

This fyftem gives a real value to the doctrine of *a refurrection from the dead*, which is peculiar to revelation, on which

alone

alone the facred writers build all our hope
of a future life, and it explains the uniform language of the fcriptures, which
fpeak of one day of judgment for all
mankind, and reprefent all the rewards
of virtue, and all the punifhments of vice,
as taking place at that awful day, and not
before. This doctrine of a refurrection
was laughed at by the conceited Athenians,
and will always be the fubject of ridicule
to perfons of a fimilar turn of mind; but
it is abundantly confirmed to us by the
well attefted refurrection of Jefus Chrift,
and the promifes of the gofpel, eftablifhed
on all the miraculous events by which the
promulgation of chriftianity was attended.

## IV. *Of Confcioufnefs.*

Since, in all metaphyfical fubjects, there
is a perpetual appeal made to *confcioufnefs*,
or *internal feeling*, that is, to what we certainly and intuitively know by reflecting
on what paffes within our own minds, and
I have hitherto contented myfelf with noticing the particular inftances in which I
apprehended

apprehended some miftake has been made
with refpect to it, as they occurred in the
courfe of my argument; I fhall here give
a more general view of the fubject, in order
to acquaint my reader what things they are
that, I apprehend, we *can* be confcious
of, and efpecially to caution him againft
confounding them with thofe things of
which we are not properly confcious, but
which we only *infer* from them.

When we fhut our eyes on the external
world, and contemplate what we find within ourfelves, we firft perceive the images,
or the ideas of the objects by which our
fenfes have been impreffed. Of thefe we
are properly confcious. They are what we
immediately *obferve*, and are not *deductions*
from any prior obfervations.

In the next place, we know by intuition,
or are confcious, that thefe ideas appear,
and re-appear, and that they are varioufly
connected with each other, which is the
foundation of *memory* or *recollection*. We
alfo fee that our ideas are varioufly *combined*
and

and *divided*, and can perceive the other re-
lations that they bear to each other, which
is the foundation of *judgment*, and confequently of *reafoning*. And laftly, we perceive that various bodily motions depend
upon ideas and trains of ideas, from which
arifes what is called a *voluntary power* over
our actions.

These particulars, I apprehend, comprize
all that we are properly confcious of; and
with refpect to thefe it is hardly poffible
we can be miftaken. But every thing that
we pretend to know that is really more
than thefe, muft be by way of *inference*
from them; and in drawing thefe inferences
or conclufions, we are liable to miftakes,
as well as in other inferences. In fact,
there is perhaps no fubject whatever with
refpect to which we have more need of
caution, from the danger we are in of
imagining that our knowledge of things
relating to ourfelves is *in the firft in-*
*ftance*, when, in reality, it is in the *fecond*,
or perhaps the *third* or *fourth*.

If

If then, as I have obferved, all that we are really confcious of be our *ideas*, and the various *affections of our ideas*, which, when reduced to general heads, we call the *powers of thought*, as *memory, judgment*, and *will*, all our knowledge of the *fubject of thought* within us, or what we call *our-felves*, muft be by way of *inference*. What we *feel*, and what we *do* we may be faid to know by intuition; but what we *are* we know only by deduction, or inference from intuitive obfervations. If, therefore, it be afferted, that the fubject of thought is fomething that is *fimple, indivifible, immaterial*, or *naturally immortal*, it can only be by way of conclufion from given premifes. Confequently, it is a decifion for which no man's word is to be taken. We may *fancy* that it is fomething that we feel, or are confcious of, but, from the nature of the thing, it can only be that a man *reafons* himfelf into that belief, and therefore he may, without having been aware of it, have impofed upon himfelf by fome fallacy in the argument.

*Feeling*

*Feeling* and *thinking* are allowed to be *properties*; and though all that we can know of any thing are its properties, we agree to fay that all properties inhere in, or belong to, fome *fubject* or *fubftance*; but what this fubftance *is*, farther than its being poffeffed of thofe very properties by which it is known to us, it is impoffible for us to fay, except we can prove that thofe known properties neceffarily imply others. If, therefore, any perfon fay he is confcious that his mind (by which we mean the fubject of thought) is *fimple*, or *indivifible*, and if he fpeak properly, he can only mean, that he is *one thinking perfon*, or *being*, and not *feveral*, which will be univerfally acknowledged. But if he means any thing more than this, as that the fubftance to which the property of thinking belongs is incapable of divifion, either having no extenfion, or parts, or that thofe parts cannot be removed from each other, I do not admit his affertion without hearing what *reafons* he has to advance for it; being fenfible that in this he goes beyond a proper confcioufnefs. I may think it more probable,

that

that every thing that exifts muft have extenfion, and that (except fpace, and the
divine effence, which fills all fpace) whatever is extended may be divided, though
that divifion might be attended with the
lofs of properties peculiar to the undivided
fubftance.

Much farther muft a man go beyond the
bounds of proper *confcioufnefs*, into thofe of
*reafoning*, to fay that the fubject of his
thinking powers is *immaterial*, or fomething different from the matter of which
his body, and efpecially his brain, confifts.
For admitting all that he can know by *experience*, or *intuition*, I may think it more
probable, that all the powers or properties
of man inhere in *one kind* of fubftance;
and fince we are agreed that man confifts,
in part at leaft, of matter, I may conclude
that he is wholly material, and may re-
fufe to give up this opinion, till I be fhown
that the properties neceffarily belonging to
matter, and thofe of feeling and thinking,
are incompatible. And before this can be
determined, the *reafons for*, and *againft* it
muft

muſt be attended to.    It is a queſtion that cannot be decided by *ſimple feeling*.

Leſs ſtill can it be determined by conſciouſneſs that the ſubject of thought is *naturally immortal*, ſo that a man will continue to think and act after he has ceaſed to breathe and move.    We are certainly conſcious of the ſame things with reſpect to ourſelves, but what one man may think to be very clear on this ſubject, another may think to be very doubtful, or exceedingly improbable; drawing different *concluſions* from the ſame premiſes.

Again, that man is an *agent*, meaning by it that he has a power of *beginning motion*, independently of any mechanical laws to which the author of his nature has ſubjected him, is a thing that is ſo far from being evident from conſciouſneſs, that, if we attend properly to what we really do feel, we ſhall, as I conceive, be ſatisfied that we have no ſuch power.    What we really do feel, or may be ſenſible of, if we attend to our feelings, is that we never come

come to any refolution, form any deliberate purpofe, or determine upon any thing whatever, without fome *motive*, arifing from the ftate of our minds, and the ideas prefent to them; and therefore we ought to conclude, that we have no power of refolving, or determining upon any thing, without fome motive. Confequently, in the proper philofophical language, motives ought to be denominated the *caufes* of all our *determinations*, and therefore of all our *actions*.

All that men generally mean by a *confcioufnefs of freedom*, is a confcioufnefs of their having a power to do what they previoufly will, or pleafe. This is allowed, and that it is a thing of which we are properly confcious. But to will without a motive, or contrary to the influence of all motives prefented to the mind, is a thing of which no man *can* be confcious. Nay every juft obfervation concerning ourfelves, or others, appears to me very clearly to lead to the oppofite conclufion, viz. that our *wills*, as well as our *judgments*, are determined by the *appearances of things* prefented sented to us; and therefore that the determinations of both are equally guided by certain invariable *laws*; and confequently that every determination of the will or judgment is juft what the being who made us fubject to thofe laws, and who always had, and ftill has, the abfolute difpofal of us, muft have intended that they fhould be. If, however, this conclufion be denied, it muft be controverted by *argument*, and the queftion muft not be decided by *confcioufnefs*, or any pretended *feeling* of the contrary.

V. *An addition to section II. on the argument for the Doctrine of Neceffity from the confideration of* CAUSE AND EFFECT.

I do not think it at all neceffary to add any thing to what I have advanced in my former treatife in illuftration of the argument from the nature of *caufe and effect.* But becaufe this is the great and moft conclufive argument for the doctrine that I contend for, proving the contrary doctrine of *philofophical liberty*, to be abfolutely *impoffible*;

*poſſible*; and I find that ſeveral perſons, of excellent judgment in other reſpects, ſeem not to feel the force of it, I ſhall attempt a farther illuſtration of it, in order to remove, as far as I am able, the only remaining objection that I can imagine may be made to it; though I muſt aſk pardon of my other readers for writing what will appear to them ſo very obvious, and ſuperfluous.

It is univerſally acknowledged, that there can be no effect without an adequate cauſe. This is even the foundation on which the only proper argument for the being of a God reſts. And the neceſſarian aſſerts that if, in any given ſtate of mind, with reſpect both to *diſpoſition* and *motives*, two different determinations, or volitions, be poſſible, it can be ſo on no other principle, than that one of them ſhall come under the deſcription of *an effect without a cauſe*; juſt as if the beam of a balance might incline either way, though loaded with equal weights.

T       It

It is acknowledged that the mechanifm of the balance is of one kind, and that of the mind of another, and therefore it may be convenient to denominate them by different words; as, for inftance, that of the balance may be termed a *phyfical,* and that of the mind a *moral* mechanifm. But ftill, if there be a *real mechanifm* in both cafes, fo that there can be only one refult from the fame previous circumftances, there will a *real neceffity,* enforcing an abfolute certainty in the event. For it muft be underftood that all that is ever meant by *neceffity in a caufe,* is that which produces *certainty in the effect.*

If, however the term *neceffity* give offence, I, for my part, have no objection to the difufe of it, provided we can exprefs, in any other manner, that property in caufes, or the previous circumftances of things, that leads to abfolute certainty in the effects that refult from them; fo that, without a miracle, or an over-ruling of the ftated laws of nature, *i. e.* without the intervention of a higher caufe, no determination

termination of the will could have been
otherwife than it has been.

To evade the force of this argument
from the nature of caufe and effect, it is
faid that, though, in a given ftate of mind,
two different determinations may take place,
neither of them can be faid to be without
a fufficient caufe; for that, in this cafe,
the caufe is *the mind itfelf,* which makes
the determination in a manner independent
of all influence of motives.

But to this I anfwer, that the mind itfelf, independent of the influence of every
thing that comes under the defcription of
*motive,* bearing an equal relation to both
the determinations, cannot poffibly be confidered as a caufe with refpect to either of
them, in preference to the other. Becaufe,
exclufive of what may properly be called
motive, there is no imaginable difference
in the circumftances immediately preceding the determinations. Every thing tending to produce the leaft degree of inclination to one of the determinations more

than

than to the other muſt make a difference in the *ſtate of mind* with reſpéct to them, which, by the ſtating of the caſe, is expreſsly excluded. And I will venture to ſay, that no perſon, let his bias in favour of a ſyſtem be ever ſo great, will chuſe to ſay in ſupport of it, that the mind can poſſibly take one of two determinations, without having for it ſomething that may, at leaſt, be called an *inclination* for it, in preference to the other; and that inclination, or whatever elſe it be called, muſt have had a cauſe producing it, in ſome previous affection of the mind.

In ſhort, let ever ſo much ingenuity be ſhown in ſtating this caſe, it is impoſſible not to come at length to this concluſion, that, in no caſe whatever, can the mind be determined to action, *i. e.* to a volition, without ſomething that may as well be called a *motive* as be expreſſed in any other manner. For the reaſon, or proper cauſe, of every determination muſt neceſſarily be ſomething either in the ſtate of the mind itſelf, or in the ideas preſent to it, immediately

diately before the determination; and thefe ideas, as they imprefs the mind, may, ftrictly fpeaking, be comprehended in what we mean by the *ftate of mind*, including whatever there is in it that can lead to any determination whatever. Or, on the other hand, the ftate of mind may be included in the meaning of the term *motive*, comprehending in the fignification of it whatever it be that can *move*, or *incline* the mind to any particular determination.

It appears to me that it may juft as well be faid that, in the cafe of the balance above-mentioned, the beam may be the caufe why, though equal weights be fufpended at the different ends of it, it may neverthelefs incline one way or the other. For, exclufive of what neceffarily comes under the defcription either of *motive*, or *ftate of mind*, the mind itfelf can no more be the caufe of its own determination, than the beam of a balance can be the caufe of its own inclination.

In the cafe of the beam it is immediately perceived that, bearing an equal relation to

T 3                          both

both the weights, it cannot possibly favour
one of them more than the other; and it
is simply on account of its bearing an equal
relation to them both that it cannot do this.
Now, let the structure of the mind be ever
so different from that of the balance, it
necessarily agrees with it in this, that, ex-
clusive of motives, in the sense explained
above (viz. including both the state of
mind and the particular ideas present to it)
it bears as equal a relation to any determination, as the beam of a balance bears to
any particular inclination; so that as, on
account of this circumstance, the balance
cannot of itself incline one way or the
other, so neither, on account of the same
circumstance, can the mind of itself incline,
or determine, one way or the other.

In fact, an advocate for the doctrine of
philosophical liberty has the choice of no
more than *two suppositions*, and neither of
them can, in the least degree, answer his
purpose. For he must either assert that, in
a given state of mind, the determination
will certainly be *a* and not *b*; or it may be

either

either *a* or *b*. If he adopts the former, he may juft as well fay at once, that the determination will *neceffarily* be *a*, and that without a miracle it cannot be *b*. For any other language that he can poffibly ufe can do no more than ferve to hide what might otherwife be obnoxious in the fentiment, and will leave it ftill true, that, without a miracle, or the intervention of fome foreign caufe, no volition, or action of any man could have been otherwife than it *has been, is,* or *is to be,* which is all that a neceffarian contends for. And if, on the contrary, he chufes to affert that, in the fame ftate of mind, the determinations *a* and *b* are equally poffible, one of them muft be *an effect without a caufe,* a fuppofition which overturns all reafoning concerning appearances in nature, and efpecially the foundation of the only proper argument for the being of a God. For if any thing whatever, even a thought in the mind of man, could arife without an adequate caufe, any thing elfe, the mind itfelf, or the whole univerfe, might likewife exift without a caufe.

T 4                     I

I own it is irkfome to me to enter into
fo minute a difcuffion of an objection that
appears to me to be fo little deferving of an
anfwer; and it is only with a view to obviate every thing that *has been*, or that I can
forefee *may be* urged, with the leaft plaufi-
bility, that I have confidered it at all. If
this do not give fatisfaction, I own I do
not think it will be in my power to give
fatisfaction with refpect to this argument,
or any other. There does not appear to
me to be, in the whole compafs of reafoning, that I am acquainted with, a more
conclufive argument, than that for the
doctrine of neceffity from the confideration
of the nature of *caufe and effect*.

VI. *Of the nature of* REMORSE OF CON-
SCIENCE, *and of* PRAYING FOR THE
PARDON OF SIN, *on the Doctrine of Ne-
ceffity*.

Several perfons firmly perfuaded of the
truth of the doctrine of neceffity, yet fay,
that it is not poffible to *act upon it*; and to
put what they think a peculiarly difficult
cafe

cafe, they afk how it is poffible for a neceffarian to pray for the pardon of fin.

I anfwer, in general, that Dr. Hartley
appears to me to have advanced what is
quite fufficient to obviate any difficulty that
can arife from this view of the fubject,
when he admonifhes us carefully to diftinguifh between the *popular* and *philofophical
language*, as correfponding to two very different views of human actions; according
to one of which the bulk of mankind refer their actions to themfelves only, without
having any diftinct idea of the divine agency
being, directly or indirectly, the caufe of
them: whereas, according to the other, we
look beyond all fecond caufes, and confider
the agency of the firft and proper caufe, exclufive of every thing fubordinate to it.

Thefe very different views of things
muft be attended with very different *feelings*; and, when feparated from each other,
they will, in feveral refpects, lead to a different *conduct*, as well as require a different
*language*. Now, fuch are the influences
                                                    to

to which all mankind, without diftinction, are expofed, that they neceffarily refer actions (I mean refer them ultimately) firft of all to themfelves and others; and it is a long time before they begin to confider themfelves and others as *inftruments* in the hand of a fuperior agent. Confequently, the affociations which refer actions to themfelves get fo confirmed, that they are never intirely obliterated; and therefore the common language, and the common feelings of mankind, will be adapted to the firft, the limited and imperfect, or rather erroneous view of things,

The Divine Being could not be unapprized of this circumftance, or unattentive to it; and he has wifely adapted the fyftem of religion that he has prefcribed to us, the modes of our religious worfhip, and every thing belonging to it, to this imperfect view of things. It is a fyftem calculated for *the bulk of mankind*, and of philofophers as partaking of the feelings of the bulk of mankind; and therefore, would, we may fuppofe, have been different if the bulk

bulk of mankind had been fpeculatively
and practically philofophers; in fome fuch
manner as the modes of worfhip varied in
the Jewifh and chriftian churches.

But it is of prime confequence in this
bufinefs, that, in whatever *fenfe*, or *degree*,
any particular fentiment or feeling is felt as
improper by a neceffarian, in the fame
fenfe and degree his principles will make
that fentiment or feeling to be of no ufe
to him. Thus, to apply this to the cafe
in hand: if the fentiments of felf-applaufe
on the one hand, and of felf-reproach on
the other be, in any fenfe or degree, impoffible to be felt by a neceffarian, in the
fame fenfe or degree (while he feels and
acts like a neceffarian) he will have no occafion for thofe fentiments; his mind being
poffeffed by a fentiment of a much higher
nature, that will intirely fuperfede them,
and anfwer their end in a much more effectual manner. And whenever his ftrength
of mind fails him, whenever he ceafes to
look to the firft caufe only, and refts in
fecond caufes, he will then neceffarily feel
the

the fentiments of felf-applaufe and felf-reproach, which were originally fuggefted by
that imperfect view of things into which
he is relapfed.

Every man's feelings will neceffarily be
uniform. To be a neceffarian in *fpeculation*,
and not in *practice*, is impoffible, except
in that fenfe in which it is poffible for a
man to be a chriftian in fpeculation and a
libertine in practice. In one fenfe a fpeculative chriftian, or neceffarian, may feel
and act in a manner inconfiftent with his
principles; but if his faith be what Dr.
Hartley calls a *practical* one, either in the
doctrine of neceffity, or the principles of
chriftianity, that is, if he really *feels* the
principles, and if his affections and conduct
be really directed by them, fo that they
have their natural influence on his mind,
it will be impoffible for him to be a bad
man. What I mean, therefore, is that *a
truly practical neceffarian* will ftand in no
need of the fentiments either of felf-applaufe, or felf-reproach. He will be under
the influence of a much fuperior principle,
*loving*

*loving God and his fellow creatures* (which is
the fum and object of all religion, and
leading to every thing excellent in conduct)
from motives altogether independent of any
confideration relating to himfelf. On this
I need not enlarge in this place, if what I
have advanced on the *moral influence of the
doctrine of neceffity*, in my Appendix, be
confidered.

It is acknowledged that a neceffarian,
who, as fuch, believes that, ftrictly fpeaking, *nothing goes wrong*, but that every
thing is under the beft direction poffible,
himfelf, and his conduct, as part of an
immenfe and *perfect whole*, included, cannot
accufe himfelf of having done wrong, in
the ultimate fenfe of the words. He has,
therefore, in this ftrict fenfe, nothing to
do with repentance, confeffion, or pardon,
which are all adapted to a different, imperfect, and fallacious view of things. But
then, if he be really capable of fteadily
viewing the great fyftem, and his own conduct as a part of it, in this true light, his
fupreme regard to God, as the great, wife,
and

and benevolent author of all things, his intimate communion with him, and de-votednefs to him, will neceffarily be fuch, that he can have no will but God's. In the fublime, but accurate language of the apoftle John, he will *dwell in love*, he will *dwell in God*, and *God in him*; fo that, *not committing any fin*, he will have nothing to repent of. He will be *perfect, as his heavenly father is perfect.*

But as no man is capable of this degree of perfection in the prefent ftate, becaufe the influences to which we are all expofed will prevent this conftant referring of every thing to its primary caufe, the fpeculative neceffarian, will, in a general way, refer actions to himfelf and others; and confe-quently he will neceffarily, let him ufe what efforts he will, feel the fentiments of fhame, remorfe, and repentance, which arife mechanically from his referring actions to himfelf. And, oppreffed with a fenfe of *guilt*, he will have recourfe to that *mercy* of which he will ftand in need. Thefe things muft neceffarily accompany one another,

another, and there is no reafon to be fo-
licitous about their feparation.

It is, alas! only in occafional feafons of
retirement from the world, in the happy
hours of devout contemplation, that, I
believe, the moft perfect of our race can
fully indulge the enlarged views, and lay
himfelf open to the genuine feelings, of
the neceffarian principles; that is, that he
can *fee every thing in God*, *i. e.* in its relation to him. Habitually, and conftantly,
to realize thefe views, would be always to
*live in the houfe of God*, and within the *gate
of heaven*, feeing the plain finger of God
in all events, and as if the angels of God
were conftantly defcending to earth, and
afcending to heaven before our eyes. Such
enlarged and exalted fentiments are fometimes apparent in the facred writers, and
alfo in the hiftories of chriftian and protef-
tant martyrs; but the beft of men, in the
general courfe of their lives, fall far fhort
of this ftandard of perfection.

We

We are too apt to lofe fight of God, and of his univerfal uncontrolled agency; and then, falling from a fituation in which we were equally ftrangers to *vice*, and *folicitude*, from a ftate truly *paradifaical*, in which we were incapable of *knowing* or *feeling* any evil, as fuch, converfing daily with God, enjoying his prefence, and contemplating his works, as all infinitely good and perfect, we look no higher than ourfelves, or beings on a level with ourfelves; and of courfe find ourfelves involved in a thoufand perplexities, follies and vices; and we now want, and ought to fly to, the proper remedy in our cafe, viz. felf abafement, contrition, and fupplication.

Moreover, well knowing what we generally are, how imperfect our *views*, and confequently how imperfect our *conduct*, it is our wifdom, and our intereft, freely to indulge thefe feelings, till they have produced their proper effect; till the fenfe of guilt has been difcharged by the feelings of contrition, and a humble truft in the Divine mercy. Thus, *gradually* attaining

to

to purer intentions, and a more upright
conduct, we fhall find lefs obftruction in
enlarging our views to comprehend the
true plan of providence; when, having lefs
to reflect upon ourfelves for, the fentiment
of reproach fhall eafily and naturally vanifh;
and we fhall then fully conceive, and rejoice in, the belief that in all things we
*are,* and *have been, fellow workers together
with God;* and that *he works all his works
in us, by us, and for us.*

The improvement of our natures, and
confequently the advancement of our happinefs, by enlarging the comprehenfion of
our minds, chiefly by means of a more diftinct view of the hand of God in all things,
and all events, is, in its own nature, a gradual thing, and our attempts to accelerate
this natural progrefs may poffibly be attended with fome inconvenience; though,
I own, I apprehend but little danger from
this quarter.

What we have moft to dread, is the almoft irrecoverable debafement of our minds
by *looking off from God, living without him,*

U

without

without a due regard to his prefence, and providence, and *idolizing ourfelves and the world*; confidering other things as *proper agents* and *caufes*; whereas, ftrictly fpeaking, there is but *one caufe*, but *one fole agent* in univerfal nature. Thus (but I feel myfelf in danger of going beyond the bounds of the queftion I am now difcuffing) all vice is reducible to *idolatry*; and we can only be completely virtuous and happy in the worfhip of the one only living and true God; the idea ufually annexed to the word *worfhip* but faintly fhadowing out what the intelligent reader will perceive I *now* mean by it.

In all this it muft be remembered that I am addreffing myfelf to *profeffed neceffarians*; and I muft inform them, that if they cannot accompany me in this fpeculation, or find much difficulty in doing it, they are no more than *nominal* neceffarians, and have no more feeling of the real *energy of their principles* than the merely nominal chriftian has of thofe of chriftianity. It requires much reflection, meditation, and
ftrength

ftrength of mind, to convert *fpeculative* principles into *practical* ones; and till any principle be properly *felt*, it is not eafy to judge of its real *tendency* and *power*. It is common with unbelievers to declaim on the fubjea of the mifchief that chriftianity has done in the world, as it is with the opponents of the doctrine of neceffity to dwell upon the dangerous tendency of it; but the real neceffarian, and true chriftian, know, and *feel*, that their principles tend to make them better men in all refpeas; and that it can only be fomething that is very improperly called either *chriftianity*, or *the doctrine of neceffity*, that can tend to make them worfe.

I think, however, that a mere fpeculatift may be fatisfied, that the feeling of re-morfe, and the practice of fupplication for pardon, have ftill lefs foundation on the doctrine of philofophical liberty, than on that of neceffity, as I prefume has been de-monftrated in my treatife. Indeed, what can a man have to blame himfelf for, when he acted *without motive*, and from *no fixed*

*principle,*

*principle*, good or bad; and what occafion
has he for pardon who never meant to give
offence; and, as I have fhewn at large,
unlefs the mental determinations take place
without regard to motive, there is no
evidence whatever of the mind being free
from its neceffary influence. But it feems
to be taken for granted, that whatever a
neceffarian cannot feel, or do, his opponent
can; whereas, in fact, the doctrine of repentance, as defined by the advocates of
liberty themfelves, has much lefs place on
their principles than on ours.

The whole doctrine of *fecond caufes* being
*primary* ones, is certainly a miftake, though
a miftake that all imperfect beings *muft* be
fubject to. Whatever, therefore, is built
upon that miftake can have no place in a
truly philofophical fyftem. But I will farther
advance, that while men continue in this
miftake, and, confequently, while their reflections on their own conduct, as well as
on that of others, fhall be modified by it,
they will derive confiderable advantage even
from an imperfect view of the true philofophical

sophical doctrine, viz. that of neceffity;
whereas a man, in the fame circumftances,
muft receive fome injury from the oppofite
fentiment of philofophical liberty; fo much
may it be depended upon, that a knowledge
of this truth can do no harm, but muft do
fome good.

Remorfe for paft mifconduct implies a
deep fenfe of depravity of heart, or a wrong
bias of mind, by which temptations to fin
will have much more influence with us
than they ought to have. This is the fentiment that will be fully felt by what I
now call the *imperfect neceffarian* (a character which, as I obferved before, applies
to all mankind). As a neceffarian he confiders his bad conduct as neceffarily arifing
from his bad difpofition. It is *bad fruit*
growing from a *bad tree*. And, as he
knows that, unlefs the tree be made good,
it will be impoffible to make the fruit
good; fo he is fenfible that unlefs he can,
by the ufe of proper difcipline, bring his
mind into a better ftate, he can never
depend upon himfelf for acting more pro-

perly

perly on future occasions. He, therefore, from that principle by which we universally seek our own happiness and improvement, labours to correct his vicious disposition; and, expecting no miraculous assistance, he applies to the proper remedies indicated by the consideration of his case.

At the same time, his regard to God, as the author of all good, and who has appointed *meditation* and *prayer* as a means of attaining it, will make him constantly look up to him for his favour and blessing. And if, as he becomes more philosophical, his devotions have in them less of *supplication*, and rather take the form of *praise, thanksgiving*, and a joyful firm *confidence* in the divine care and providence, respecting equally the things of time and eternity, it will not contribute the less to his moral improvement and happiness. But the best of men will not, in fact, get beyond that state of mind, in which direct and fervent *prayer*, properly so called, will be as *unavoidable* as it will be *useful* to them. What I now say will not be well under-
stood

ſtood by all perſons, but I ſpeak to thoſe who have ſome experience in matters of religion, and who are accuſtomed to re-flection on their natural feelings.

Let us now conſider what the doctrine of philoſophical liberty can do for a man in the circumſtances abovementioned. He, like the neceſſarian, finds himſelf involved in guilt, and he alſo begins to ſpeculate concerning the cauſes of it; but, overlook-ing the ſecret mechaniſm of his mind, he aſcribes the whole to the mere *obſtinacy of his will*, which, *of itſelf*, and not neceſſarily influenced by any motives, has turned a deaf ear to every thing that better principles could ſuggeſt. But, in what manner can ſuch mens *uncontrollable will* be rectified? As far as we have recourſe to *motives*, and *principles*, we depend upon the doctrine of *mechaniſm*; and without that we have no-thing to do but ſit with folded hands, wait-ing the arbitrary deciſions of this ſame *ſo-vereign will*.

If he ſpeculates farther, and conſiders how little his real temper and character are

U 4 con-

concerned in fuch unaccountable motions of his felf-determined will, I fhould think him in fome danger of making himfelf very eafy about his vices. And this would be the cafe, if men were not neceffarily influenced by founder principles than they always diftinctly perceive. Now, it appears to me, that if a man's fpeculations take this turn, it would have been much better for him never to have fpeculated at all, and that they only tend to bewilder, and hurt him.

Again, fuppofing a man to have attained to fome degree of a virtuous character and conduct, his farther progrefs will be accelerated by the belief of the doctrine of neceffity, and retarded by that of philofophical liberty.

The conviction that God is the author of all *good* will always much more readily take firm hold of the mind than the idea of his being, likewife, the author of all *evil*, though all evil ultimately terminates in good; becaufe it requires more ftrength of mind to fee and believe this. A long time, therefore,

therefore, before we fufpect that our evil difpofitions come from God, as well as our good ones, and that all things that exift, ultimately confidered, equally promote the divine purpofes, we fhall afcribe all evil to ourfelves, and all good to God; and this perfuafion will be fo riveted, in a long courfe of time, that after we are convinced that God is really and truly the author of *all things*, without diftinction, we fhall afcribe evil to him only in an unfteady and confufed manner, while the perfuafion that he is the fole author of all good will have received a great acceffion of ftrength, from our new philofophical principles coinciding with, and confirming, our former general notions.

Now no fentiment whatever is fo favour-able to every thing amiable, good, and great, in the heart of man, as a fpirit of *deep humility*, grounded on difclaiming all our excellencies, and referring them to their proper fource, that feeling which Dr. Hart-ley very expreffively calls *felf-annihilation*, joined with that which naturally and ne-ceffarily accompanies it, *joy and confidence in God,*

*God,* as *working all our good works in us and for us.* This is the difpofition that infpires all the writers of the books of fcripture, and is obfervable in all truly ferious and devout perfons to this day, whether their fpeculative opinions be favourable to it or not. Nay, it has given fuch a turn to the *eftablifhed language of devotion* in all countries, and all ages, that the contrary fentiment, or that of claiming the merit of our good works to ourfelves, would have the appearance of fomething abfolutely impious, and blafphemous. Now it muft be acknowledged that this difpofition of mind, viz. that of afcribing every thing that is good in us to God, is greatly favoured and promoted by the belief of the doctrine of neceffity. It may even operate this way, to the greateft advantage, at the fame time that, through our imperfect comprehenfion of things, we continue to afcribe evil to ourfelves, and are affected with the deepeft fentiments of remorfe and contrition.

On the contrary, as far as the doctrine of philofophical liberty operates, it tends

to

to check humility, and rather flatters the pride of man, by leading him to confider himfelf as being, independently of his maker, the primary author of his own good difpofitions and good works. This opinon, which, without being able to perceive *why*, every truly pious perfon dreads, and cannot bring himfelf exprefly to avow, is apprehended to be juft, * according to the doctrine of philofophical liberty, which reprefents man as endued with the faculty of free will, acting independently of any control from without himfelf, even that of the Divine Being; and that juft fo far as any fuperior being, directly· or indirectly, influences

---

* I fay *apprehended* to be juft, which is all that my argument requires, though, ftrictly fpeaking, as I have fhewn at large, the claim of *merit*, or *demerit*, is equally ill-founded on the doctrine of philofophical liberty. The fentiments of merit and demerit are certainly *natural*, and found in all mankind; but they have not, therefore, any connection with the doctrine of philofophical liberty. On the contrary, I maintain that the *common opinion* is the doctrine of neceffity, though not come to its proper extent. No man, for inftance, has any idea but that *the will is always determined by fome motive*, which is the great hinge on which the doctrine of neceffity turns; nor has any man in common life any idea of *virtue*, but as fomething belonging to *character* and *fixed principle*, conftantly *influencing the will*.

Influences his will, he can pretend to no
such thing as real virtue, or goodness;
though the virtue that answers to this de-
scription is certainly not that which animated the prophets of the Old Testament,
or our Saviour and the apostles in the New,
but is mere heathen *Stoicism.*

When this temper is much indulged, it
is even possible, contradictory as it seems,
to ascribe all moral good to a man's self,
and all moral evil to the instigation of the
Devil, or some other wicked spirit that has
access to our minds: whereas, without the
intervention of this doctrine of the *indepen-
dency of the will,* and especially with a little
aid from the doctrine of *mechanism,* we
should rather, as was shewn before, though
inconsistently still, ascribe all good to God,
and all evil to ourseves.

Constantly to ascribe *all* to God is an at-
tainment too great for humanity. To be
able to do it *at intervals,* in the seasons of
retirement and meditation, but so as con-
siderably to influence our general feelings,
and conduct in life, is a happy and glorious
advantage,

advantage. Sweet, indeed, are the moments in which thefe great and juft views of the fyftem to which we belong can be fully indulged. But if we cannot habitually afcribe *all* to God, but a part only, let it be (and fo indeed it naturally will be) that which is *good*, and if we muft afcribe any thing to ourfelves, let it be that which is *evil*.

Thus have I given a frank and ingenuous account of my own ideas and impreffions on this fubject. How far they will give fatisfaction to others I cannot tell.

ADDITIONAL

# ADDITIONAL OBSERVATIONS

BY

## Dr. PRICE,

ON A

REVIEW of the whole CONTROVERSY,

AND OF

Dr. PRIESTLEY's LETTERS and ILLUSTRATIONS,

As printed in the preceding Parts of this Work.

# L E T T E R

## TO

## DR. PRIESTLEY.

NEWINGTON-GREEN, Sept. 19, 1778.

DEAR SIR,

THE defire you have expreffed that
I would give you my fentiments of
the Controverfy between us, *on a view of
the whole of it as now printed*, has induced
me once more to apply my thoughts to it.
I have done this with care and attention;
but am not fure that any thing which you
will judge of great importance has occurred to me. It might, therefore, have been
right to refolve to fay no more; and indeed,
I am fo much afraid of perplexing by a
multiplicity of words, and of giving difguft by too many repetitions, that this
would have been my refolution, had I not

X                    thought,

thought, that the *Additional Observations*
which you will receive with this letter,
contain fome *new* matter; and place feveral
of the arguments already infifted on, in a
light that may render them to fome perfons more intelligible and ftriking. I
have now faid the beft I can; and I leave
our readers to judge between us, hoping
that whether they decide in your favour or
mine, they will be candid, and believe
that we are both of us governed alike by
a fincere love of truth and virtue. I feel
deeply that I am in conftant danger of
being led into error by partial views, and
of miftaking the fuggeftions of prejudice
for the decifions of reafon; and this, while
it difpofes me to be candid to others, makes
me ardently wifh that others would be
candid to me.

I am, in a particular manner, fenfible of
my own blindnefs with refpect to the nature of matter and fpirit, and the faculties
of the human mind. As far as I have gone
in this difpute I am pretty well fatisfied;
but I cannot go much further. You have
afked

afked me fome queftions (and many more may be afked me) which I am incapable of anfwering.

I cannot help taking this opportunity of repeating to you, that I diflike more than I can eafily exprefs, the malevolence ex-preffed by moft of the writers againft you. I have myfelf, as you well know, been long an object of abufe for a publication which I reckon one of the beft actions of my life, and which events have fully juftified. The confcioufnefs of not deferving abufe has made me perfectly callous to it; and I doubt not but the fame caufe will render you fo.

It is certain that, in the end, the intereft of truth will be promoted by a free and open difcuffion of fpeculative points. What-ever will not bear this muft be fuperftition and impofture. Inftead, therefore, of being inclined to cenfure thofe who, with honeft views, contribute to bring about fuch a dif-cuffion, we ought to thank and honour them, however miftaken we may think them, and however facred the points of

X 2 difcuffion

difcuffion may be reckoned. I wifh I
could fee more of this difpofition among
the defenders of religion. I am particularly
forry to find that even Mr. Whitehead does
not perfectly poffefs this temper. Had
he avoided all uncandid infinuations, and
treated you conftantly with the fame juft
refpect that he does in general, his book
in my opinion would have done him much
honour.

Dr. Horfley is, I fancy, the only perfon who, in oppofing your opinions, has
difcovered a juft liberality. This is worthy of an able Philofopher; and you have,
therefore, very properly diftinguifhed him
from your other antagonifts, by addreffing
him, in your letter to him, with particular refpect. His method of arguing agrees
very much with mine. There is, likewife, an agreement between fome of Mr.
Whitehead's arguments and thofe I have
ufed. But this agreement has been acci-
dental; for our correfpondence was begun
and finifhed long before I knew any thing
of

of either Dr. Horſley's or Mr. Whitehead's publications.

Wiſhing you every possible bleſſing,

I am,

With the moſt affectionate reſpect,

Yours,

RICHARD PRICE.

X 3 ADDITIONAL

# ADDITIONAL OBSERVATIONS

## BY

## Dr. PRICE.

### Sect. I. *Of the Human Soul.*

DR. PRIESTLEY acknowledges that the foul is a *fingle* being or fub-ftance. But at the fame time he fpeaks of the *parts* of a foul; of its being a *fyftem*; and, in p. 119, of the *materials* of which Chrift confifted before his birth. Has he yet proved this to be confiftent? (\*) His

X 4      doctrine

(\*) Page 86, " I believe I am a *being* or *fubftance*; " alfo, that I am a *fingle* being; and that my limbs and " fenfes are not *myfelf*."—P. 279, " Man, who is *one* be- " ing, is compofed of *one kind* of fubftance, made of the " duft of the earth."—To the fame purpofe Dr. Prieftley fays in p. 284, " that the mind, the fubject of thought, is

" one

doctrine is, that, as a number of corporeal
fubftances put together in a particular manner, become, when put into motion, that
*meafurer of time* which we call a *clock* or
a *watch*; fo a number of corporeal fubftances put together in a particular manner
in the brain become *of courfe*, when circulation begins, that thinking being we call
a *man*. And his doctrine further is, that
both are alike machines, the operations of
the one in meafuring time, and of the
other in thinking, perceiving, willing, &c.
being equally brought about by mechanical
laws, and the neceffary refult of particular
motions and vibrations. This, I imagine,
is as concife and juft an account as can be
given of his fyftem. See particularly, the
fecond

" *one* thinking perfon, or one being;" but afterwards (in
the next page) he fays, " that the fubject of thought, is the
" body, efpecially the brain; and that its powers inhere in
" *one kind* of fubftance."—Thefe paffages compared lead me
to fufpect, that when he fays, in the firft of them, that he
is *one* being or fubftance; his meaning is, that he is *many*
fubftances of *one kind*. I can think of no other method of
making thefe paffages confiftent. For I fuppofe he cannot
poffibly mean, that the mind, though one *being*, is many *fubftances*. This would imply, that a fubftance, numerically
different from all others, is not a being

fecond fect. of his Additional Illuftrations.
P. 256, &c.

Not to fay any thing at prefent of the
latter part of this fyftem, I would beg
leave again to remind him that, according to
his own conceffion, it is *one* fubftance that
*thinks*; that, on the contrary, it is a number of fubftances that *meafure time*; and
that, confequently, thefe cafes cannot be
parallel.

I know not how to believe Dr. Prieftley will adhere to the only obfervation
he has made in anfwer to this objection;
I mean, the obfervation (in p. 100) " that
" a *number* of unthinking fubftances may
" make *one* thinking fubftance." Would
he not wonder were I to maintain that a
number of *un*learned men may make one
learned *fociety*? But what would he think
were I to maintain, that a number of *un*-
learned men may make one learned *man*?

But difmiffing this difficulty. According to Dr. Prieftley, certain particles in
the

the brain are the *fubject* of thought and confcioufnefs ; and their arrangement, order and motion are *actual* thought and intelligence. Thefe particles, it fhould be obferved, muft be fome *definite* number: For were they an *indefinite* number, the *man*, or the *fubject of thought*, could not continue always the fame. Any particles added would *increafe* the man, in proportion to the number added. Any taken away would *leffen* him, in proportion to the number taken away. Or, in other words, the man would become fo far *different* ; and fo many particles might be added or taken away, as would make him, in any given proportion, a *different* or *another* being.

All this is manifeftly abfurd and contradictory. The foul we know, amidft all changes and through every period of its exiftence, maintains a precife and unvaryed famenefs and individuality. If, therefore, the foul is the brain, it muft be, not that grofs and ever-varying mafs of fubftances commonly fo called, but fome certain *ftaminal* parts of it which have exifted from
the

the firſt creation of matter, (*) but were put
together at conception ſo as to form
thought; and which continue without in-
creaſe or diminution during the life of
man; are only diſarranged at death; will
be put together again at the reſurrection ſo
as to form an improved conſciouſneſs; and
will remain preciſely the ſame, except
in their order and vibrations, through all
eternity.

Can Dr. Prieſtley ſatisfy himſelf with
ſuch a notion of the human ſoul? Is it
poſſible this ſhould be a right account of
that ſimple and indiviſible eſſence, which
every

(*) When Dr. Prieſtley ſays (in p. 191) " *The ſentient*
" *principle* in man, I ſuppoſe to be the brain itſelf," he
means probably not the whole brain, but (agreeably to what
is above obſerved) ſome *ſtaminal* parts of it. He ſometimes,
indeed, calls the *ſentient principle* " a *reſult* from the orga-
" nization of the brain;" but his meaning muſt be, not
that the ſoul itſelf is nothing but a *reſult* from the form and
arrangement of the materials of the brain, for he has acknowledged it (p. 86) to be a *ſubſtance*; but that its conſciouſneſs and reaſon are ſuch a reſult. See the reaſoning
from p. 113, to p. 116. It is not, he ſays (p. 76) *myſelf*,
but my *power of thought*, that is the reſult of figure, motion, &c.

every man calls *himfelf*; and of thofe faculties by which we inveftigate truth, and are capable of growing for ever in knowledge and blifs ? Does he, in particular, feel no difficulty in conceiving that a number of particles, difpofed in *one* order and moved in *one* way, fhould be nothing but torpid matter; but, difpofed in *another* order and moved in *another* way, fhould become perception, judgment and reafon ? (†)

I

(†) Dr. Prieftley (in p. 258) intimates, that the power of thinking may as well be the refult of the organization of the brain, as the attraction of iron be the refult of the ftructure of a magnet. But the attraction of iron by a magnet is the action, not of the magnet itfelf, but of *another* caufe. It would be ftrange indeed if a mafs of matter could be fo put together as to become capable of moving a body at a diftance without touching it. The truth, in this cafe, feems to be, that there are caufes or powers in nature operating according to ftated laws which unite themfelves to fubftances formed as iron and a magnet are, and drive them towards one another. Perhaps, therefore, this fact might be mentioned as moft fimilar to the union of a foul to the brain in confequence of its organization. Some affert that magnetifm is caufed by the emiffion of *effluvia*, or the intervention of a fubtle fluid; and if this is true, it is only an inftance of the communication of motion by impulfe from matter to matter.

Dr. Prieftley has obferved, (fee p. 124) that a compound may have properties which the component parts have

I muſt leave every one to make his own
reflections on what Dr. Prieſtley ſays from
page 268, to 270.  I think it ſcarcely
worthy of him.  Why might I not ſay
that ſpirit is not *extended?* He ſays ſo, if I
underſtand him, of matter; and yet maintains (p. 248, 249,) that it exiſts in place,
poſſeſſes a ſphere of action, and is moveable,

have not.  This is true only of ſuch properties as denote
merely an *order* or *relation* of parts.  For inſtance.  Though
no *one* of the component parts of a circle is *circular,* the
whole compound is ſo.  What can be plainer?—A number of
things may be ranged into the order of a circle, but one thing
cannot.  Does this warrant us to conclude, that, though no
one of the particles in a maſs of matter is conſcious, yet all
taken together may be ſo?  As well might we conclude that
though no one of the particles moves, yet the whole compound may move.  Such, however, is the concluſion we are
directed to draw by Dr. Prieſtley; and alſo by Mr. Collins in
his diſpute with Dr. Clarke.

I will beg leave to remark further in this place, that Dr.
Prieſtley's account of the ſoul has no ſuch tendency as hede-
ſcribes in the Introduction, from p. 16, to p. 19.  If he is
right, we ſhall, in the *future ſtate,* have no ſeparate ſouls.
But this will give us no reaſon for *then* concluding, that we
had not pre-exiſted in a conſcious and active ſtate.  Juſt as
little reaſon, in my opinion, does it give us *now* for drawing
ſuch a concluſion.  But this obſervation may be carried much
farther.—Our exiſtence after death, according to Dr. Prieſtley, will be only the exiſtence of the materials, ſeparated and
diſperſed,

able. But I have repeatedly acknowledged my ignorance on this fubject. I
pretend to know no more than that, whatever my foul is in refpect of *locality*, it is
*indivifible*, the idea of a *part* of a felf, or of
a *felf* divided into *two felves* being contradictory. Of this I think myfelf fure.
See p. 62, 96, and 106.

## Sect. II. *Of the Nature of Matter.*

Dr. Prieftley denies that matter is impenetrable, becaufe there is no experiment
in which we are fure that we have found
it to be fo. I have given a reply to
this in p. 51. What I would obferve
here

difperfed, of which we now confift. But this is an exiftence
which belonged to us equally before we were born. Our
*pre-exiftence*, therefore, is no lefs certain than our *poft-exift-
ence.*—It is true, Dr. Prieftley teaches, that fome time after
death our fcattered parts are to be brought into union, and
to be made again confcious. But will he fay fuch an union
might not have alfo taken place fometime or other before we
were born?—Little then certainly is the fupport which *Socinianifm* receives from *Materialifm.*—See what is faid to this
purpofe in p. 125. The remembrance of pre-exiftence cannot be neceffary; or, if it is, Chrift might have poffeffed
it.

here is, that, according to Dr. Prieftley's doctrine, there is alfo no experiment in which we have found that any one thing *caufes* or *produces* another; the only proper caufe in nature, as he afferts, being that power of the Deity which is not an object of our fenfes. When a body in motion gives motion to another, all that we ob-ferve (and all that is true, if Dr. Prieftley is right) is a *conjunction*, not a *connection* of two events; or one motion *going before* another, not one motion *producing* a-nother; the body moved having really received its motion not from the *ap-parent*, but from an *invifible* caufe. This, if I underftand Dr. Prieftley, is the truth in every inftance. Even the determi-nations of the will are the actions of the Deity; and motives are properly no more than certain perceptions that con-ftantly *precede* them. Since then experi-ments do not furnifh us with the ideas of *caufation* and *productive power*, how came we by thefe ideas? And how does Dr. Prieftley know they have any exiftence?

How

How, in particular, does he avoid the fcep-
tical fyftem which Mr. Hume has advanced
in his Philofophical Effays, and which he
founds entirely on this obfervation ? I have
fhewn how I avoid it in my *Review* of the
Difficulties in Morals. P. 29, 30, &c.

In p. 245, Dr. Prieftley repeats a former
obfervation ; namely, that " it is no lefs
" proper to afk what remains of matter after
" folidity and extenfion are taken away,
" than to afk what remains of it after at-
" traction and repulfion are taken away."
I have anfwered, that folidity and extenfion
are *inherent* properties ; but that attraction
and repulfion, fignifying only *fomething that
is done to matter*, convey no idea of it;
Were he to afk me what *fpirit* is, and
I was to give him no other anfwer, than
that it is *fomething* that is moved, he would
probably be much diffatisfied.

In the firft fect. of the *Additional Illuftrations*, Dr. Prieftley has given a new account of matter, according to which it is
only

only a number of centers of attraction and repulfion; or, more properly, of centers (not divifible, p. 249) to which divine agency is directed.  I would here afk, wherein do fuch centers differ from mathematical points? Is not a mathematical point merely the *end* or *termination* of a line, as a line is the termination of a furface, and a furface of a folid? Can any one of thefe be conceived to fubfift feparately from the reft? What conception can be formed of a point or center which has no figure, nor is the termination of a line, but is capable of moving and being moved? Is the whole univerfe nothing but a collection of fuch points acted upon by divine power? Are thefe points *fubftances*? If not, can they be *matter*? Or can they be the *fouls* of men? Does not divine agency require an object different from itfelf to act upon? What then can Dr. Prieftley mean when he intimates that there is nothing in nature but God's agency?

At the beginning of this controverfy Dr. Prieftley denyed *folidity* to matter, but allowed it extenfion. He feems now inclined to deny it *both*, and to be for reducing it (and confequently all fentient beings) to nothing but points to which God's agency (in attracting and repelling I know not what) is directed.

In p. 250, &c. he obferves, that fince the conftituent parts of matter do not touch one another, it can *do* nothing, (every thing being really done by divine power) and confequently is of no ufe, and, if created, muft have been created in vain. (‡) The obvious inference from hence is, that there is no fuch thing as matter. And, accordingly, influenced by this reafon, he fays, that " it is nothing but the divine agen- " cy." The whole creation, then, being matter

(‡) Dr. Prieftley intimates (p. 252) that he fhould prefer to his own hypothefis, an hypothefis, could he find it, which fhould make provifion for the ufe of created matter without refolving it into the divine agency. I think I can inform him of fuch an hypothefis. *Solid* matter (that is, the matter hitherto believed in by all mankind) is capable of moving other matter by contact and impulfe. It can, therefore, *do* fomewhat, and be of ufe. Why then fhould he not admit it?

matter according to Dr. Prieftley's doctrine, the whole creation is nothing but the divine agency; and confequently it muft be nothing at all.   For what idea can be formed of the *creation* of the divine agency; or of an agency that acts upon itfelf?

But, perhaps, it is not proper to urge thefe objections, becaufe Dr. Prieftley in the very paffage (p. 253) which contains this account of matter, afferts that " though " every thing *is* the divine power, and all " action is his action," yet every thing is not the *Deity himfelf*; and becaufe, like-wife, he has very candidly (p. 252) ex-preffed a doubt whether he has not loft himfelf on this fubject.   It will, however, be proper to put him in mind (and I wifh I could prefs it on his attention) that he ought not to lay fo much ftrefs as he does on the doctrine of materialifm, till he is better able to inform us what matter is.

SECT. III.   *Of the Doctrine of Necessity.*

Dr. Prieſtley, in his letter to Dr. Horſe-ley, endeavours to prove, that there is no difference between him and the Neceſſa-rians.   His reaſon for this aſſertion is, that Dr. Horſeley acknowledges a *certain*, and (in one ſenſe) a *neceſſary* influence of mo-tives on the will.   Now, it ſhould be re-collected, that the whole controverſy has been reduced to this ſhort queſtion.  " Has " man a power of *agency*, or *ſelf-determi-* " *nation?*  Dr. Prieſtley has denyed this. He has maintained that ſuch a power is an impoſſibility ; (p. 129 and 241) that we are miſtaken when we refer our actions to our-ſelves ; that our volitions are *perfectly me-chanical things* ; that motives influence *ex-actly as weights operate on a ſcale* ; (§) and that

(§) See Treatiſe on Neceſſity, Dedication p. 12 ; and Il-luſtrations, p. 30, 36, &c.   See likewiſe this Volume, p. 306.

that there is only *one agent* in nature. (||)
It is only as far as he means to maintain
fuch affertions that he oppofes the doctrine
of liberty as explained by Dr, Clarke and
others,

The influence of motives has never been
denied. The point in difpute is, the *nature* of that influence; and with refpect to
this, I have long ago obferved, (fee Review
of Morals, p. 351, 2d edit.) that *no* influence
of motives, which is fhort of making them
*phyfical efficients* or *agents*, can clafh with
liberty. May I then afk him whether he
ftill adheres to the affertions I have mentioned? If not, our controverfy is at an
end. But if he does, then he and I (and
Y 3 probably

---

(||) Dr. Prieftley has fometimes called man an *agent*. In
p, 86, he fays, that " man is a *voluntary agent*, though
" not poffeffed of a felf-moving power." There feems to
me an evident contradiction in thefe words. For an agent
that does not put himfelf in motion, is an agent that is always acted upon, or an agent that never acts. In p. 178, he
even allows that man may be called a *free* agent; but his
meaning plainly is, that man is moved only by *internal*
fprings; and this no more makes him truly free than it makes
a watch free.

342 ADDITIONAL OBSERVATIONS

probably alſo he and Dr. Horſeley) ſtill
differ. He ſhould not ſay here, as he does
p. 221, &c. that, provided the influence of
motives is allowed, it makes no difference
whether they influence in one way or in a-
nother; or whether we reckon them *phyſical cauſes* or *moral reaſons*. This has been
already anſwered in p. 138, &c. That
kind of influence which I allow to motives implies, that man is a *ſelf-moving* being. The other implies, that he is nothing but a machine. The one implies,
that motives are only certain reaſons on the
view of which, or certain rules and perceptions according to which, the mind *determines itſelf*. The other implies, that
they are *ſubſtances* which operate mechanically on the mind, and leave it no dominion
over its determination. In ſhort, the one
is conſiſtent with *moral agency*. The other,
deſtroying *all* agency, deſtroys of courſe all
*moral* agency. Is it poſſible there ſhould be
any greater difference? See p. 143.

I have in the courſe of this controverſy
ſometimes appealed to common ſenſe. Dr.
Prieſtley

Prieſtley will, I hope, allow me again to
do this on the preſent occaſion. Let us
ſuppoſe a common man, who knows nothing of thoſe refinements on plain points
which have diſgraced human learning, and
turned ſo much of it into rank folly; let
us, I ſay, ſuppoſe ſuch a man aſked whether,
in all his actions, he does not determine
himſelf? He would certainly anſwer, without heſitation, in the affirmative. Suppoſe
him told, that he was miſtaken; and that
very wiſe men had diſcovered, that he no
more determined himſelf in any of his
actions than a ſtone determines itſelf when
thrown from a hand. Would he not wonder greatly?

Suppoſe him farther aſked, whether there
is not a *certainty* that he would accept a
good eſtate if it was offered to him fairly?
He would anſwer in the affirmative. Suppoſe it objected to him, that there could
be no ſuch *certainty*, becauſe, being a ſelf-
determiner, he would be free not to accept. Would there be a poſſibility of
puzzleing him by ſuch an objection?

Y 4

Dr.

344 ADDITIONAL OBSERVATIONS

Dr. Prieſtley ſays, " that a determi-
" nation of the mind in caſes in which
" a regard to different motives is equal, is
" an impoſſibility." (*) The following
caſe will prove the contrary, and may,
I hope, help a little to illuſtrate this ſubjeƈt.

Suppoſe an *agreeable* propoſal made to
a perſon which ſhocks his moral feelings, but which he muſt immediately re-
ſolve, either to accept, or not. If he
*accepts*, he gratifies his paſſions. If he
does not accept, he follows his ſenſe of
duty. This brings him into circumſtances
in

(*) There are numberleſs caſes in which there is a reaſon
for aƈting *in general*, but no reaſon for any preference of one
way of aƈting to another. It appears to me very wrong to
ſay, that in theſe caſes aƈtion becomes impoſſible. I may
have a reaſon for going to a certain place, but it may be indifferent in which of two ways I go. Do I, in theſe circumſtances, loſe the power of going at all? Suppoſing the uni-
verſe finite, it was indifferent where in infinite ſpace it was
placed. But was it, on this account, impoſſible to place it
any .where? Suppoſing it to conſiſt of only two ſyſtems, there
could have been no reaſon for placing one of them on *one* ſide
of the other, rather than at an equal diſtance on the *oppoſite*
ſide.

in which he muſt act upon a motive; and alſo upon *one* or *other* of two given motives. Nothing is more conceivable, than that theſe motives may be equal in their influence. In that caſe, would determination be (as Dr. Prieſtley ſays) impoſſible ? To ſay this, would be to ſay, that a perſon, when tempted, may neither comply with the temptation, nor reject it. Without all doubt, his power in ſuch a ſituation is to do *either*, not to do *neither*.

In general, I would obſerve here that, in circumſtances of temptation, there are always two motives which influence the will;

ſide. But would it, on this account, have been impoſſible to create them ?

In forming this earth, there could have been no reaſon againſt the tranſpoſition of any *ſimilar* particles on its ſurface. Was it, therefore, impoſſible (as Mr. Leibnitz contended) that there ſhould have been any ſuch particles ? See the beginning of Dr. Clarke's, 3d, 4th, and 5th Replies in the Collection of papers which paſſed between Dr. Clarke and Mr. Leibnitz.

When I ſay there are caſes in which there can be no reaſon for any *preference* of one way of acting to another, I mean by *preference,*

346 ADDITIONAL OBSERVATIONS

will; and that the effence of moral merit
and demerit confifts in the free refolution
of the will (or in its *felf-determination*) to act
on one of them rather than on the other.
Dr. Prieftley, therefore, fhould not have
faid, that the doctrine of liberty implies
that a man in acting wickedly or virtuoufly,
acts without a motive. I cannot conceive
of a more groundlefs affertion.

But let us again confider the cafe I have
put.

Paffion and intereft draw us one way.
Confcience and duty order us another. In
thefe circumftances, we may determine as
we

*preference*, the judgment of the mind concerning the beft
way of acting. I mention this, becaufe there is a *preference*
included in the idea of volition; and which fignifies merely
the determination to act in one way, and not in another.
Preference in the former fenfe, is a perception of the underftanding, and, therefore, *paffive*. In the latter fenfe, it is
the exertion of the felf-moving faculty, and therefore *active*.
Thefe, though *commonly* united, are *often* feparated; and it is
chiefly inattention to the difference between them, or the not
diftinguifhing (as Dr. Clarke obferves) between the *perceptive* and *active* faculties, that has produced the difputes about
liberty and neceffity.

we *pleaſe*. Thus far Dr. Prieſtley and I
would ſpeak the ſame language, but we
ſhould mean differently. By determining
*as we pleaſe*, he would mean our being
ſubject, without the power of reſiſtance, to
the mechanical influence of that motive
which happens to be ſtrongeſt. But I
ſhould mean, our poſſeſſing a power to
make *either* of the motives the ſtrongeſt ;
that is, to make either of them the motive that *ſhall* prevail, and on which we
*ſhall pleaſe* to determine. Unhappily for
us, we are continually finding ourſelves in
theſe circumſtances. Let every one examine himſelf, and conſider which of theſe
accounts is right. Has a man, urged by
contrary inclinations, (by paſſion on one
hand and a regard to virtue on the other)
no controuling power over his inclinations
to make one of them, preferably to the
other, the inclination that he will follow.
Or is he then exactly in the condition of a
body impelled by contrary forces, which
muſt be carried along by the ſtrongeſt ? If
this is the truth, there is no *action* of the
man, when a temptation overcomes him ;

nor

nor confequently, if there is any meaning in words, can there be any guilt, or ill-defert. I intreat Dr. Prieftley to remember, that this is the doctrine, and the *only* doctrine of neceffity that I mean to oppofe.

Dr. Prieftley fays, at the conclufion of his letter to Dr. Horfeley, that there is no medium between acknowledging the will to be fubject to the influence of motives, and afferting an effect without a caufe; and that confequently, " there is no choice but " of the doctrine of neceffity, or abfolute " nonfenfe." I am very fenfible, that it is nonfenfe to deny the influence of motives, or to maintain that there are no fixt principles and ends by which the will is guided; but, at the fame time, I muft fay, that this nonfenfe is fcarcely equal to that of confounding *moral* with *phyfical* caufes, making motives fubftances, afferting that we are not the caufes of *our own* determinations, and denying that we are free merely becaufe we have reafons for acting.

In

. In Difquifitions, vol. II. p. 77, he fays,
" that in all cafes where the principle of
" freedom from the influence of motives
" takes place, it is *exactly an equal chance*
" whether rewards and punifhments will
" determine or not, the felf-determining
" power being not at all of the nature of
" any mechanical influence, that may be
" counteracted by influence equally me-
" chanical." Does not this imply, that
if the will is not fubject to a *mechanical* influence, it can be fubject to *no* influence; and that, if there is not a *certainty* of its following a particular motive
in any cafe, there cannot be even a *probability* ?

Dr. Prieftley lays great ftrefs on the obfervation " that felf-determination implies
" an effect without a caufe." I have taken
fome notice of this objection in p. 136.
It evidently implies that it is impoffible a
" felf-moving power fhould be *itfelf* a
" caufe," and " that there muft be an
" endlefs progreffion of caufes and effects
" without

" without any firſt cauſe." (†)   I cannot,
therefore, but wonder at this objection;
and I am diſpoſed the more to wonder at it,
becauſe Dr. Prieſtley, though he urges it
ſo repeatedly, has at the ſame time been ſo
candid as to acknowledge that the Deity is
a ſelf-determining being.   But in anſwer
to this he obſerves, that the Deity is alſo
*ſelf-exiſtent*, and that it does not follow,
becauſe he is ſo, that his creatures may be
ſo.   See what is ſaid to this in p. 102,
and 157.   Let the impartial reader judge
here.

(†) Mr. Leibnitz maintained, that in all caſes of ſuch abſolute indifference as thoſe referred to in the note, p. 345, there
could be *no* determination of the will; becauſe it would be a
determination for which no reaſon could be given.   Undoubtedly ſays Dr. Clarke in anſwering him, (ſee 3d Reply,
ſect. 2d.)  " Nothing is without a ſufficient reaſon why it *is*
" rather than *not*, and why it is *thus* rather than otherwiſe.
" But in things in their own nature indifferent, mere will,
" without any thing external to influence it, is alone a ſuf-
" ficient reaſon; as in the inſtance of God's creating or
" placing a particle of matter in one place rather than in
" another, when all places are originally alike."

" A balance (5th Reply, 1ſt ſect.) for want of having in
" itſelf a principle of action, cannot move at all when the
" weights are equal.   But a free agent, when there appears
" two or more perfectly alike reaſonable ways of acting, has
" ſtill

here. Would not one think that if God is
a felf-moving being, felf-motion cannot
imply an effect without a caufe? What
analogy is there between faying " God is
" felf-exiftent, (that is, *underived*;) there-
" fore, his creatures may be fo," and faying, " God is an *agent*; therefore, his
" creatures may be *agents*." Did God's
felf-exiftence mean, that he is the caufe of
his own exiftence, or that he produced
himfelf, it would be no lefs abfurd to apply

" ftill within itfelf, by virtue of its felf-moving principle a
" power of acting, and it may have very ftrong reafons for
" not forbearing to act at all, when yet there may be no
" poffible reafon to determine any particular way of doing the
" thing to be better than another. To affirm, therefore,
" that fuppofing two different ways of placing certain par-
" ticles of matter were equally good and reafonable, God
" could neither wifely nor poffibly place them in either of
" thofe ways for want of a fufficient weight to determine him
" which way he fhould chufe, is making God not an active,
" but a paffive being, which is not to be a God or governor
" at all." But the objection that liberty implies an effect
without a caufe, has been more particularly anfwered by
Dr. Clarke, in his Remarks on Mr. Collins's *Philofophical
Enquiry concerning Liberty*. It is indeed with fome pain I reflect, that much of this difcuffion is little more than a re-
petition of Mr. Collins's objections on one fide, and Dr.
Clarke's Replies on the other.

ply this attribute to him than to any other
being; but moſt certainly it has a very different meaning. It means, that being underived, he exiſts (as Dr. Clarke ſpeaks)
" by an abſolute neceſſity in the nature of
" the thing;" or (as I ſhould chuſe to
ſpeak) that the *account* of his exiſtence is
the ſame with the account of the exiſtence
of ſpace and duration, of the equality of
the three angles of a triangle to two right
angles, or of any abſtract truth.

Dr. Prieſtley's arguments, in the 6th
ſection of his *Additional Illuſtrations*, (p.
296) plainly lead to, and imply the following concluſions. That, ſince no action or
event could poſſibly have been different
from what it *has been, is,* or *will* be; and
ſince there is but one cauſe, one will, one
ſole agent in nature; our proneneſs to look
off from this one cauſe, and to refer our
actions to ourſelves, is an inſtance of
vicious weakneſs in us, leading us to
*idolize ourſelves and others;* (p. 305, 306)
and that had we *fortitude* enough to con-
quer

quer this weakneſs, and *wiſdom* enough to lay aſide all fallacious views, or were perfect philoſophers and *neceſſarians,* we ſhould aſcribe to God our evil diſpoſitions no leſs than our good ones, (p. 313) and conſider ourſelves as fellow-workers with him in our vices as well as our virtues; and, therefore, ſhould never reproach our-ſelves for having done wrong, never think we have need of repentance, and never pray to God for pardon and mercy, or addreſs him in any of the forms of confeſſion and ſupplication.

If this is a juſt account, and Dr. *Prieſt-ley* really means to acknowledge theſe to be proper inferences from his doctrine; I muſt ſay that he cannot be ſufficiently ad-mired for his fairneſs in the purſuit of truth. He believes he has found it in the doctrine (the great and glorious doctrine, as he calls it) of neceſſity; and he follows it into all its conſequences, however fright-ful, without attempting to evade or palli-ate them. For my own part, I feel here my own weakneſs. I ſhudder at theſe

Z con-

confequences, and cannot help flying from them. I think it impoffible a doctrine fhould be true, from which fuch an apólogy for vice can be fairly deduced; and which oppofes fo ftrongly the conftitution of nature and our neceffary feelings, as not to be capable of being applied to practice, or even of being *believed* without particular fortitude. I am fully perfuaded, however, that fo found is Dr. Prieftley's conftitution of mind, and fo excellent his heart, that he can drink this deadly potion, and find it falutary. But fuch powers and fuch integrity are given to few.

I muft farther confefs to Dr. Prieftley, that I am in fome degree rendered averfe to his doctrine, by my pride. I had been ufed to think of my foul as fo real and fubftantial, as to be the very principle that gives reality to the fenfible qualities of bodies, and confequently to the whole drefs of the external world; as an effence of heavenly origin, incorporeal, un-

com-

compounded, felf-determining, immortal and indeftructible except by the power that created it; poffeffed of faculties which (however the exercife of them may be fubject to interruptions) make it an image of the Deity, and render it capable of acting by the fame rule with him, of participating of his happinefs, and of *living* for ever, and *improving* for ever under his eye and care. But if Dr. Prieftley is right, my foul is literally the offspring of the earth; a compofition of duft; incapable of all agency; a piece of machinery moved by mechanical fprings, and chained to the foot of fate; all whofe powers of thought, imagination, reflection, volition, and reafon, are no more than a *refult* from the arrangement and play of a fet of atoms, all unthinking and fenfelefs.——What can be more humiliating than this account?——How low does it bring the dignity of man?——I cannot help feeling myfelf degraded by it unfpeakably?——Were it to be received univerfally, it would, I am afraid, operate like a dead

weight

weight on the creation, breaking every
afpiring effort, and producing univerfal
abjectnefs. The natural effect of believing (§) that nothing is left to depend on
ourfelves, and that we can *do* nothing,
muft be concluding that we have *nothing to
do*; and refolving to leave every thing to
that being who (as Dr. Prieftley fays,
p. 303, 314) works *every thing in us, by us,
and for us.*

That SELF-ANNIHILATION, therefore,
which he mentions as one of the happy
effects

(§) Dr. Prieftley frequently fpeaks of the dependence of
events on *ourfelves*; but I cannot fee the confiftency of fuch
language with his principles. Events, it is true, depend
on our *determinations*; but our *determinations*, no more depending on *ourfelves*, than the motion of a wheel depends
on *itfelf* when pufhed by another wheel, no events derived
from fuch determinations, can be properly faid to depend on
*ourfelves*. Dr. Prieftley's fyftem allows no one to be the
maker of his own *volitions*. How then can it, as he fays it
does, (Difquifitions, vol. 2d. p. 99) allow every one to be
the maker of his own *fortune?* In truth, the ufe which he
finds unavoidable of fuch expreffions as thefe and many others
implying liberty, is a ftrong argument againft him. For it
proves, that fo incompatible is his fyftem with the whole
frame of *language* as well as *nature*, that it is impoffible even
to *fpeak* agreeably to it.

effects of his doctrine, is no great re-
commendation of it.  On the contrary.
That SELF-REVERENCE, which is taught
by the opposite doctrine, inspiring high
designs and a disdain of mean passions and
vicious pursuits, is, in my opinion, a far
more useful and noble principle.

Dr. Priestley takes notice of the serenity
and joy which the doctrine of necessity
inspires by causing us to view every thing
in a favourable light, by shewing us the
hand of God in all occurrences, and by
teaching us that there is nothing wrong in
nature.  But these sources of joy are by
no means confined to the doctrine of necessity.  The contrary doctrine supplies
them on better ground, and with more
safety and purity.  There are no ideas of
free agency which do not allow of such a
dependence of events on the circumstances
of beings and the views presented to their
minds as leaves room for *any* direction of
events by superior wisdom.  And though I
believe that vice is an *absolute evil* productive of infinite losses to the individuals

Z 3                                who

who practice it; and that the permiſſion of
it is to be accounted for chiefly by the impoſſibility of producing the greateſt good
without giving *active powers*, (‡) and allowing ſcope for exerciſing them. Though, I
ſay, I believe this; yet I believe at the
ſame time, that no event comes to paſs
which it would have been proper to exclude; and that, relatively to the divine
plan and adminiſtration, *all is right*. Under this perſuaſion, I can view the courſe
of events with ſatisfaction; and commit
joyfully the diſpoſal of my lot to that
ſelf-exiſtent reaſon which governs all things;
not doubting but that the order of nature
is in every inſtance wiſe and good beyond
the poſſibility of amendment; that infinitely more takes place in the creation than
my

(‡) See p. 174. The beſt that I can ſay on this ſubject,
may be found in my Diſſertation on Providence, ſect. 4th.

*Active* powers, *ſelf-determining* powers, and *voluntary* powers, are, according to my ideas, the ſame. But according
to Dr. Prieſtley, a *voluntary* power (or the power of willing)
is a *paſſive* power. That is, it ſignifies only (like *moveable-
neſs* in bodies) the capacity of being acted upon, or the neceſſity of yielding to an impreſſed force.

my warmeſt benevolence can wiſh for ; and
that, if I practice righteouſnefs, I ſhall
(according to the promiſe of God by Jeſus
Chriſt) riſe again after ſinking in death ;
and, together with all the upright of all
nations and opinions, be at laſt happy for
ever.

## POSTSCRIPT.

At the end of the ſecond paragraph of the note beginning
in p, 332, add the following words.——In ſhort ; conſciouſ-
nefs, not being a mere order of parts, or an external denomination, but a quality *inhering* in its ſubject, it ſeems the
plaineſt contradiction to ſay, that it can inhere in the *whole*,
without inhering in the *parts*.

Alſo: After the words, *effect without a cauſe*, in p. 351,
add—And that, if our acting with a view to ends and reaſons proves we do not begin motion in ourſelves, it muſt much
more prove the ſame of the Deity ; and, conſequently, that
there can be no *beginner* of motion, or *firſt cauſe ?*

In the laſt line of p. 330, add a reference to Dr. Prieſtley's
words in p. 83.—" No particle of the man being loſt, *as
" many as were eſſential to him,* will be collected and revivified
" at the reſurrection."

To the reference in p. 341, add p. 85, 145, and 241.

For the words quoted in p. 344, ſee p. 160.

# R E P L I E S

T O

Dr. P R I C E's

ADDITIONAL OBSERVATIONS,

W I T H

A LETTER addreſſed to him

B Y

Dr. P R I E S T L E Y.

# REPLIES

### TO

### Dr. PRICE's

## ADDITIONAL OBSERVATIONS.

### Sect. I. *Of the Human Soul,*

P. 327, 328. I CANNOT fee any real in-consiftency between calling *the mind*, or *the man*, *one being*, or even *one substance*, and yet faying that this one sub-ftance, or being, confifts of many parts, each of which, feparately confidered, may likewife be called a diftinct being, or fub-ftance; * having again and again obferved, what

* That all the *unity* or *fimplicity* of which we can be con-fcious with refpect to ourfelves, is that each perfon is *one*, and not *two* confcious intelligent beings; but that confcioufnefs can give us no information whatever concerning the *fubftance* to which thefe powers belong, as whether it be *fimple* or *com-plex*, *divifible* or *indivifible*, &c. has, I prefume, been fuf-ficiently fhown in the *Additional Illuftrations* under the article of *Confcioufnefs*, efpecially p. 284; and yet this feems to be the thing on which Dr. Price lays the greateft ftrefs.

what I believe will be univerfally admitted, that by the words *being, fubftance,* or *thing,* we only mean the unknown, and perhaps imaginary *fupport of properties,* fome of which may belong to the parts, though others may be peculiar to the whole.

Dr. Price, indeed, fays, (p. 333) that "this "is only true of fuch properties as denote "merely *an order or relation of parts,* as "that no one of the component parts of "a circle is circular, though the whole "compound is fo." But I fee no reafon for this limitation. It is well known that chemical compounds have powers and properties which we could not have deduced from thofe of their component parts, or their new arrangement; as the power of *aqua regia* to diffolve gold, when neither the fpirit of nitre, nor the fpirit of falt, of which it is compofed, will do it. It may be faid, that a being of competent knowledge of the nature of gold, and that of the two acids, feparately confidered, might foretel that gold would be foluble in a mixture

ture of them. But I alfo may fay that a
being of fufficient knowledge might have
foretold, that when God had made a human body, even of the *duft of the earth*, or
*mere matter*, the refult of the animation of
this organized fyftem would have been his
*feeling* and *thinking*, as well as his *breathing*
and *walking*; or, in the words of Mofes,
that when the mere *breath of life* was imparted, nothing more remained to be done
to make a complete man. There was no
*feparate foul* to be communicated.

Even Dr. Price's own example, viz. that
of *a clock*, or *watch*, will fuit my purpofe
tolerably well. A watch, as he properly
fays, is a *time-meafuring machine*, as man is
a *thinking machine*. But what connection
is there between the ideas of the brafs,
or fteel, &c. of which the watch is made,
or even of the feparate parts of which
it confifts, as the wheels, pinions, fpring,
or chain, &c. and the idea of *meafuring
time*? Has not the whole, in this cafe, a
property, or power, which does not, in the
leaft degree, belong to any of the parts.
Nay

Nay the whole machine, when properly put together, has no more power of measuring time than any of its separate parts, or the rough materials of which they are made, till the spring is wound up; but then its power and office of measuring time takes place *of course.* Why then should it be thought not to be within the compass of almighty power to form an organized body of mere matter, so that by simply giving it *life* the faculty of *thinking* shall be the necessary result.

It is of no consequence, however, whether we be able to find any proper illustration of this case, or not, since, as I have shewn both in the *Disquisitions,* and in the course of this correspondence, that it is as evident from fact, that the brain thinks, as that the magnet attracts iron. See p. 92, &c.

Dr. Price says, p. 330, " The soul, we " know, amidst all changes, and through " every period of its existence, maintains " a precise and unvaried sameness and in-
" divi-

" dividuality; and, p. 334, he calls it a
" *fimple and indivifible effence.*" Now I
am fatisfied that a man continues fufficiently the fame being through the whole
courfe of his life, and will be fo after
the refurrection; but I do not think that
our imperfect knowledge of the nature
of organized bodies will authorize the
very ftrong language above quoted. I
confider *man* as preferving his individuality, or identity, in the fame manner as a
*tree* does; and if we confider the lofs of
memory, the change of difpofition and
character, and the impairing of all the human faculties in old age, there will be no
more argument from *fact* of his having
continued the fame from his birth to his
death, than of an old, fhattered, and dif-
membered tree being the fame that it was
when firft planted, and during its vigour.

Dr. Price thinks, (fee p. 333) that what
I have faid on the fubject of *extended fpirit*
is *fcarcely worthy of me.* Now I cannot
help thinking that what I have advanced
on that fubject is both perfectly *juft,* and
likewife

likewife *proper.* In my *Difquifitions* I had
confidered principally the moft refined and
proper kind of fpiritualifm, if I may ufe
that expreffion, as appearing to me to be
the only confiftent fyftem; according to
which, fpirit has neither extenfion nor relation to fpace. This Dr. Price acknowledges (p. 25) to be *an abfurdity and contradiction that deferves no regard.* He fays,
" That matter is incapable of confciouf-
" nefs and thought, not becaufe it is *ex-
" tended,* but becaufe it is *folid,*" p. 57,
" That Dr. Clarke," whofe ideas he
feems to adopt, " was not for excluding
" expanfion from the idea of immaterial
" fubftances," p. 55, and together with
myfelf, and Dr. Clarke, he always fuppofes the divine effence to have proper extenfion, filling all fpace.

It certainly then behoved me to examine
this opinion of *extended human fouls,* and I
think I have fhewn it to be no lefs abfurd
than the former. Dr. Price himfelf does
not chufe to defend it, but rather feems
willing to adopt a new and middle opinion;
fup-

fuppofing the foul to have *locality,* without *extenfion.* But this idea I have noticed, and I think fufficiently, in my *Difquifitions,* referring to Dr. Watts, who confutes it more at large. I prefume, therefore, that *in no form whatever* can the hypothefis of a foul feparate from the body be maintained,

As to what I advanced in my random fpeculation concerning the *centers of attraction and repulfion,* of which I fuppofed that what we call *matter* might poffibly confift, it was a mere voluntary excurfion into the regions of hypothefis. I do not at prefent fee any thing amifs in it, but I am confident that had I been more in earneft, and determined to abide by that hypothefis, there is nothing in it of which Dr. Price could materially avail himfelf in fupport of his doctrine of a feparate foul.

The fact of the exiftence of *compound ideas* in the mind, ftill appears to me decifive againft the opinion of fuch an abfolute *fimplicity* and *indivifibility* of its effence,

A a

as

as Dr. Price contends for. See *Difquifitions*, p. 37, and this Correfpondence,
p. 51, 95.

Since I wrote the *Additional Illuftrations*,
I have had the curiofity to make fome inquiry into the actual ftate of opinions concerning the foul, and I fee reafon to think
that, excepting Dr. Clarke, and perhaps a
few others, the opinion that has moft generally prevailed of late, is that which I
have principally combated in my *Difquifitions*, viz. that it is a thing that has *no
extenfion, or relation to fpace*. Dr. Watts
afferts this opinion, and defends it very
largely and ably againft Mr. Locke, and it is
the opinion that is advanced and proved, in
all the forms of geometrical demonftration,
by Dr. Doddridge in his *Lectures*. Thefe Lectures are now read in all our diffenting acade-
mies, where perhaps one half of the metaphyficians in the nation are formed; for the
clergy of the eftablifhed church do not, in
general, feem to have fo much of this turn.
Now I do not remember that any of my fellow ftudents ever entertained a different idea,
and

and many of us were very much intent upon metaphyfical inquiries. We held very different opinions on other points, and were pretty eager difputants. I have alfo inquired of many other perfons, and hitherto they have all told me, that their idea of fpirit was that which I have confidered. It will be obferved, however, that all the arguments on which I lay the moft ftrefs refpect the notion of a feparate foul *in general*, without regard to any particular hypothefis about the nature of it.

Mr. Baxter, feems to deny extenfion to fpirits, but not *locality*, fo that probably neither Dr. Price nor myfelf have been exactly right in our idea of his opinion. It rather feems to have been that middle opinion to which Dr. Price now reverts. As to the doctrine of immaterial fpirits having real *fize*, and confequently *form*, or *fhape*, though I ought perhaps to have refpected it more, as the opinion of fo great a man as Dr. Clarke, I really confidered it as an hypothefis univerfally abandoned, till Dr. Price's feeming avowal of it made me

give

give it the degree of attention which I have done, and which produced what I have advanced on the fubject in the *Additional Illuftrations* to which he refers.

In his *Additional Obfervations*, (p. 332) Dr. Price fuggefts an idea of a foul, and of its union to the body, that I own I fhould not have expected from his general fyftem; comparing it (as " that to which," he fays, " it is perhaps the moft fimilar") to " thofe caufes and powers in nature, " operating according to ftated laws, which " unite themfelves to fubftances formed " as iron and a magnet are."

Is then the foul nothing more than a *power* or *property*, neceffarily refulting from the organization of the brain? This has been *my* idea, and not *his*. I therefore fup- pofe him to mean that whenever a body is completely organized, there is a general law in nature, by which, without any particu- lar interpofition of the Deity, a foul im- mediately attaches itfelf to it. But this fuppofes what Dr. Price will excufe me for calling

calling *a magazine of fouls* ready formed for that purpofe, or the pre-exiftence of all human fouls; which, indeed, was the original doctrine of a foul, and what I think is neceffary to make the fyftem complete, and confiftent.

Dr. Price fays, *note* p. 334, " It is cer-" tainly very little fupport that Socinianifm " receives from Materialifm," becaufe the refurrection being nothing more than the re-arrangement of the fame particles that compofed a man before death, the fame may have compofed a man in a ftate prior to his birth.

I anfwer, that this is certainly *poſſible*, and had I the fame *authority* for believing it, that I have to believe the refurrection, I fhould have admitted it; but having no *evidence* at all for it, it is a notion fo far within the region of mere poffibility, that it is in the higheft degree incredible. For none of the natural arguments for the future exiftence of men, which are derived from the confideration of the moral government of God, can be alledged in favour of

A a 3                                      a

a pre-exiftence of which we have no knowledge.

It is likewife poffible that, in a former re-
mote period, not only myfelf, but every
thing with which I am connected, and the
whole fyftem of things, may have been juft
as it now is, that Dr. Price then wrote remarks on my *Difquifitions*, &c. and that I
replied to him in a joint publication, the
very fame as the prefent; that there have
been infinite revolutions of the fame fyftem, and that there is an infinity of them
ftill to come, which was the opinion of
fome of the antient philofophers.

But it is not the mere *poffibility* of fuch a
fcheme that can entitle it to any degree of
credit. If, therefore, the failure in the
fupport that the doctrine of Materialifm
gives to the doctrine of Socinianifm be only
in proportion to the probability of the pre-
exiftence of man on the fyftem of materialifm (which excludes the notion of a feparate foul) I think it may be put down as
an *evanefcent quantity*, or nothing at all. In
other

other words, the doctrine of materialifm is a fufficient, and effectual fupport of the So-cinian hypothefis.

So much confidence have I in the tend-ency that the doctrine of materialifm has to favour Socinianifm, that I doubt not but the moment it is believed that men in ge-neral have no fouls feparate from their bo-dies, it will be immediately and univerfally concluded, that Chrift had none. And as to the mere poffibility of his, and our *bo-dies*, having had a pre-exiftence in an or-ganized and thinking ftate, I fhould enter-tain no fort of apprehenfion about it. Or, if this odd opinion fhould gain ground, it will have nothing in it contrary to the *pro-per principle* of Socinianifm, which is, that Chrift was a *mere man*, having no natural pre-eminence over other men ; but that all his extraordinary powers were derived from divine communications after his birth, and chiefly, if not wholly, after his baptifm, and the defcent of the holy fpirit upon him. This kind of pre-exiftence can alfo afford no fupport to any other of thofe cor-

ruption$

ruptions of chriftianity which have been derived from the notion of a feparate foul, fuch as the doctrine of *purgatory*, and the *worſhip of the dead*, &c. &c.

## SECT. II.  *Of the Nature of Matter.*

On what I advanced concerning the con-ftitution of matter, as confifting of mere *centers of attraction and repulfion,* which I gave as a mere *random fpeculation,* and not at all neceffary to my purpofe, but accord-ing to which it may be faid that every thing is the *divine agency,* Dr. Price afks, (p. 337) " Does not the divine agency re-" quire a different object from itſelf to " act upon," and, (p. 338) " What idea " can we form of the creation of the di-" vine agency, or of an agency that acts " upon itſelf." I anfwer, that the diffi-culty confifts in *terms* only; for that on the random hypothefis to which this argument refers, the *exertion of the divine agency* may properly enough be called *creation,* and the *modification* of that exertion, the *action* of the Deity upon that creation.

Dr.

Dr. Price fays, in the note p. 338, that *folid matter can do fomewhat*, and *be of ufe*. But is it not rather unfortunate for this hypothefis, and thofe who maintain it, that they are not able to fay *what it does*, there being no *effect*, or *appearance* in nature, to the explication of which it is neceffary; all that is *actually done*, where matter is concerned, being probably effected by fomething to which folidity cannot be afcribed. There is certainly no conceivable connection between *folidity* and *attraction*. Solidity, indeed, might account for *refiftance at the point of contact*, but I challenge any philofopher to ftand forth, and produce but one clear inftance of actual *unqueftionable contact*, where matter is concerned. In moft cafes of repulfion it is undeniable that proper contact is not at all concerned, and therefore there can be no reafon *from analogy* to lead us to conclude that it is, in *any cafe*, the proper caufe of repulfion; but, on the contrary, that the true caufe, as *certainly in moft cafes*, fo *probably in all*, is fomething elfe. The cafe the moft like

to

to real contact is that of the component parts of solid bodies, as gold, &c. but even this cannot be any thing more than a certain *near approach*, becaufe they are brought *nearer* together by cold; and it will hardly be pretended that any body merely impinging againft a piece of gold comes nearer to its fubftance than the diftance at which its own component parts are placed from each other.

On this fubject Dr. Price refers to what he has advanced p. 31. But all that he fays there is that, in fome cafes, the reafon why bodies cannot be brought into contact *may be* their *folidity*, at the fame time allowing that, in other cafes, it is *certainly* a *repulfive power*. In the fame fection he refers to his *Treatife on Morals* for another origin of the idea of folidity. But this I have fully confidered in the third of the *Effays* prefixed to my edition of *Hartley's Theory of the Human Mind*. See particulairly p. 37.

However,

However, the whole of what I have advanced concerning *the penetrability of matter*, is a thing on which I lay no great ſtreſs. I do not ſee any reaſon to be diſſatisfied with it; but admitting matter to have all the ſolidity that is uſually aſcribed to it, I have no doubt of its being compatible with the powers of thought; all the phenomena demonſtrating to me that man is a being compoſed of *one kind of ſubſtance*, and not of *two*, and theſe ſo heterogeneous to each other as has been generally ſuppoſed.

It is within the limits of this ſection that Dr. Price puts the following queſtion to me, (p. 335.) " Since experiments do
" not furniſh us with the idea of *cauſation*,
" and *productive power*, how came we by
" thoſe ideas, and how does Dr. Prieſtley
" know they have any exiſtence? How,
" in particular, does he avoid the ſcep-
" tical ſyſtem which Mr. Hume has ad-
" vanced ?"

I anſwer that my idea of *cauſation*, and of its *origin* in the mind, is, as far as I
know;

know, the very fame with that of other perfons; but we all diftinguifh between *primary* and *fecondary caufes*, though fpeaking ftrictly and philofophically, we call fecondary caufes mere *effects*, and confine the term *caufe* to the primary caufe. Thus we fay that the caufe of moving iron is in the magnet, though the magnet is not the primary, but only the proximate, or fecondary caufe of that effect; deriving its power, and all that can be faid to belong to it from a higher caufe, and ultimately from God, the original caufe of all things. So alfo I formerly confidered man as the original caufe of his volitions and actions, till, on farther reflection, I faw reafon to conclude that like the magnet, he is no more than the proximate, immediate, or fecondary caufe of them; himfelf, his conftitution, and circumftances, and confequently his actions, having a prior caufe, viz. the fame firft caufe from which the powers of the magnet, and all the powers in nature, are derived.

SECT,

SECT. III. *Of the Doctrine of Necessity.*

On this subject Dr. Price refers me, (p. 342) to the decisions of what he calls *common sense,* or the notions of the vulgar. These I have observed, as far as they go, are uniformly in favour of the doctrine of necessity. For if men were properly interrogated, they would admit all that I require in order to a proper demonstration of the doctrine; though, not being used to reflection, they do not *pursue* or even *apprehend* the consequences. See my *Treatise on Necessity,* p. 103, &c.

As to the consistency of the *popular language* with the doctrine of necessity, I have again and again made observations upon it, which I think it unnecessary to repeat, in answer to the conclusion of Dr. Price's note, p. 356.

Dr. Price says, (p. 345) that he " cannot conceive a more groundless assertion, " than that the doctrine of liberty implies " that a man can act wickedly or virtuously " without a motive." But after putting a case in which he supposes motives to be
exactly

exactly equal, viz. the combination of *paſſion* and *intereſt* on one ſide, and of *conſcience* and *duty* on the other, he makes liberty to conſiſt in our poſſeſſing *a power of making either of them the motive that ſhall prevail.*

Now it appears to me to require very little power of analization to ſee that before the mind can decide to which of the motives it ſhall give this preference, it muſt form a previous real, and moſt ſerious *determination,* and that this previous determination requires a motive as much as the final determination itſelf, eſpecially as Dr. Price expreſsly acknowledges, (p. 348) that " it is nonſenſe to deny the influence of " motives, or that there are no fixed prin- " ciples or ends by which the will is " guided." In the caſe above mentioned I have the choice of two things, viz. either to give the preponderance to the *motives of intereſt,* or to *thoſe of duty,* which, being by ſuppoſition exactly equal, are themſelves out of the queſtion, and therefore cannot at all contribute to the deciſion. Now this being a real determination of the mind, it muſt,

muſt, by Dr. Price's own confeſſion, require ſome motive or other.

This argument I own is quite new to
me, and therefore I preſume that it is, in
part, the *new matter* which Dr. Price obſerves (p. 322,) is contained in theſe *Additional Obſervations*; but I know he will
excuſe my franknefs if I tell him that it
appears to me to be the laſt retreat of the
doctrine of philoſophical liberty, and not
at all more tenable than any of thoſe out
of which it has been already driven. For
when *all argument* fails, he will hardly
take refuge in the *common ſenſe* of my
Scotch antagoniſts. I could ſay more on
the ſubject of this new idea of *the mind
chuſing the motive on which it will decide*,
but I think what I have now ſaid may be
ſufficient.

I would take this opportunity of ob-
ſerving that if the motives, in the caſe
abovementioned, be not of a *moral* nature,
(and ſince both the motive of *intereſt* on
one ſide, and that of *duty* on the other, are
expreſsly excluded, every thing elſe of a
moral nature ſeems to be excluded along
with

with them) the determination cannot with
propriety be denominated *moral*, or be faid
to be either *virtuous* or *vicious*.

Dr. Price, on this occafion, fuppofes
that a ftrict equality of motives is a very
common cafe. I anfwer that we are, indeed, fometimes fenfible of it, but that
then the determination always remains in
fufpence. For it appears to me that, if
we give attention to the ftate of our minds,
we fhall fee reafon enough to conclude
that we never come to an actual determination without a fufficient preponderance
of motive. And if we confider that the
force of a motive depends upon *the ftate
of the mind* to which it is prefented, as
well as upon what it is in itfelf, that the
ftate of mind is in perpetual fluctuation,
and that the point of light in which we
view the fame thing is continually varying, we fhall not be at all furprifed that, in
ordinary cafes, when nothing of much
confequence is depending, we determine
with fuch readinefs, and from motives fo
evanefcent, that we are not able to trace
the progrefs of our thoughts, fo as diftinctly

tinctly to recollect the real caufes of our
choice, after the fhorteft interval of time.
If it were poffible to make a balance which
fhould fupport a thoufand pounds weight,
and yet turn with one thoufandth part of
a grain, would it be any wonder that a
perfon fhould not be able eafily to bring
it to an equipoife? But what is even this
to the exquifite ftructure of the mind?

Dr. Price acknowledges, as above, that
" it is nonfenfe to deny the influence of
" motives, or to maintain that there are
" no fixed principles by which the will is
" guided;" but at the fame time he fays
(p. 348) that " this nonfenfe is fcarcely
" equal to that of confounding *moral* and
" *phyfical caufes.*" Now if what I have
faid on this fubject both in my *Treatife on
Neceffity,* and in my *Letter to Dr. Horfeley* be not fatisfactory, I fhall defpair of
ever being able to give fatisfaction with refpect. to any thing. I will even grant
moral and phyfical caufes to be as different,
in their nature and operation, as Dr. Price
himfelf can poffibly fuppofe them to be;
B b                                    but

but if they be really *caufes*, producing *certain effects*, that is, if we be fo conftituted, as that one definite determination fhall always follow a definite ftate of mind, it muft be true that, without a miracle, no volition, or action, could have been otherwife than it *has been*, *is*, or *is to be*; and this is all that, as a neceffarian, I contend for. If any perfon can pleafe himfelf with calling this *liberty*, or the refult of the *mind's determining itfelf*, I have no fort of objection, becaufe thefe are mere *words* and *phrafes*.

Dr. Price calls the doctrine of neceffity, according to which all events, moral as well as natural, are ultimately afcribed to God, a *deadly potion* (p. 354) and yet he hefitates not to fay (p. 358) that he believes " no event comes to pafs which " it would have been proper to exclude, " and that, relatively to the divine plan " and adminiftration, all is right." Now, between this doctrine, and thofe naked views of the doctrine of neceffity at which Dr. Price is fo much alarmed, I fee no real

real difference. When a perfon can once bring himfelf to think that there is no wickednefs of man which it would have been proper to exclude, and that the divine plan *requires* this wickednefs, as well as every thing elfe that actually takes place (which is the purport of what Dr. Price advances, and very nearly his own words) I wonder much that he fhould hefitate to admit that the Divine Being might ex-prefsly *appoint* what it would have been improper to exclude, what his plan ab-folutely required, and that without which the fcheme could not have been right, but muft have been wrong.

May not this view of the fubject, as given by Dr. Price, be reprefented as an *apology for vice,* and a *thing to be fhuddered at,* and to be *fled from,* which is the language that he ufes (p. 354) with refpect to the doctrine of neceffity? If to make vice *neceffary* be deadly poifon, can that doc-trine be innocent which confiders it as a thing that is *proper,* and, relatively to the divine plan and adminiftration, *right?* The

two

two opinions, if not the same, are certainly very near *akin*, and must have the same kind of operation and effect.

If Dr. Price will attend to *facts*, he may be satisfied that it *cannot* require that great *strength* and *soundness of constitution* that he charitably ascribes to me, to convert the doctrine of necessity, poison as he thinks it to be, into wholesome nourishment, and that he must have seen it in some very unfair and injurious light. I am far from being singular in my belief of this doctrine. There are thousands, I doubt not, who believe it as firmly as I do. A great majority of the more intelligent, serious, and virtuous of my acquaintance among men of letters, are necessarians, (as, with respect to several of them, Dr. Price himself very well knows) and we all think ourselves the better for it. Can we *all* have this peculiar strength of constitution? It cannot be surely deadly poison which so many persons take, not only without injury, but with advantage, finding it to be, as Dr. Price acknowledges

with

with refpect to myfelf (p. 352) even *fa-lutary*.

We are all, no doubt, conftituted much alike, how different foever may be the opinions that we entertain concerning the principles of our common nature. I, therefore, infer that Dr. Price himfelf, if it were poffible for him to become a neceffarian, would think it not only a very harmlefs, but a great and glorious fcheme, worthy of a chriftian divine, and philofopher, and that he would fmile, as I myfelf now do, at the notions which we firft entertained of it.

Dr. Price alfo imagines (p. 355 and 356) " that the belief of the doctrine of neceffity " muft operate like a dead weight upon " the creation, breaking every afpiring ef- " fort, and producing univerfal abjectnefs. " The natural effect of believing that no- " thing is left to depend upon ourfelves, " and that we can *do* nothing, and *are* " nothing, muft be concluding that we " have nothing to do."

B b 3

But

But I have obſerved in my *Treatiſe on Neceſſity* (p. 96, &c.) that, in the only ſenſe in which the conſideration of it can operate as a motive of action, *every thing depends upon ourſelves*, much more ſo than upon any other ſcheme; and therefore that the neceſſarian muſt feel himſelf more ſtrongly impelled to an exertion of his faculties than any other man.

By a man's *making his own fortune*, I mean that his *ſucceſs* depends upon his *actions*, as theſe depend upon his *volitions*, and his volitions upon the *motives* preſented to him. Suppoſing a man, therefore, to have *propenſities* and *objects of purſuit*, as his own happineſs, &c. &c. of which no ſyſtem of faith can deprive him, he will neceſſarily be rouſed to exert himſelf in proportion to the ſtrength of his propenſity, and his belief of the neceſſary connection between his *end* and his *endeavours;* and nothing but ſuch an opinion as that of philoſophical liberty, which deſtroys that neceſſary connection, can poſſibly ſlacken his endeavours.

With

With refpect to this also, let Dr. Price confider whether his *theory* has any correfpondence with *facts*. Let him confider thofe of his acquaintance who are neceffarians. To fay nothing of myfelf, who certainly, however, am not the moft torpid and lifelefs of all animals; where will he find greater ardour of mind, a ftronger and more unremitted exertion, or a more ftrenuous and fteady purfuit of the moft important objects, than among thofe of whom he knows to be neceffarians? I can fay with truth (and meaning no difparagement to Dr. Price, and many others, who, I believe, unknown to themfelves, derive much of the excellence of their characters from principles very near akin to thofe of the doctrine of neceffity) that I generally find *chriftian neceffarians* the moft diftinguifhed for active and fublime virtues, and more fo in proportion to their fteady belief of the doctrine, and the attention they habitually give to it. I appeal to every perfon who has read *Dr. Hartley's Obfervations on Man*, whether he can avoid having the fame conviction with refpect to him.

It

It is at *names* more than *things* that
people in general are moft frightened.   Dr.
Horfeley is clearly a neceffarian, in every
thing but the name.   He avows his belief
that every determination of the mind certainly follows from previous circumftances,
fo that without a miracle, no volition, or
action, could have been otherwife than it
*has been, is,* or *is to be,* and yet he dif-
claims the doctrine of neceffity.   Dr. Price
does not properly maintain the doctrine,
but he ftands on the very brink of that
tremendous precipice ; believing that the
mind cannot act without a motive, but
thinking to fecure his liberty on the fuppofition that the mind (I fuppofe, without any motive whatever) has the power
of chufing what motive it will act from;
and believing with the neceffarian, that
every thing is *as it fhould be,* and *as the divine plan required it to be.*

Upon the whole, both he and Dr. Horfeley appear to me to want nothing more
than what is called *courage* fully to adopt,
and boldly defend, the doctrine of neceffity
in

in *its proper terms,* and to *its full extent.*
I well remember to have had the fame
fears and apprehenfions about the doctrine
of neceffity that they now exprefs; but
being compelled, by mere *force of argument,* to believe it to be *true,* I was by
degrees reconciled to it, and prefently found
that there was nothing to be dreaded in it,
but, on the contrary, every thing that can
give the greateft fatisfaction to a well difpofed mind, capable of any degree of comprehenfion, or extent of view. I think it
much better, however, to admit the doctrine of neceffity explicitly, and with all
its confequences, than be compelled to admit the fame confequences, in other words,
and in conjunction with principles that are
quite difcordant with it.

To take off the dark cloud that Dr.
Price has in thefe laft obfervations thrown
over the doctrine of neceffity, I fhall not
here repeat what I have on former occafions advanced in its favour, but fhall leave
it to make whatever impreffion it may on
our readers.

What

What Dr. Price says of *the soul* (p. 355) that, " it is possessed of faculties which " make it an image of the deity, and ren- " der it capable of acting by the same rule " with him, of participating of his hap- " piness, and of living for ever, and im- " proving for ever under his eye and care," I can say of *man*. But I do not think that, for this purpose, it is at all necessary that the mind should be *incorporeal*, *un-compounded* or *self-determining*, arrogating to ourselves the attributes of *little independent gods*. To whatever kind of substance, though it should be the humblest *dust of the earth*, that the truly noble prerogatives of man be imparted, it will appear to me equally respectable. For it is not the *substance*, but the *properties*, or *powers*, that make it so.

I also *reverence myself*, but not in the character of a being *self-determined*, or *self-existent*, but as the rational offspring of the first great and only proper cause of all things. By his power I am animated, by his wisdom I am conducted, and by his bounty

bounty I am made happy. It is only from the idea I have of my near relation to this great and glorious being, and of my intimate connection with him, that my exultation arifes; far from founding it upon the idea that I have a will that is not ultimately his, or a fingle thought that he cannot controul. *Of him, and through him, and to him, are all things. To him, therefore, and not to ourfelves, be glory.*

Dr. Price lays great ftrefs on the confideration of God being a *felf-determining,* and *felf-moving* being, as a proof that man *may* be fo too (p. 349 & 350) and confidering *felf-determining* as equivalent to *felf-moving,* and this as equivalent to what we mean by *a felf-exiftent,* or *firft caufe,* I have not objected to applying that appellation to the Divine Being; but I would obferve that in this I mean nothing more than to exprefs my total want of conception concerning the *caufe,* or *reafon,* of the *exiftence,* and if I may fo fay, of the *original action,* of the Deity. For, confidering the Divine Being as *actually exifting,* I have no more idea of the

the poffibility of his acting without a motive (if there be any analogy between the
divine mind and ours) than of any created
being doing fo; and to afcribe this felf-
determining power to the Divine Being,
meaning by it that *he acts without a motive*,
or *reafon*, is certainly fo far from exalting
the Deity, that we cannot form any idea
of him more degrading, It is to diveft
him at once of all his moral perfections,
For to act invariably from good principles,
or motives (in whatever it be that we make
goodnefs, or virtue, to confift) is effential
to moral excellence.

As to the *caufe*, or *account*, as Dr. Price
expreffes it, of the divine exiftence, I profefs to have no idea at all. That there
muft be a neceffarily exifting being, or a
firft caufe, follows undeniably from the exiftence of other things; but the fame difpofition to inquire into the caufes of things
would lead us on *ad infinitum*, were it not
that we fee a manifeft abfurdity in it; fo
that, confounding as it is to the imagination, we are under an abfolute neceffity of
acqui-

acquiefcing in the idea of a *felf-exiftent being*.

Every thing that I have yet feen advanced with refpect to the proper *caufe,* or *reafon* of the divine exiftence appears to me either to fuggeft no ideas at all, or to give falfe ones. Dr. Clarke fays, that *the Deity exifts by an abfolute neceffity in the nature of things*, but this expreffion gives me no proper idea; for, exclufive of that neceffity by which we are compelled to admit that fuch a being exifts, which may be called neceffity *a pofteriori*, I am fatisfied that no man, let his reafoning faculties be what they will, can have the leaft idea of any neceffity. Of neceffity *a priori* it is impoffible we fhould know any thing. Let any perfon only exclude all idea of creation, which is not difficult, and confider whether, in thofe circumftances, he can difcover a caufe of any exiftence at all. To talk of *the nature of things*, in this cafe, is, to my underftanding mere jargon, or a cloak for abfolute ignorance.

Dr.

Dr. Price himself does not seem to be satisfied with this explanation of the cause of the divine existence, and therefore suggests a different idea; saying (p. 351) that " the account of the divine existence " is the same with the account of the ex- " istence of space, and duration, of the " equality of the three angles of a triangle " to two right angles, or of any abstract " truth." Now, as Dr. Clarke's language gives me no idea at all, this account appears to me to suggest a false one.

The reason, or the account, of the existence of the *divine being* cannot be the same with that of the existence of *space*, or *duration*, for this plain reason. I can, in any case, form an idea of the non-existence both of all *effects*, and of all *causes*, and consequently both of the creation, and of the creator, and of the non-existence of the latter, just as easily as of that of the former; but still the ideas of *space* and *duration* remain in the mind, and cannot be excluded from it. To say that space is an *attribute of the deity*, or that it necessarily
implies,

implies, and draws after it, the idea of his exiftence, appears to me to have no foundation whatever, and to have been affumed without the leaft face of probability. For this I appeal to what paffes in any perfon's mind.

Again, the reafon of the divine exiftence, and that of an abftract truth, as that the three angles of a triangle are equal to two right angles, appear to me to have no fort of analogy. They agree in nothing but that both of them are true, but with refpect to the *reafon*, or *caufe of their being true*, no two things, in my opinion, can be more unlike.

An abftract truth is no *being*, *fubftance*, or *reality* whatever. It implies nothing more than the agreement of two ideas, whether the archetypes of thofe ideas have any exiftence or not, and of this agreement we have the moft perfect comprehenfion. Nothing can be more intelligible. Now, if our perfuafion of this abftract truth was of the fame nature with our perfuafion concerning the exiftence of God, we fhould

have

have the fame perfect comprehenfion of the latter that we have of the former. But can any perfon ferioufly fay this, when of the former we know *every thing*, and of the latter abfolutely *nothing*? Let any perfon exclude from his mind all idea of the creation, and confider whether there be any thing left that will compel him to believe the exiftence of any *thing*, *being*, or *fubftance* whatever. A *creation* neceffarily implies a *creator*, but if there be no creation, the only proof of the exiftence of a creator is cut off.

The caufe of the exiftence of a *thing*, *fubftance*, or *being*, cannot, in the nature of things, be the fame with that of a mere abftract hypothetical truth. The caufe of a being, or fubftance, muft be a being or fubftance alfo, and therefore, with refpect to the divine being we are obliged to fay that he has *no proper caufe whatever*. The agreement of two ideas is a thing fo very different in its nature from this, that the term *caufe* is not even applicable to it; as, on the other hand, I fee no meaning what-

whatever in the word *account* as applicable to the divine exiftence. In this cafe there muft either be *a caufe*, or *no caufe*. Account, here, is to me a word without meaning.

If by the word *account*, we mean the fame with *reafon*, the cafes are clearly the fartheft in the world from being parallel. If I be afked the reafon why the three angles of a triangle are equal to two right angles, I anfwer, that the quantity of the three, and that of the two, is the fame, or that the ideas, when rightly underftood, exactly *coincide*. But if I be afked why the divine being exifts (I fay *why he exifts*, not why I *believe* him to exift) can I fatisfy any body, or myfelf, by faying that the two ideas in the propofition *God exifts* are the fame, or coincide? Is the idea of *God*, and that of mere *exiftence* the fame idea? The two cafes, therefore, have nothing in them at all parallel. How then can the *reafon, account*, or *caufe* of an *abftract truth*, be of *the fame nature* with that of the reafon, account, or caufe of the *divine exiftence*?

C c                                    I

I ſhall now conclude the whole controverſy with mentioning what appear to me
to be the things on which the principal arguments in each part of it turn, and the
miſconceptions that Dr. Price ſeems to me
to have laboured under.

On the ſubject of the *penetrability of
matter*, he has never produced what I have
repeatedly called for, viz. *one caſe of real un-
queſtionable contact*, without which the doctrine of proper impenetrability cannot be
ſupported.   And till this be produced, I
am obliged to conclude, from analogy, that
*all* reſiſtance is owing to ſuch cauſes as we
both agree that, in *many*, if not in *moſt
caſes*, it does certainly ariſe from, and this
is *not ſolidity*, or impenetrability, but ſomething very different from it.

With reſpect to the doctrine of *a ſoul*,
Dr. Price appears to me to have been
miſled principally by his notion of the *abſolute ſimplicity*, or *indiviſibility* of the mind,
or the thinking principle in man; as if it
was

was a thing of which we could be *confcious*; whereas I think I have fhown fufficiently that we cannot be confcious of
any thing relating to the *effence of the mind*;
that we are properly confcious of nothing
but what we *perceive*, and what we *do*.
As to what we *are*, it is a thing that we
muft learn by way of *inference*, and *deduction* from obfervations, or confcioufnefs;
and I think the *arguments* are decifively
againft fuch a fimplicity and indivifibility
as Dr. Price fuppofes.

On the fubject of the doctrine of *neceffity*, Dr. Price agrees with Dr. Horfeley
in admitting that our volitions *certainly*,
and invariably depend upon the preceding
ftate of mind; fo that, without a miracle,
there was a real neceffity of every thing
being as it *has been*, *is*, or *is to be*; and
imagines that the controverfy depends on
what I think to be the mere verbal diftinction,
of motives being the *moral*, and not the
*phyfical caufes* of our volitions and actions;
or, as he fometimes expreffes himfelf, that
it is not the motives that determine the

C c 2                    mind,

mind, but that the mind determines itfelf according to the motives; which I maintain to be the doctrine of neceffity, only difguifed in other words. Indeed, how any man can boaft of his liberty, merely becaufe he has a power of determining himfelf, when, at the fame time, he knows that he cannot do it in any other than *in one precife and definite manner*, ftrictly depending upon the circumftances in which he is placed, and when he believes that, in no one action of his life, he could have determined otherwife than he has done, is to me a little difficult of comprehenfion.

As to *real liberty*, or the power of acting independently of motives, he exprefsly confines it to thofe cafes in which the motives for and againft any particular choice are *exactly equal*. Such cafes, I think, feldom, or never, occur; fo that a man could have but few opportunities of fhewing fuch a liberty as this. If they fhould occur, and any determination take place in thofe circumftances, it appears to me to be attended with the *abfurdity* (as Dr. Price
himfelf

himſelf calls it) of determining without a motive; and I ſhould think that after ſuppoſing it poſſible that the mind might determine *without* a motive, it might alſo determine *contrary* to all motive. For the ſame conſtitution of mind that could enable it to do the one, would enable it to do the other.

A LET-

A

# L E T T E R

TO

Dr. P R I C E.

Dear Sir,

WITH this letter you will receive a
few remarks on your *Additional
Observations*, which I have read with that
*attention* which every thing from you de-
mands. That it has not been with *conviction*, your candour, I know, will not
impute to any peculiar *obstinacy*, but to my
unavoidably seeing the subjects of our discussion in a light different from that in
which you see them. We have not the
same idea of the nature of the human

mind,

mind, or of the laws to which it is fubject, but we are both fufficiently aware of
the force of *prejudice*, and that this may
equally throw a biafs on the fide of *long
eftablifhed*, or of *novel* opinions. Alfo,
equally refpecting the chriftian maxim of
*doing to others as we would that others fhould
do to us*, we are each of us ready to give to
others that liberty which we claim ourfelves ; while we equally reprobate thofe
rafh fentiments which proceed from a decifion without a previous difcuffion of the
reafons for and againft a queftion in debate.

I am not a little proud of your commendation of me for my " fairnefs in the
" purfuit of truth, and following it in all
" its confequences, however frightful, with-
" out attempting to evade or palliate
" them" (p. 352.) It is a conduct that
I hope I fhall always purfue, as the firft of
duties to that God who has given me whatever *faculties* I poffefs, and whatever *opportunity of inquiry* I have been favoured with;
and I truft I fhall continue to purfue this
con-

conduct at all rifks. As he is properly no
chriftian, who does not *confefs Chrift before
men;* or who is *afhamed* of his religion in
an unbelieving age, like the prefent; this
maxim, which the author of our religion
inculcates with refpect to chriftianity in
general, the reafon of the thing requires
that we extend to every thing that effentially
affects chriftianity.

So long, therefore, as I conceive the
doctrine of a *feparate foul* to have been the
true fource of the groffeft corruptions in
the chriftian fyftem, of that very *antichrif-
tian fyftem* which fprung up in the times of
the apoftles, concerning which they entertained the ftrongeft apprehenfions, and delivered, and left upon record, the moft
folemn warnings, I muft think myfelf a
very lukewarm and difaffected chriftian if
I do not bear my feeble teftimony againft
it.

With refpect to the private conduct of
individuals, as affecting our happinefs after
death, I do not lay any ftrefs upon this,

or

or upon *any opinion whatever*, and there
is no perfon of whofe chriftian temper and
conduct I think more highly than I do of
yours, though you hold opinions the very
reverfe of mine, and defend them with fo
much zeal; a zeal which, while you maintain the opinions at all, is certainly com-
mendable. But with refpect to the *general
plan of chriftianity*, the importance of the
doctrines I contend for can hardly, in my
opinion, be rated too high. What I contend for leaves nothing for the manifold
corruptions and abufes of popery to faften
on. Other doctrinal reformations are partial things, while this goes to the very
root of almoft all the mifchief we complain of; and, for my part, I fhall not
date the proper and complete downfal of
what is called *antichrift*, but from the general prevalence of the doctrine of materialifm.

This I cannot help faying appears to me
to be that fundamental principle in true
philofophy which is alone perfectly confo-
nant to the doctrine of the fcriptures; and
being

being at the fame time the only proper
deduction from natural appearances, it
muft, in the progrefs of inquiry foon *appear to be fo*; and then, fhould it be
found that an unqueftionably true philofophy teaches one thing, and revelation
another, the latter could not ftand its
ground, but muft inevitably be exploded,
as contrary to *truth and fact*. I therefore
deem it to be of particular confequence,
that philofophical unbelievers fhould be
apprized in time, that there are chriftians,
who confider the *doctrine of a foul* as a tenet
that is fo far from being *effential* to the
chriftian fcheme, that it is a thing quite
*foreign* to it, derived originally from heathenifm, difcordant with the genuine principles of revealed religion, and ultimately
fubverfive of them.

As to the doctrine of *neceffity*, I cannot,
after all our difcuffion, help confidering it
as *demonftrably true*, and the only poffible
foundation for the doctrines of a *providence*,
and the *moral government of God*.

Con-

Continuing to fee things in this light, after the clofeft attention that I have been able to give to them, before, or in the courfe of our friendly debate (and you will pardon me, if I add, feeing this in a ftronger light than ever) you will not be difpleafed with the *zeal* that I have occafionally fhewn ; as I, on my part, intirely approve of yours, who confider yourfelf as defending important and long received truth, againft fundamental and moft dangerous innovations.

We are neither of us fo far blinded by prejudice as not to fee, and acknowledge, the wifdom of conftituting us in fuch a manner, as that every thing *new* refpecting a fubject of fo much confequence as *religion*, fhould excite a great alarm, and meet with great difficulty in eftablifhing itfelf.    This furnifhes an occafion of a thorough examination, and difcuffion of all new doctrines, in confequence of which they are either totally exploded, or more firmly eftablifhed.    The flow and gradual

progrefs

progrefs of chriftianity, and alfo that of the
reformation, is a circumftance that bids
fairer for their perpetuity, than if they
had met with a much readier reception in
the world. You will allow me to indulge
the hope of a fimilar advantage from the
oppofition that I expect to this article of
reformation in the chriftian fyftem, and
that the truth I contend for will be the
more valued for being dearly bought, and
flowly acquired.

As to the *odium* that I may bring upon
myfelf by the malevolence of my oppofers,
of which, in your letter to me, you make
fuch obliging mention, I hope the fame
confcioufnefs of not having deferved it,
will fupport me as it has done you, when
much worfe treated than I have yet been,
on an occafion on which you deferved the
warmeft gratitude of your country, whofe
interefts you ftudied and watched over,
whofe calamities you forefaw, and faith-
fully pointed out; and which might have
derived, in various refpects, the moft folid
and

and durable advantages from your labours. But we are no chriftians, if we have not fo far imbibed the principles and fpirit of our religion, as even to *rejoice that we are counted worthy of fuffering* in any good caufe.

Here it is that, fuppofing me to be a defender of *chriftian truth*, my object gives me an advantage that your excellent *political writings* cannot give you. All your obfervations may be juft, and your advice moft excellent, and yet your country, the fafety and happinefs of which you have at heart, being in the hands of infatuated men, may go to ruin; whereas chriftian truth is a caufe *founded upon a rock*, and though it may be overborne for a time, we are affured that the *gates of death fhall not prevail againft it.*

Having now, each of us, defended, in the beft manner that we can, what we deem to be this important truth, we are, I doubt not, equally fatisfied with ourfelves, and fhall chearfully fubmit the refult

fult of our difcuffion to the judgment of our friends, and of the public; and to the final and infallible determination of the *God of all truth.*

I am, notwithftanding this, and every other poffible difference in *mere opinion,* with the moft perfeſt efteem,

Dear Sir,

Yours moft affeſtionately,

J. PRIESTLEY.

Calne, Oſt. 2, 1778.

A NOTE

# NOTE to DR. PRIESTLEY.

DR. PRICE defires DR. PRIESTLEY's acceptance of his gratitude for the expreffions of his kindnefs and regard in the preceding letter; and affures him in return of his beft wifhes and ardent efteem. The controverfy between them having grown much too tedious, he thinks there is a neceffity of now dropping it. He cannot therefore perfuade himfelf to enter farther into it; or to fay any more than that his fentiments are undefignedly miifreprefented, when in page 387, Dr. Prieftley fuggefts, that he confiders wickednefs as *a thing that is proper*, and thinks the *plan of the Deity abfolutely required it*. He has never meant to fay more, than that the PERMISSION of wickednefs is *proper*; and that (for the reafons mentioned in p. 173, 174, and 358) the divine plan required the communication of powers rendering beings capable of perverfely *making themfelves* wicked, by acting, not as the divine plan requires, (for this, he thinks, would be too good an excufe for wickednefs) but, by acting in a manner that oppofes the divine plan and will, and that would fubvert the order of nature; and to which, on this account, punifhment has been annexed.

ANSWER

ANSWER by DR. PRIESTLEY,

DR. PRIESTLEY will always think himself happy in having an opportunity of ex-
pressing the very high and affectionate regard he entertains for Dr. Price, notwith-
standing their difference of opinion on subjects of so much moment as those discussed
in the present Correspondence. He is confident that Dr. Price needs no assurance
on the part of Dr. Priestley, that his sen-
timents have not been *knowingly* misrepre-
sented; but must take the liberty to say,
that he cannot help considering the voluntary *permission* of evil, or the *certain cause*
of it, by a being who foresees it, and has
sufficient power to prevent it, as equivalent
to the express *appointment* of it.

A N

# A N

# ALPHABETICAL INDEX

## TO THE

DISQUISITIONS ON MATTER AND SPIRIT, the TREATISE ON NECESSITY, and this CORRESPONDENCE, which is here confidered as the third volume in the Set,

*N. B.* Where no Roman numeral is ufed, the firft volume, or the *Difquifitions*, is underftood,

## A

*AGOBARD,* his account of opinions concerning the foul, 213.

*Abfence of mind,* an argument for a feparate foul, 99.

*Abftract ideas,* compatible with materialifm, 84.

*Accountablenefs,* explained on the doctrine of neceffity, iii. 149.

*Agency,* how underftood, ii. 50.

*Alexandrian School,* the fource of great corruptions in chriftianity, 292.

*Ammonius,* his philofophy, 292.

*Animal Spirits,* by whom brought into vogue, 217.

*Anfelm,* his opinion of the ftate of the dead, 227.

*Anthropomorphites,* a chriftian fect, 187.

*Aquinas,* his opinion concerning the divine effence, 190.—Of the foul, 214.

*Arabians,* who believed that the foul died with the body, 226.

*Arianifm,* termed *the low,* reafons againft it, 332.

*Arians,* did not platonize, 305.

*Ariftotle,* his opinion concerning the foul, 198.

*Arnobius,* his opinion concerning the foul, 206.

*Athanafius,* his reafons why the apoftles did not preach the divinity of Chrift, 309.

D d 2

*Atheifm,*

*Determi-*

D d 4

*Liberty,*

*Self-motion*, whether it belongs to the foul, 96.—Mr. Locke's difficulties with refpect to it, 111.

*Sentient Principle*, in the brain, 24, 33.

*Simon Magus*, how reckoned the parent of herefy, 297.

*Sleep*, a puzzling phenomenon on the doctrine of a foul, 80.

*Socinianifm*, Dr. Price's opinion concerning it, iii. 144.—Dr. Prieftley's, iii. 165.—Whether fupported by Materialifm, iii. 334, note 373.—The fubordination of the doctrines of the penetrability of matter, and of materialifm to it, iii. 239.

*Solidity*, whether to be afcribed to matter, iii. 31.

*Soul*, in what manner prefent with the body, 52.—The original philofophical doctrine concerning it, 53.—Confidered as a mathematical point, 55.—Its vehicle, 74.—Its unwearied nature, 97.—The meaning of the word in the fcriptures, 115.—What our Saviour meant by it, 129.—The origin of the doctrine, 166.—The hiftory of opinions concerning it, 192.—The confequence of its being compounded, iii. 69.—In what fenfe it is naturally immortal, iii. 69.—Of what ufe between death and the refurrection, on the fuppofition of its fleeping in that interval, iii. 76, 80, 108.—In what fenfe its powers may be faid to be extinct at death, iii. 80.—Queries relating to it by Dr. Price, iii. 87.—Others propofed to Dr. Price, iii. 167.—A general view of the progrefs of opinions concerning it, iii. 260.—Arguments againft its being extended, iii. 268. Whether ftrictly indivifible, iii. 327, 366, 402.

—— *and Body*, their mutual influences, 60.

*Space*, whether an attribute of the Deity, iii. 68, 103.

*Spirit*, the vulgar notion of one, 52, 173.—The term applied to any invifible power, 170.—Whether it bears any relation to fpace, iii. 54, 96, 98, 106.—Whether matter might not have been fo called on the doctrine of the penetrability of matter, iii. 190.

*Stoics*, their opinion concerning the divine effence, 181.—Concerning the foul, 200.

*Synefius*, a Platonift, 295.

*Syftem*, in what fenfe man may, or may not be one, iii. 99, 112, 123, 327.

## T

*Tertullian*, his opinion concerning the divine effence, 186.—Concerning the foul, 205.

*Thales*, his opinion concerning the foul, 195.

*Thinking,*

*F  I  N  I  S.*

# E R R A T A.

Introduction, p. vi. l. 2, for *capable*, read *as capable*.
———————— xxxiii. l. 16, for *retraction*, r. *retractation*.

---

P. 39. l. 4, for *a force of bodies*, r. *or force of bodies*.
51. l. 7, for *and juft*, r. *juft*.
59. l. 16, for *writings*, r. *other writings*.
113. l. 16, for *man*, r. *men*.
143. l. 1, for *cafuality*, r. *caufality*.
160. l. 2, dele *and*.
226. l. 18, for *thefe*, r. *thofe*,
274. l. 16, for *tolerable*, r. *tolerably*.
284. l. 14, for *and if*, r. *if*.
401. l. 3, from the bottom, dele *that of*.

# A CATALOGUE of BOOKS,

## WRITTEN BY

# Dr. PRICE,

### AND SOLD BY

## T. CADELL, in the STRAND.

1. OBSERVATIONS on REVERSIONARY PAY-
MENTS; on Schemes for providing Annuities for
Widows, and Perfons in Old Age; on the Method of calcu-
lating the Values of Affurances on Lives; and on the National
Debt. To which are added, FOUR ESSAYS on different
Subjects in the Doctrine of Life, Annuities and Political
Arithmetic. Alfo, AN APPENDIX, containing a complete
Set of Tables, fhewing the Probabilities of Life in London,
Norwich, and Northampton, and the Values of two joint
Lives. The Third Edition, with a SUPPLEMENT, contain-
ing (befides feveral new Tables) additional Obfervations on
the Probabilities of Human Life in different Situations; on
the London Societies for the Benefit of Widows, and of Old
Age; and on the prefent State of Population in this King-
dom. Price 6s. Bound.

2. A REVIEW of the principal QUESTIONS and DIFFI-
CULTIES in MORALS; particularly, thofe relating to the
Original of our Ideas of Virtue, its Nature, Foundation, Reference to the Deity, Obligation, Subject, Matter, and Sanc-
tions. The Second Edition, Price 6s. Bound.

3. FOUR DISSERTATIONS. 1ft. On Providence. 2d. On
Prayer. 3d On the Reafons for expecting that virtuous Men
fhall meet after Death in a State of Happinefs. 4th. On the
Importance of Chriftianity, the Nature of hiftorical Evidence,
and Miracles. The Fourth Edition, Price 6s. Bound.

4. An APPEAL to the PUBLIC on the Subject of the NA-
TIONAL DEBT. Second Edition; with an APPENDIX, containing explanatory Obfervations and Tables; and an Account of the prefent State of Population in Norfolk. Price
2s.

5. TWO TRACTS on CIVIL LIBERTY, the WAR with
AMERICA, and the DEBTS and FINANCES of the KING-
DOM; with a GENERAL INTRODUCTION and SUPPLEMENT.
Price 5s. in Boards.

A

A CATALOGUE of BOOKS written by
JOSEPH PRIESTLEY, L.L.D.F.R.S.
AND PRINTED FOR
J. JOHNSON, BOOKSELLER, at No. 72, ST. PAUL'S
CHURCH-YARD, London.

1. THE HISTORY and PRESENT STATE of ELECTRI-
CITY, with original Experiments, illuſtrated with
Copper-Plates, 4th Edition, correćted and enlarged, 4to. 1l. 1s.
Another Edition, 2 vols. 8vo. 12s.

2. A Familiar INTRODUCTION to the STUDY of ELEC-
TRICITY, 4th Edition, 8vo. 2s. 6d.

3. The HISTORY and PRESENT STATE of DISCOVERIES
relating to VISION, LIGHT, and COLOURS, 2 vols. 4to. illuſtrated with a great Number of Copper-Plates, 1l. 11s. 6d.
in Boards.

4. A COURSE of LECTURES on ORATORY and CRITI-
CISM, 4to. 10s. 6d. in Boards.

5. A Familiar INTRODUCTION to the Theory and Praćtice
of PERSPECTIVE, with Copper-Plates, 5s. in Boards.

6. Experiments and Obſervations on different Kinds of Air,
with Copper-Plates, 3 vols. 18s. in Boards.

7. PHILOSOPHICAL EMPIRICISM : Containing Remarks
on a Charge of Plagiariſm reſpećting Dr. H————s, inter-
ſperſed with various Obſervations relating to different Kinds
of Air, 1s. 6d.

8. A New CHART of HISTORY, containing a View of the
principal Revolutions of Empire that have taken Place in the
World ; with a Book deſcribing it, containing an Epitome of
Univerſal Hiſtory, 4th Edition, 10s. 6d.

9. A CHART of BIOGRAPHY, with a Book, containing
an Explanation of it, and a Catalogue of all the Names inſerted
in it, 6th Edition, very much improved, 10s. 6d.

10. OBSERVATIONS relative to EDUCATION : more eſpecially as it reſpećts the MIND. To which is added, an Eſſay
on a courſe of liberal Education for Civil and Ańive Life,
with Plans of Lećtures on, 1. The Study of Hiſtory and general Policy. 2. The Hiſtory of England. 3. The Conſtitution
and Laws of England, 4s. ſewed.

11. An EXAMINATION of Dr. REID's Inquiry into the
Human Mind on the Principles of Common Senſe, Dr. BEAT-
TIE's Eſſay on the Nature and Immutability of Truth, and Dr.
OSWALD's Appeal to Common Senſe in Behalf of Religion.
2d Edition, 5s. ſewed.

13. HART-

12. Hartley's Theory of the Human Mind, on the Principle of the Association of Ideas, with Essays relating to the Subject of it, 8vo. 5s. sewed.

13. Disquisitions relating to Matter and Spirit. To which is added, The History of the philosophical Doctrine concerning the Origin of the Soul, and the Nature of Matter; with its Influence on Christianity, especially with respect to the Doctrine of the Pre-existence of Christ. Also, The Doctrine of Philosophical Necessity illustrated, 2 vols. 8vo. sewed. 8s. 6d.

14. The Rudiments of English Grammar, adapted to the Use of Schools, 1s. 6d.

15. The above Grammar with Notes and Observations, for the Use of those who have made some Proficiency in the Language, 4th Edition, 3s.

16. An Essay on the First Principles of Government, and on the Nature of Political, Civil, and Religious Liberty, 3d Edition, much enlarged, 4s. sewed.

17. Institutes of Natural and Revealed Religion, Vol. I. containing the Elements of Natural Religion; to which is prefixed, An Essay on the best Method of communicating religious Knowledge to the Members of Christian Societies, 2s. 6d.—Vol. II. containing the Evidences of the Jewish and Christian Revelations, 3s. sewed.—Vol. III. containing the Doctrines of Revelation, 2s. 6d. sewed.—The Fourth and last Part of this Work will contain an Historical Account of the Corruptions of Christianity.

18. A Harmony of the Evangelists, in Greek: To which are prefixed, Critical Dissertations, in English, 4to. 14s. in Boards.

19. A Free Address to Protestant Dissenters, on the Subject of the Lord's Supper, 3d Edition, with Additions, 2s.

20. The Additions to the above may be had alone, 1s.

21. An Address to Protestant Dissenters on the Subject of giving the Lord's Supper to Children, 1s.

22. Considerations on Differences of Opinion among Christians; with a Letter to the Rev. Mr. Venn, in Answer to his Examination of the Address to Protestant Dissenters, 1s. 6d.

23. A Catechism for Children, or Young Persons, 2d Edition, 3d.

24. A Scripture Catechism, consisting of a Series of Questions, with References to the Scriptures, instead of Answers, 3d.

25. A

BOOKS written by JOSEPH PRIESTLEY, LL. D.

25. A SERIOUS ADDRESS to MASTERS of Families, with Forms of Family Prayer, 2d Edition, 6d.

26. A VIEW of the PRINCIPLES and CONDUCT of the PROTESTANT DISSENTERS, with refpect to the Civil and Ecclefiaftical Conftitution of England, 2d Edition, 1s. 6d.

27. A FREE ADDRESS to PROTESTANT DISSENTERS, on the Subject of CHURCH DISCIPLINE; with a Preliminary Difcourfe concerning the Spirit of Chriftianity, and the Corruption of it by falfe Notions of Religion, 2s. 6d.

28. A SERMON preached before the Congregation of PROTESTANT DISSENTERS, at Mill Hill Chapel, in Leeds, May 16, 1773, on Occafion of his refigning his Paftoral Office among them, 1s.

29. A FREE ADDRESS to PROTESTANT DISSENTERS, as fuch. By a Diffenter. A new Edition, enlarged and corrected, 1s. 6d.—An Allowance is made to thofe who buy this Pamphlet to give away.

30. LETTERS to the Author of Remarks on feveral late Publications relative to the Diffenters, in a Letter to Dr. Prieftley, 1s.

31. An APPEAL to the ferious and candid Profeffors of Chriftianity, on the following Subjects, viz. 1. The Ufe of Reafon in Matters of Religion. 2. The Power of Man to do the Will of God. 3. Original Sin. 4. Election and Reprobation. 5. The Divinity of Chrift; and, 6. Atonement for Sin by the Death of Chrift, 5th Edition, 1d.

32. A Familiar Illuftration of certain Paffages of Scripture relating to the fame Subject, 4d. or 3s. 6d. per Dozen.

33. The TRIUMPH of TRUTH; being an Account of the Trial of Mr. Elwall for Herefy and Blafphemy, at Stafford Affizes, before Judge Denton, 2d Edition, 1d.

34. CONSIDERATIONS for the USE of YOUNG MEN, and the Parents of YOUNG MEN, 2d Edition, 2d.

*Alfo, publifhed under the Direction of Dr. PRIESTLEY.*

THE THEOLOGICAL REPOSITORY:

Confifting of Original Effays, Hints, Queries, &c. calculated to promote religious Knowledge, in Three Volumes, 8vo. Price 18s. in Boards.

In the Firft Volume, which is now reprinted, feveral Articles are added, particularly Two Letters from Dr. THOMAS SHAW to Dr. BENSON, relating to the Paffage of the Ifraelites through the Red Sea.